Tom Wolfe

Twayne's United States Authors Series

Frank Day, General Editor

Clemson University

TUSAS 650

TOM WOLFE
Donald Levan

Tom Wolfe

William McKeen

University of Florida

Twayne Publishers
An imprint of Simon & Schuster Macmillan
New York

Prentice Hall International
London Mexico City New Delhi Singapore Sydney Toronto

Grateful acknowledgment is made to the publishers listed below for permission to reprint from the following works:

Reprinted by permission of Farrar, Straus & Giroux, Inc: Excerpts from *The Bonfire of the Vanities*. Copyright © 1987 by Tom Wolfe. Excerpts from *The Electric Kool-Aid Acid Test* by Tom Wolfe. Copyright © 1968 by Tom Wolfe. Exerpts from *From Bauhaus to Our House* by Tom Wolfe. Copyright © 1981 by Tom Wolfe. Excerpts from *The Kandy-Kolored Tangerine-Flake Streamline Baby* by Tom Wolfe. Copyright © 1965 and renewed © 1993 by Tom Wolfe. Excerpts from *Mauve Gloves & Madmen, Clutter & Vine* by Tom Wolfe. Copyright © 1976 by Tom Wolfe. Excerpts from *The Painted Word* by Tom Wolfe. Copyright © 1975 by Tom Wolfe. Excerpts from *The Pump House Gang* by Tom Wolfe. Copyright © 1968 by Tom Wolfe. Excerpts from *Radical Chic & Mau-Mauing the Flak Catchers* by Tom Wolfe. Copyright © 1978 by Tom Wolfe. Excerpts from *The Right Stuff* by Tom Wolfe. Copyright © 1979 by Tom Wolfe.

Excerpts from *"Rolling Stone* Interview: Tom Wolfe" by Chet Flippo. From *Rolling Stone*, August 21, 1980. By Straight Arrow Publishers, Inc. 1980. All Rights Reserved. Reprinted by Permission.

Twayne's United States Authors Series No. 650

Tom Wolfe
William McKeen

Twayne Publishers
An Imprint of Simon & Schuster Macmillan
866 Third Avenue
New York, N.Y. 10022

Library of Congress Cataloging-in-Publication Data

McKeen, William, 1954–
    Tom Wolfe / William McKeen
        p.   cm.—(Twayne's United States authors series; TUSAS 650)
    Includes bibliographical references and index.
    ISBN 0-8057-4004-X
    1. Wolfe, Tom—Criticism and interpretation. I. Title. II. Series.
PS3573.0526Z78 1995
818'.5409   95-2284
                                                                              CIP

The paper used in this publication meets the minimum requirements of American National Standard for Information Sciences—Permanence of Paper for Printed Library Materials. ANSI Z3948–1984. ∞ ™

10 9 8 7 6 5 4 3 2 1 (hc)

Printed in the United States of America

For my children
Sarah, Graham, and Mary
with love

Contents

Preface

Twenty years ago, I was a reporter for a daily newspaper in Indiana. One night I went to a sock hop on the local college campus and wrote a story about the phenomenon of children of the 1970s rediscovering the dry old 1950s.

The next morning, when I saw the piece in the paper, I began to have doubts about what I had done. It was an odd little feature, the language was loose, and parts of it might be deemed downright insulting to readers. I concluded it had been a monstrous mistake to write the story and a heinous crime against journalism to print it.

That was my day off. I did, however, get a message that our earnest young publisher had called and very much wanted to talk to me. I did not return the call. The next day, when I came into the office, I hoped he would have forgotten yesterday's news. Unfortunately, he blocked my path into the newsroom; he had been waiting for me.

To my surprise, he did not upbraid me for the insouciance of my piece. He began praising it, urging me to cut loose more often. Finally, he offered me this: "Looks like we have our own little Tom Wolfe on the staff."

Not hardly. But I tell this story because there was no greater praise for a reporter of that era than to be compared, in any small way, with the Great Emancipator of Journalism. Tom Wolfe was the man who had, with his collegium of innovative New Journalists, made newspaper work more than just the path to some other goal. Journalism began to attain what respectability it has because of Wolfe and his compatriots.

After a few more years in daily journalism, I was off to graduate school and teaching, working only six-month stints here and there on newspapers, mostly as a copy-desk editor. I was obviously *not* a Tom Wolfe. Yet I repeat: there was no greater praise for a reporter in that era. Back then, at our newspaper parties, where we talked shop for hours, poked fun at the city officials we were forced to cover, and derided the competing newspaper, we chanted Wolfe's name like a mantra. He was it. We saw him as the leader of a journalistic revolution, as an individual whose work could single-handedly raise the level of the newspaper business. (And we did say "newspaper business." This was before we were instructed in the intricacies of "media" and "information flow.")

Now, after years of reading Wolfe and then, through this project, reexamining his minor work along with his well-known books, my admiration for his feat grows. To look again at what Wolfe and Gay Talese, Truman Capote, Joan Didion, and the others did is humbling. Without any sort of plan, they changed the rules of the game. Thank God they did not stop to analyze their anarchistic activities. They just wrote.

This book about that writing naturally includes some information about Wolfe's life (a general outline comprises chapter 1), but it is largely concerned with his writing for newspapers, magazines, and books.

Many people have helped me with advice and support. I am extremely grateful to my friend and former colleague, Harry L. Allen of Western Kentucky University. When he shared with me his many insights into literary journalism, he was in fact introducing me to his teachers at the University of Florida, who, years later—I am happy to report—are now my colleagues: Jean Chance, Rob Pierce, Jon Roosenraad, John Griffith, and Buddy Davis.

Several students offered research help when I needed it. I am especially grateful to Pamela Biggs, Rebecca Brauner, Adrian Dennis, David DiSalvo, Bob Litwins, Ted Lund, Kristin Rosevear, Derek Willis, and John Young. I also wish to thank Geoff Boucher, James Dubriel, and Milo Thomas. Professor Frank Day of Clemson University is the academic editor of this series, and Mark Zadrozny, Cindy Buck and Lesley Poliner of Twayne made it all work. I appreciate their efforts.

I also want to acknowledge the love and support of my family, particularly my children, Sarah, Graham, and Mary. Thanks to Vicky for buying me all of those Tom Wolfe books so long ago.

I also thank my students who have offered advice and encouragement and have been understanding when I was preoccupied with the book during our advisement sessions. One of the pleasures of teaching is introducing young writers to artists such as Tom Wolfe.

Chronology

1931	Wolfe is born 2 March in Richmond, Virginia, to Helen Hughes and Thomas Kennerly Wolfe.
1951	Graduates from Washington and Lee University with honors.
1951–1956	Attends Yale University. Leaves campus before completing work on Ph.D. dissertation in American studies.
1956	After a brief stint as a truck loader, joins the staff of the *Springfield Union* in Massachusetts as a general assignment reporter.
1957	Completes his dissertation, "The League of American Writers," and is awarded doctorate.
1959	Moves to the "City Life" staff of the *Washington Post*.
1962	Leaves the *Post* for the *New York Herald-Tribune*.
1963	Writes "There Goes (Varroom! Varroom!) That Kandy-Kolored Tangerine Flake Streamline Baby" for *Esquire*. His "breakthrough" is both hailed and reviled.
1964	Covers the arrival of the Beatles for the *Herald-Tribune*.
1965	*The Kandy-Kolored Tangerine-Flake Streamline Baby* is published. A one-man show of his drawings is exhibited at the Maynard Walker Gallery in New York.
1966–1967	Researches and writes extended piece on the fugitive novelist Ken Kesey. Regular contributor to *Esquire* and the *Herald-Tribune*'s Sunday magazine, *New York*.
1968	*The Electric Kool-Aid Acid Test*, his book about Kesey, and his second collection of magazine articles, *The Pump House Gang*, are published on the same day. The *World Journal Tribune*, successor to the *Herald-Tribune*, has gone out of business, but its Sunday magazine lives on as *New York*, an independent publication for which Wolfe becomes a contributing editor.
1970	Publication of *Radical Chic and Mau-Mauing the Flak Catchers*.

1971   Receives an honorary doctorate from the Minneapolis College of Art.

1973   Series on the astronauts appears in *Rolling Stone*. Wins Frank Luther Mott Award for research in journalism. *The New Journalism* is published.

1974   One-man show of drawings at the Tunnel Gallery in New York. Receives honorary doctor of letters degree from Washington and Lee University.

1975   *The Painted Word* is published.

1976   *Mauve Gloves and Madmen, Clutter and Vine* is published. His phrase characterizing the 1970s, the "Me Decade," comes into the language.

1977   Named Virginia Laureate for Literature.

1978   Marries Sheila Berger, a magazine art director, on 27 May.

1979   *The Right Stuff* is published.

1980   *In Our Time*, a collection of drawings, verse, and short prose, is published. Wins Harold D. Vursell Memorial Award for Excellence in Literature from the American Institute of Arts and Letters. Daughter Alexandra is born.

1981   *From Bauhaus to Our House* is published.

1983   Film version of *The Right Stuff* is released. Awarded honorary doctorate from Virginia Commonwealth University.

1984   Begins serializing his long-discussed novel *The Bonfire of the Vanities*, being written under deadline pressure for *Rolling Stone*.

1985   Son Thomas is born.

1986   Awarded the Washington Irving Medal for Literary Excellence from the Nicholas Society.

1987   *The Bonfire of the Vanities* is published to tremendous critical acclaim.

1990   Disastrous film version of *Bonfire of the Vanities* is released.

Chapter One

The Man in the White Suit

Like a protoplasmic Red Sea, the crowd parted when the Distinguished Visitor came into the room. Cocooning him, the group of eager, young hangers-on beheld a thin, pink-skinned man in a white suit. A high antique collar gripped a delicate neck that supported a vaguely aristocratic face with its aquiline nose and fine, precise hair. The eyes were sharp and liquid, and the voice was lilting yet seemed to work in starts and stops, jerking the listeners along through his sentences.

The crowd was young: students who had eschewed jeans and sweatshirts for the evening to attend this reception for the Distinguished Visitor—someone they had heard of, or were *supposed* to have heard of. They were the gods of student government at this university; when Distinguished Visiting Muckety-mucks came to speak to the plebeian masses in the basketball arena, these students were the ones who got a postlecture chance to schmooze in private with the great ones: Ollie North . . . C. Everett Koop . . . Bill Buckley. . . .

And now.

So they donned their suits and pulled prom dresses out of their cellophane prisons, styled their hair, and sculpted their makeup for the reception. The Distinguished Visitor was a writer of some sort, so the young gods and goddesses now clutched to their bosoms copies of his latest book, most having hunted down and purchased the cumbersome volume that very afternoon. Could they pull it off? they wondered. Could they feign some knowledge of his work? The previous weekend they had rented the film of this fat book and cheered when Tom Hanks nailed that villainous Melanie Griffith in the courtroom scene. She sure got what was coming to her! They had vowed to read the book, but faced with its 623 pages, they ran off like curs, claiming to find the opening a bit dense, the story kind of, well, like, *dull*. Now here he was, the Distinguished Visitor, just a few feet away. Would he be able to tell they knew nothing about him?

There were a few, well, *others* in attendance—vermin! Look at them, huddled in the corner, ruffians in cheap suits from Sears, escorting their low-life wenches sans mascara, in those icky, inappropriate miniskirts.

Oh, aren't we thoughtful, the student clerisy thought. This man had something to do with journalism, so we have invited those vermin from the campus newspaper. They congratulated themselves on their largesse.

The vermin had reacted visibly when the man in the white suit entered, but now they hung back by the safety of the refreshments table, scarfing the Free Food. When the Visitor walked in, squired by the earnest chairman of the student speakers' bureau, the vermin contracted, bracing as if for a massacre by savages, while the student governors flocked to the writer like groupies to a rock 'n' roll star. The student journalists (young scribes!) were shut out, preparing for a lifetime of being on the outside. Life's symbolism was so obvious!

Soon after the Distinguished Visitor's arrival, another head-turner walked into the room. He was the editor of the student newspaper (King of the Vermin!), usually clothed in cutoffs and a Miami Dolphins cap. But not now! Look at the shine on those lapels! On his arm was a stunning young vixen in a gown worthy of an inaugural ball. The editor could not get near the Distinguished Visitor just yet, so he made his way to the safety of his troops near the refreshments table. In answer to the obvious question, the editor reminded them that he had just been representing their fine publication at another (and more formal) affair, an AIDS benefit—hence the nifty tux. He had therefore missed the speech by his hero, but he rushed to the reception as soon as the benefit ended, desperately wanting to meet the Visitor, now nearly buried under blond explosions of bouffants and blinded by capped teeth.

The editor had actually read several of the Visitor's books and could quote favorite passages at length. The crush of thick-necked frat boys and lacquered sorority women around the writer and their forced peals of high-decibel laughter at first annoyed the editor, then amused him. He's toying with them, the editor thought. For him, this reception is priceless research.

The student journalists still huddled, desultory and waiflike, by the rapidly disappearing food. The Distinguished Visitor was one of *them*, they shared the kinship of journalism, and yet he was surrounded by that crush of hair and cologne, suffocating amid the aroma of the young scribes' mortal enemies, the student governors, the apprentices to the State's power structure—the people they, as journalists, would be required to dog throughout their lives. Both camps were now merely in rehearsal, playing out their roles on a campus stage in preparation for careers of mutual antagonism. It seemed fitting to the young scribes that they had been invited to gaze upon this great man, then shut out by the worms that ran student government. Members only—you can't join this club. The young scribes sighed. C'est la vie!

The editor immediately recognized the situation. Here was one of the gods of journalism, a hero to those of his breed, and they were in the same room yet separated. It was like raw meat dangled just out of a pit bull's reach. The morale of the troops was suffering. Laughter would soothe them, perhaps turn the extravagantly coiffed heads encircling the Visitor, freeing him from the Polo stench. Yes! The student editor realized he needed to care for his crestfallen pups, these journalists of the twenty-first century. They need entertainment, the editor thought, gazing upon his dispirited charges. It is my duty, he concluded.

"So," the editor said, straightening his tie, nodding toward the crowd across the room. "Which one's Wolfe?"

Knowing full well.

The man in the white suit is unmistakably Tom Wolfe, as much a cultural icon as a brilliant cultural observer. For the last half of the twentieth century, he has held a fun-house mirror up to the pandemonium that is America. Jaded and cynical (the required mind-set of the journalist), he has also been openly sentimental, adoring heroism and the values for which others have given their lives. His work exalts the higher principles and long ago transcended the superficial observations that constitute much of everyday journalism. He helped move journalism, the bastard child of literature, to a higher plane, putting it on a par with The Novel, making it no longer the means to an end but an end in itself. Before Wolfe came along, claiming literary status for journalism would have provoked a symphony of guffaws. After Wolfe, no one is laughing—not about *that* claim at least.

And yet, Wolfe has said he had nothing revolutionary in mind when he entered the newspaper business. He just wanted to be a reporter. It looked like so much fun.

Wolfe's Early Life

Thomas Kennerly Wolfe, Jr., was born 2 March 1931, in Richmond, Virginia, the son of his namesake, a scientist and business executive, and Helen Hughes Wolfe, a woman who bequeathed to her son her wide-ranging interest in art, teaching him to sketch. She helped her son, while he was still a toddler, to appreciate the subtleties of color. She also read to him frequently and urged him to adopt reading as a way of life.

Wolfe has described his childhood as one of near-academic serenity. Schooling was vital to the family, and therefore a premium was placed on classroom performance at St. Christopher's, a private day school. He did not disappoint.

Although his mother had provided the conscious tutorial in the arts, it was Thomas Wolfe, Sr., who may have most influenced his son. He too was a journalist, editor of the *Southern Planter*, an agronomy journal. He would also publish books, including *Production of Field Crops*, a textbook published in 1953. "To my mind he was a writer," Wolfe said of his father. "My first memories are when he was editing *The Planter*. He would write in longhand and it seemed magical to me. I once went to the New York Public Library, and he had more entries in the card catalog than I did."[1]

The elder Wolfe also was influential in shaping his son's attitudes toward clothing, yet he refrained from the pretensions normally associated with more elegant dressing. "He had his clothes all custom-made," Wolfe said, "but I never saw him choosing fabrics, or talking about fashion. There was never any social emphasis. The big thing in Richmond was the Country Club of Virginia, but you couldn't have dragged my father in there with a chain."[2]

Wolfe came to realize that growing up in the South was a "good career move." It infused his thought and speech with a richness he wouldn't have found elsewhere. At an early age, he began listening carefully, storing up idiosyncrasies that he would drop into his writing like the key ingredient of a secret recipe. As he once told an interviewer:

> I like the way people talk in rural areas—homey phrases, it's a richer speech and phrasing. . . .
>   I like to slip them [into my articles]. Sometimes it'll be a thing that I'm probably the only one aware of. Like in one piece I say the way they pass a Saturday in Georgia is to go down to the railroad tracks and watch the Seaboard sleeper barrelling through to New York City. I mean nobody in *New York* calls it New York City. "Just plain-long tired" is a phrase that's been cut out of every piece I've tried to use it in.[3]

For five years, Wolfe had the undivided attention of his parents. Then a sister was born. Life continued in Richmond, civilized and refined. "I had a very happy childhood," Wolfe once told an interviewer.[4] He had varied (one might even say controversial) interests for a child, including tap dancing and ballet, but he cast these aside as an adolescent for the more conventional pursuit of sports. Wolfe excelled in baseball and developed a slider, a sinker, and several varieties of breaking pitches that made him a sought-after pitcher on youth league teams. (Eventually he earned a tryout with the New York Giants in 1952, but he was cut after three days in spring training.)

Wolfe's close family and his genteel upbringing made him different in many ways. Although he chronicled the many weirdnesses of the 1960s, Wolfe's manner—exemplified by his vaguely formal and anachronistic dress—made him stand out from his colleagues in journalism.

Clay Felker, Wolfe's editor at *New York* and *Esquire*, said: "I think it's very hard for people in the East to read exactly what it means to be a Virginia gentleman. That background shapes character in a way that people who have grown up without roots might not appreciate."[5]

Wolfe left home, but not Virginia, for college. Accepted at Princeton and Washington and Lee, he selected the institution in his home state because "the people seemed nicer."[6] At college, he found that his diverse interests in the arts were not entirely satisfied in the constraining English Department. The intensely bookish Wolfe—certain that he would write novels after graduation—cofounded the prestigious literary quarterly *Shenandoah* and served for a time on its editorial board. He also began dressing unconventionally while in college. He went to a local theater and saw the tough-guy actor Richard Widmark in *Kiss of Death*. Widmark and his smarmy pals wore black shirts with white ties. The look appealed to Wolfe, who soon adopted it.

Yet his most vital instruction as an undergraduate occurred outside of his major. He learned at the feet of the reigning guru of popular culture at Washington and Lee—a dynamic young professor named Marshall Fishwick—that there was a broader field in academe than he had been shown by the elbow-patch brigade in the English Department.

"[Fishwick] gave a course," Wolfe said, "which in effect was all of American studies pressed into one year—American architecture, American art, theories in psychology, history, across the board." For his part, Fishwick saw Wolfe as prime material for graduate work. "I tried to baptize the proletarian," he said. "Tom immediately took the bait. He saw through the facade of this small, elite college and demonstrated that everyone was of the same pattern."[7]

Fishwick's instruction included field trips and practical work experience (in building construction, for example), as well as exposure to those aspects of proletarian life largely disdained by the university clerisy, country music shows being a prime example. The experience with

Fishwick helped broaden Wolfe's horizon, and after the flirtation and heartbreak with the New York Giants, Wolfe enrolled in Yale University's American studies program.

God and Tom Wolfe at Yale

The move to Yale was difficult. "It was the one time in my life I was really stuck," Wolfe recalled. "I couldn't stand out because everybody was eccentric in graduate school. They had everything from genuine dirty-neck bohemians to true British fops."[8] Nevertheless, Wolfe vowed to make an attempt to embrace a different lifestyle.

In New Haven, he became proletarian and bohemian at once and planned to pursue a teaching career, to fashion his life somewhat in the manner of his Washington and Lee mentor.[9] The American studies program expanded Wolfe's reading list far beyond the usual favorites of literature programs, and his reading of the sociologist Max Weber enlightened him to the dynamics of status in modern society. Studiously bohemian, Wolfe dressed in black turtlenecks, embracing some of the less unhygienic elements of the beatnik movement, along with some of the high points of that subculture's reading list. He admired Jack Kerouac's "momentum,"[10] although he never professed much admiration for any of the other writers of the Beat Generation.

He began work on his dissertation, a study of communist influences on American literature. Wolfe delivered "The League of American Writers" to the Yale graduate faculty in 1957, by which time he was already a year into his career as a journalist.

Wolfe had maintained his academic fantasy of a teaching career throughout his three years in New Haven, but finally, he said, "I couldn't face the academic life any more, because I'd been in it too long. I pushed it to its furthest boundaries."[11] Conveniently, he finished his course work—if not his dissertation—too late in the year to get a teaching job.

Moreover, as he wrote, "I was in the twisted grip of a disease of our times in which the sufferer experiences an overwhelming urge to join the 'real world.'"[12] His first job in the real world was as a truck loader. He decided he would embrace bohemianism. "Jack London, of all people, was my model," he said. "I got myself a cloth cap and became a furniture mover for a trucking firm. But I could see that the girls in the offices were not impressed. . . . Believe me, there is *no* insight to be gathered from the life of the working-class milieu."[13]

The working-class life was a little "too real" for Wolfe, and he tired of it after a couple of months of exhausted evenings drinking beer and watching television, with the unfinished dissertation manuscript moldering on his desk. The furniture mover's life was not the real world of which he had dreamed.

Journalism certainly seemed like part of the "real world," and not as physically taxing as loading boxes into trucks. He first tried out his résumé on the New York newspapers. The *Daily News* editors, delighted at the thought of hiring their first Ph.D. copyboy (standard procedure at the *New York Times*, but novel at the *Daily News*), offered Wolfe $40 a week to be at the beck and call of the news desk.

Yet it was the *Springfield Union* in Massachusetts—the only one of the 120 newspapers he had leafleted with his résumé to offer a real job— where he began his career. On the way back home on the train after the successful job interview, Wolfe sang to himself, "I'm-a-member-of-the-working-press."[14]

His first year on the staff as a $55-a-week city hall reporter baptized him into the ways of the newspaper craft. He also learned more about other inhabitants of the real world in which he wanted so desperately to participate. Springfield, Wolfe said, was a revelation. "It was the first time I realized that a city could be made up of more than one ethnic group that was politically powerful, that had its own way of life and its own restaurants," he said.[15]

While at the *Union*, Wolfe found the motivation not only to labor on but to finish his dissertation, which was finally completed and defended in 1957. The dissertation carried an impressively academic title: "The League of American Writers: Communist Organizational Activity among American Writers, 1929–1942." The writing is livelier than that usually found in academic tomes, yet still within the stodgy and acceptable mainstream of university writing style. It allowed Wolfe to conclude that American writers were not always what they seemed. "My theory was that writers, who think of themselves as loners in pursuit of a great goal . . . actually are lonesome," Wolfe said. "It's a socializing influence to join these organizations."[16]

The dissertation was a historical survey of the attempts of the Communist party to infiltrate the ranks of the American literati; it shows the kernel of Wolfe's interest in status, which was to become one of the unifying themes in his perspective on American culture. The dissertation allowed Wolfe to focus on the peculiar nature of status among the literary crowd.

The most sought-after reward within the writing craft was literary prestige rather than high income, a social motivation that held true even
among screen writers at a high-income level. This premium upon the
economically non-rational goal of literary prestige seems to have been
anchored in a centuries-old tradition which characterized the writer as a
creative artist with superior or even supernatural powers of perception.
. . . The pursuit of this economically non-rational goal led to the
formation within the writing craft of a unique inter-personal status system, centered within New York City. This status system, in turn, resulted in a hierarchy divided, roughly, into a small literary elite at the top
and a large "commercial" mass at the bottom.[17]

Wolfe's dissertation, though most immediately concerned with the
problem of examining communist influence on American writers, gave
him the opportunity to outline the social strata of the American literary
community, a pursuit that would become his raison d'être for a couple of
decades before he threw himself in with the writers of fiction in the
1980s.

Writing his dissertation also allowed Wolfe to meet some of the literary world's old guard; as part of his research, he interviewed the influential critic Malcolm Cowley, the poet Archibald MacLeish, and the author
of *Studs Lonigan*, James T. Farrell. In defending his extensive use of interviews in researching the dissertation, Wolfe said the sessions were
extremely valuable and, despite the passing of years, his interviewees'
memories of communist activity in the early 1930s were sharp and vivid.
"Virtually no conflicting data was [*sic*] received," Wolfe wrote in an after-
word.

The dissertation also led Wolfe to question his goal of becoming the
great American novelist. Like many of his colleagues in the undergraduate program in English, he had assumed he would write important novels that would explain human existence. Now he began to wonder.
There was something undignified about displaying one's regrets, fears,
doubts, and broken hopes through the guise of fiction. As he practiced
journalism, he began to think that reality might be a better device than
imagination for dealing with the complexities of human life.

Degree finally in hand, Wolfe had become a rarity in the world of
small-city newspapers: a reporter with a Ph.D. The three-year apprenticeship continued, but Wolfe longed for a career at a big-city paper.
Eventually, his work at the *Union* gave him an impressive portfolio,
which allowed him to jump to the *Washington Post* in 1959. Wolfe was a
star of the *Post*'s "City Life" section and contributed a number of offbeat

features and sketches (in both senses of the word). The *Post* in the early 1960s was not a good enough paper to hold on to Wolfe, and so he went on to the *New York Herald-Tribune* in 1962.

The *Herald-Tribune* was the premier writer's paper in New York and, therefore, a showplace for some of the nation's best journalistic talent. The *Times* may have had the reputation of being the "newspaper of record" and played perhaps a greater part in upholding the nation's conscience, but the *Herald-Tribune* was the fun newspaper with an army of great writers.

Wolfe in New York

As Wolfe wrote about his arrival in the newsroom, "This must be the place! I looked out across the city room of the *Herald-Tribune*, 100 moldering yards south of Times Square, with a feeling of amazed bohemian bliss. . . . Either this is the real world, Tom, or there is no real world."[18]

Things began to happen fast. Immersed in the competitive world of New York journalism, Wolfe began to branch out. He'd managed to enliven several of his *Washington Post* assignments with his adventurous wordplay, though his efforts may not have been appreciated by his editors (see chapter 2). At the *Herald-Tribune*, however, the story was different. Wolfe's talent was recognized, and he was soon promoted to the staff of the Sunday magazine supplement, *New York*. His *Herald-Tribune* colleagues included talented writers like Jimmy Breslin, Dick Schaap, and Charles Portis, yet Wolfe felt most in competition with a *New York Times* reporter, Gay Talese. Talese had managed to publish some of his quirky, idiosyncratic pieces in the great gray *Times* and had published a selection of them in a book, *New York: A Serendipiter's Journey*.[19] Talese frequently wrote for *Esquire*, and when Wolfe returned from a lunchtime break in the fall of 1962 with the new issue, he nearly exploded with festering admiration for the Talese article it carried, a profile of the former heavyweight boxing champion of the world, Joe Louis. It began:

> "Hi, sweetheart!" Joe Louis called to his wife, spotting her waiting for him at the Los Angeles airport.
>
> She smiled, walked toward him, and was about to step up on her toes and kiss him—but suddenly stopped.
>
> "Joe," she said, "where's your tie?"
>
> "Aw, sweetie," he said, shrugging, "I stayed out all night in New York and didn't have time—"

"All *night!*" she cut in. "When you're out here all you do is sleep, sleep, sleep."[20]

Wolfe's reaction to the piece was "*What inna namea christ is this.*"[21] Talese's article was not the standard magazine profile: volleying routine questions and answers with the subject or some "here I am with the Great One" disposable feature. Talese had written his observations of Louis with the detail and insight of a short-story writer.

That article opened Wolfe's eyes to the possibilities of a new form of journalism that incorporated the techniques of fiction. He wanted to play that game too. Wolfe immediately secured an assignment from *Esquire*, the most vital magazine in America during the 1960s, and set to work, after initial troubles finding his voice and tone, to capture the essence of the times in the style Talese had demonstrated, a form soon dubbed the New Journalism (see chapter 3).

Soon Wolfe was the leading figure of the movement, occasionally deified, but more often reviled. The literary establishment attacked Wolfe frequently, but he usually responded—if at all—with wit.

It was difficult, however, to take all of the literary community's virulent attacks with humor. After publishing Wolfe's two-part dissection of the *New Yorker* in 1965, *New York* was deluged with letters of protest. The *New Yorker*'s fabled fact-checking department went to work on Wolfe's piece—largely seen as an attack on the legendary *New Yorker* editor William Shawn—and sent the *Columbia Journalism Review* a list of "errors" in the articles.

Wolfe survived the criticism, of course, aided by the blurring lines between fiction and nonfiction. George Plimpton, a bona fide literary figure as editor of the *Paris Review*, published a book-length experiment in literary journalism called *Paper Lion* (1966). And one of the *New Yorker*'s own, a contributor and former copy clerk, Truman Capote, published a masterpiece of the new form in, of all places, the *New Yorker*. Capote called *In Cold Blood* (1966) a new art form, a "nonfiction novel," to distance it from the trendiness of New Journalism, but it was clearly another example of work Wolfe and Talese were doing: using some of the techniques and insights of the novelist on the nonfiction form.

The publication of several of Wolfe's *New York* and *Esquire* pieces in book form gave his writing a level of respectability and permanence. *The Kandy-Kolored Tangerine-Flake Streamline Baby* received generally good reviews, and Wolfe's insouciance was suddenly available to a large, mass audience.

Wolfe became a character in the 1960s madness he was so effectively chronicling. In photographs and on talk shows, he could be seen in his distinctive white suits and high-necked shirts, a dandy from an earlier age somehow dropped into the middle of a tumultuous decade that celebrated denim, not worsted wool, that smelled more of patchouli oil than Pinaud, and that saw the necktie as a corporate yoke, not a statement of sartorial defiance.

Indeed, an article on Wolfe that does not comment upon his clothing is rare. The white suits that had always been a part of his wardrobe began to multiply in his closets during his tenure at the *Herald-Tribune*. He had a white wool suit tailored but found it too hot to wear in the summer. He began wearing it in the fall, long after the traditional Labor Day cutoff point for wearing white. "It annoyed people enormously," Wolfe said. "Why I enjoyed that, I don't know. But after that, it became fun dressing every day. People were so easy to disturb through dress in those days."[22] Indeed, clothing became one of Wolfe's favored methods to outrage people. "I discovered I had this marvelous, harmless form of aggression going for me."[23] The clothing represented something else to Wolfe—his concern with status:

> Just think of how clothes conscious American males are. Often it's negative. One of the greatest male fears in America today is the fear of seeming pretentious in dress. That is status consciousness. That's why I have so much fun being pompous in dress—high collars, faux spats, things like that. I consider that very daring because it's status consciousness in another fashion.[24]

Soon Wolfe's was a household name, sometimes for the wrong reasons. He received many letters from admirers who professed admiration for his journalism as well as his earlier literary works, *Look Homeward Angel* and *Of Time and the River*. The letter writers often wondered why there had been such a long gap between publication of his books.

Wolfe continued his profitable association with *New York* and *Esquire* but soon embarked on a larger project: a book-length examination of the disintegrating career of the novelist Ken Kesey. Kesey had skyrocketed to literary stardom with *One Flew over the Cuckoo's Nest* (1962) and *Sometimes a Great Notion* (1964), then, just as suddenly, appeared to burn out. Joining a group of bohemians who called themselves the Merry Pranksters, Kesey had begun a long cross-country odyssey on a multicolored school bus driven by Neal Cassady, the god of the Beat

Generation. Cassady had been one of the inspirations for the Beat writer
Jack Kerouac in the 1950s. Now, in the mid-1960s, he drove a bus with
a destination plate that read "furthur" (spelling was never a strong point
of the Merry Pranksters) and, with Kesey, led young followers down the
corridors of LSD.

Wolfe, with his natty attire, would have seemed totally out of place
with the tie-dye-and-denim crowd. Indeed he was. But immediately
upon its publication in 1968, *The Electric Kool-Aid Acid Test* was recognized as one of the definitive books about America in the 1960s. And
Wolfe, as flamboyant professionally as he was in his attire, outraged the
literary community by having the audacity to publish his second collection of articles, *The Pump House Gang*, on the same day *The Electric Kool-
Aid Acid Test* appeared. Some appreciated the joke. The critic C. D. B.
Bryan's review in the *New York Times Book Review* was titled "The SAME
Day: heeeeeewack!!!"[25]

Wolfe was firmly established as an author by the time his newspaper,
the *Herald-Tribune*, folded. By 1967 a corporate shotgun wedding had
created the *World Journal Tribune*, the result of merging the once-great
New York newspapers established by James Gordon Bennett, Horace
Greeley, Joseph Pulitzer, and William Randolph Hearst—four characters
who would have been revolted to learn what happened to their newspaper progeny.

Despite the inconvenience of its parent newspaper ceasing publication, the Sunday magazine *New York* lived on. Clay Felker, editor of the
supplement, bought the rights to the name and launched *New York* as a
separate publication in 1968, so Wolfe's dual association with it and
Esquire continued. Indeed, Wolfe remained a prolific contributor to both
publications through the mid-1970s. He also remained a popular author,
collecting two lengthy articles as *Radical Chic and Mau-Mauing the Flak
Catchers* in 1970.

Wolfe first began making noises about writing a novel in the early
1970s. His statements carried the taste of spite, as if he intended to
show a self-indulgent literary community how to "do it right." But other
projects intervened.

Where *Esquire* had provided the best cultural record of the 1960s, the
San Francisco magazine *Rolling Stone* served that function for the 1970s.
A whole new breed of Wolfe-weaned New Journalists were publishing
wild and innovative (and tremendously long) articles in the magazine.
Originally perceived as a publication devoted to rock and roll and the
drug culture, *Rolling Stone* was publishing investigative reports on the

Vietnam War, the FBI's abuses of power, and undercover drug informants. The most famous of its reporters was Hunter S. Thompson, whom Wolfe admired greatly. Thompson had established himself as a writer before going to *Rolling Stone*—he rode with an outlaw motorcycle gang for a year in order to write *Hell's Angels* (1967),[26] a classic of New Journalism—but he flowered at *Rolling Stone* with the freedom and open pages that the editor, Jann Wenner, lavished upon him. Thompson brought the magazine great acclaim, which attracted more good writers. When Wolfe was commissioned to write a piece on the astronauts for *Rolling Stone*, the contract made headlines.

The *Great* Tom Wolfe

Jann Wenner knew his little magazine—barely five years old—had arrived the day he signed Tom Wolfe. Wenner openly idolized Wolfe and once altered the writer Grover Lewis's passing reference to Wolfe in an article to read "the *great* Tom Wolfe."[27] Wolfe's article on the astronauts expanded into a series of three pieces and finally grew into a project that would consume much of his time for the next decade. Along the way, Wolfe published a few smaller books: an anthology called *The New Journalism* (1973) allowed him to expound as the professor he had trained to be at Yale; an extended essay on art called *The Painted Word* (1975) drew the ire of the fine arts community; and his third collection, *Mauve Gloves and Madmen, Clutter and Vine* (1976) introduced his phrase "the Me Decade" to the era. Finally, in the last two months of the Me Decade, Wolfe published his magnum opus on the astronauts, a look back to a period when the heroism since wiped out by cynicism had flourished. *The Right Stuff* was Wolfe's most mature work of journalism and a testament that was fiercely and unabashedly patriotic. When finally he was free of the burden of the astronauts' story, he began to consider once again the possibilities of the novel.

During the hoopla surrounding the publication of *The Right Stuff*, Wolfe frequently told interviewers that he longed to write the great novel of New York—fertile territory, Wolfe said, since the self-indulgent American literary lions were not bothered much by narrative or the concept of the social novel. The book would be called *Vanity Fair*, he said, and it would in fact parallel the work by William Makepeace Thackeray.

While he worked on the novel, Wolfe published a collection of drawings and poems, *In Our Time* (1980), and another essay on the arts, *From Bauhaus to Our House* (1981). He sanctioned a collection of "greatest hits"—short articles and bits from his books—called *The Purple Decades* (1982). Finally, feeling he needed some of the creative pressure of journalism to help him write his novel, Wolfe again joined forces with *Rolling Stone*. He began to serialize his novel in the magazine, writing fiction on deadline the way Charles Dickens had done in nineteenth-century London.

The technique worked—too well, in fact. Eventually, reality began to intrude on Wolfe's fiction, and before book publication, he had to revise several sections of his novel that were too strangely parallel to the madness of New York City in the 1980s. When it was published in 1987, *The Bonfire of the Vanities* was immediately a popular and critical success. Wolfe, having reestablished the concept of the social novel, was unwilling to sit back and bask in smugness. He hit the lecture circuit and essayed in *Harper's* on the subject of the modern novel, as if to rub the noses of the literati in the fact that he had, nearly single-handedly, restored the realistic social novel to prominence.

Journalism had not been a detour to the life Wolfe envisioned as an undergraduate. The novelist he became—and he began referring to himself as such—was one who needed the nearly 30 years he spent in journalism. Had he turned to fiction earlier, he could not have written *The Bonfire of the Vanities*. It would not have had the grounding that came naturally to Wolfe after writing journalism for so many years.

And yet Wolfe's greatest accomplishment has probably little to do with his career as a novelist. He gave modern journalism a face-lift. When he entered the newspaper business, many of his contemporaries regarded it merely as the means to an end. A group of journalists changed that, making journalism itself a respectable end. Wolfe's name is at the top of the list of those who altered the nature of journalistic writing: Gay Talese, Truman Capote, Norman Mailer, Joan Didion, George Plimpton, Gloria Emerson, John Sack, Michael Herr, and other, younger writers who first saw, in the works of Wolfe and Talese, the expanding possibilities of nonfiction writing. His career in the newspaper and magazine businesses not only revolutionized journalism but was necessary to his development as a writer. "I enjoyed the cowboy nature of journalism," he said. "The idea that it wasn't really respectable, and yet it was exciting, even in a literary way. I loved the fact that this was something a literary person could dismiss, and yet couldn't dismiss."[28]

Though perhaps not retired from journalism, the novelist Tom Wolfe remains a social critic and elder (though by no means elderly) statesman of American letters. Married for the first time at 47, he still has young children at home when many of his contemporaries are observing their grandchildren from afar.

Wolfe watches his children grow as he works at home in his office on the second floor of his New York townhouse. In his colorful work room (lavender lounge chairs, lime-green carpeting, mustard-yellow walls), Wolfe sits at his desk, at home in suit (frequently white) and tie. He dresses formally, even if he does not plan to leave his house. He once said, wearing a stiff collar, that there is no allowance for sloth. He *must* work. "I dress so formally," he once told a reporter, "so that I can feel what I do is important."[29] Thus attired, he turns out his quota of ten pages a day. His work, he reports, is also his pleasure. And it is indeed important—to him and to the culture he has documented in fact and fiction for nearly 40 years.

"I've created my own little church in literature," Wolfe once said. "I regard myself in the first flight of writers but I don't dwell on this. If anything, I think I tend to be a little modest. . . . But I have been able to derive strength from the writing I've done that I know is good, no matter how many eminences have told me it's awful."[30]

Chapter Two
The Real World

By the summer of 1957, Tom Wolfe had overdosed on the academic life—through his undergraduate work at Washington and Lee University and then through his Ivory Tower baptism at Yale. He was now *Dr.* Tom Wolfe, perfectly prepared for a teaching position at a major university—but his timing was bad. He finished at Yale a bit too late to apply for any reputable teaching position. Community colleges might still be hiring in the humid days of midsummer, but any university worthy of a recent Yale Ph.D. had long since assembled its faculty for the fall.

Wolfe was not terribly disappointed by his bad timing. He was not sure that he wanted to remain in the insular university environment. Like many college students since the dawn of time, he had thought of his time in school as an experience quite different from what would follow—the unknown out there in the "real world." That was Life. (Did that make time on campus Not Life?)

Wolfe yearned for the real world. It being the mid-1950s, bohemianism was attractive. The Beat Generation was in full flower, and the popular press was jeering at the so-called beatniks. Yet that lifestyle, however caricatured, was appealing to Wolfe. He tried being a delivery man for a trucking company for a while but found the hard labor a little too toxic for his creative soul.

Journalism—now that was the real world, and no heavy lifting was required. Wolfe, a child of popular culture, had grown up on movies that made newspaper reporters out to be lovable louses with swell jobs that allowed plenty of time to meet interesting people, mutter smart-aleck comments, and toss back a few brews after work. The kind of journalism portrayed in *The Front Page*, the classic play by Ben Hecht and Charles MacArthur—that's what appealed to Wolfe.

Unfortunately, his attempts to get hired by a newspaper were largely futile. He was ready for the real world, but the real world did not appear to be ready for him. This future revolutionary journalist found that only one newspaper was willing to take a chance on him.

The *Springfield Union*

Wolfe joined the staff of the *Springfield Union* in 1957 as a "general assignment" reporter—meaning, he did whatever needed to be done. Unlike a beat reporter, who covers, for example, the police, the local government, or the schools and who knows generally what to expect on a daily basis, Wolfe arrived at the newspaper office each morning, relatively ignorant of what lay ahead. If there was a two-car collision, he would report it. If a visiting dignitary came to make a speech, Wolfe was in the audience. If one of the beat reporters needed a helping hand on an assignment, Wolfe pitched in.

The newspaper rarely granted bylines, so very little paper trail exists that could be followed to get a look at Wolfe's work through his years at the *Union*. His stories did not distinguish themselves above those of any other reporter at the *Union*, its sister paper the *Daily News*, or the combined Sunday edition, the *Springfield Republican*. The *Republican* was the namesake survivor of the great nineteenth-century—and early-twentieth-century—newspaper whose reputation was still so great by the 1960s that Wolfe often claimed his first job was with the legendary *Republican*. Technically, he did write for the *Republican* whenever his stories appeared on Sunday, but the *Union* was his employer.

Wolfe wore white suits even then at the beginning of his newspaper career. But they were of the worn and somewhat dingy variety any son of the South might wear, quite unlike the tailored, English-style suits he began to sport in the mid-1960s.

That was to be expected. Tailoring was something Wolfe could ill afford on his *Union* salary. His budget did not allow for many luxuries, so the suits were well used, as was the green book bag he lugged into the newsroom every day and carried with him on assignments. The other reporters—some of whom were put off by Wolfe's elitist tendencies, which were a bit out of place among the hard-drinking, chain-smoking crew in the city room—were curious about the bag's contents. Wolfe would not reveal what was within. Realizing the bag held a mystery to his fellow staffers, Wolfe fertilized their imaginations, intimating that the bag contained wonders to which they would not be privy.

Once when Wolfe was out of the room, some of the reporters coaxed a female staff member to open the bag and describe the contents. She did and found only a couple of newspapers and copies of *Time* magazine. Wolfe, returning to his desk while the search was still in progress, was furious. Later he would admit that he was studying *Time* to teach himself to write in a less academic, more engaging style.

Though Wolfe made efforts to "be one of the guys" (and it was a nearly all-male staff), his occasional lapses into academic elitist or Virginia squire alienated his fellow reporters. As one of his colleagues recalled:

> He always had that Virginia charm. . . . You don't have to be among the first families of Virginia to have it. He always had a very nice way about him.
>
> One thing that irritated the other guys on the staff: His parents came up to visit one time. He marched them through the city room [to the editor's office]. He introduced them to [the editor] and they chatted with him. [Wolfe] didn't introduce them to one single colleague. What were they? Just a group of peasant journalists.[1]

The newspaper may not have paid well, but Wolfe did not complain. The old suits, a beat-up car, the small apartment—it was all preparation for something larger. If nothing else, Wolfe exuded confidence. He knew he would be at the *Union* for a short time. Wolfe may have known that, but his colleagues did not suspect that greatness lay ahead for him. One of them said it was clear that Wolfe—like most of the ambitious reporters on the staff—harbored an ambition to write a novel. "When he left," the colleague said, "he was just an ordinary reporter leaving. He was not a dolt, but he was certainly not someone who had shown to anybody there great promise in writing. Everyone was happy for him [getting the job at the *Washington Post*], without thinking, 'He will now rise to the top.'"[2]

The *Washington Post*

The newspaper that Tom Wolfe joined in 1959 was not the same newspaper that would be credited with bringing down President Richard Nixon 15 years later. It had the same name (actually its full name in 1959 was the *Washington Post and Times Herald*), but little else about it was similar to the later, more famous incarnation.

The *Post* had had some good days. The famous marching-band tune that bears its name dates from the nineteenth century, and so it was not without renown. It had been saved from bankruptcy in the late 1930s by the businessman Eugene Meyer. Meyer had good intentions but no firm idea what to do with the newspaper.[3]

Then his daughter, Katherine Meyer, fell in love with a young hay-seed-gone-to-the-city, Philip Graham. As a young child, Graham had lived on a houseboat in the Everglades and was schooled by his mother, who offered a home course in Western civilization. By the time he was an adult, his father, Ernest Graham, had secured himself a place in the world and was able to support his son at the University of Florida and Harvard Law School.

Young Graham was over 6 feet tall and barely 120 pounds, but he overcame his classmates' derision over his unusual appearance by sheer force of personality and intelligence. He overcame the physical odds (gangliness) as well as the social ones (rural background) to become the star student at the center of American learning.

He was, specifically, the star student of the law professor Felix Frankfurter, and when President Franklin Roosevelt appointed Frankfurter to the Supreme Court in 1940, Graham followed his mentor to Washington to serve two terms as a clerk, for Frankfurter as well as for Justice Stanley Reed. He had been red-shirted (to use a modern expression from athletics and given an additional year of eligibility) with Reed and played out his senior clerkship with Frankfurter.

He met Katherine Meyer at a party, and after a short romance they were married. Eugene Meyer also fell in love with Graham and pursued him until the young man agreed to take over the *Washington Post* and do what Eugene Meyer could not do—turn it into a great newspaper.

Philip Graham assumed a major role at the *Post* after his return from service in World War II. He ascended the throne of publisher in the early 1950s and set his sights on making the *Post* the number-one newspaper in the nation's number-two city. Along the way, the *Post* gobbled up the competition—the *Times Herald*—and began a long battle with the pre-eminent newspaper in the capital, the *Washington Star*.

Tom Wolfe was joining a newspaper, then, that was on its way up. In 1959, when he was hired for the city staff, the *Post* was still decidedly the also-ran paper in a small southern city that happened to be the capital of the free world. The front pages were frequently devoted to a budget of robberies, rapes, car wrecks, and the usual carnalities of urban life. The *Post* was a surprisingly sloppy newspaper, with each page offering a new editing gaffe. Philip Graham may have been a charming man and a friend of presidents—John Kennedy and Lyndon Johnson were his buddies—but his newspaper had a long way to go to achieve greatness. It would be Katherine Graham, who became publisher after her husband's death, who would make it into a great institution of American journalism.

Tom Wolfe was hired just four years before Graham's suicide in August 1963. His four years' service at the *Springfield Union* was deemed adequate preparation for a career on the *Washington Post*'s city desk. Wolfe was 28—still young to be hired as a reporter by the *Post*, which rarely employed recent graduates—when the managing editor, Al Friendly, decided the young man would be a nice addition to the staff.

The *Post* editors came to realize, however, that they did not quite know what to make of the soft-spoken young Virginian with the skewed vision of the world and the mordant eye for detail. The *Post* historian Chalmers Roberts, himself a colleague of Wolfe's during his stint at the newspaper, said that the city editor Ben Gilbert "never knew what to do with Wolfe's offbeat talent."[4] Wolfe found himself frustrated, like a leashed animal: "A typical story would be nine inches, about 360 words," he told an interviewer. "Writing to that length was really bad for you, for your mind."[5] Another writer ably summed up Wolfe's frustration with the newspaper: "Every time he turned out something fresh and original, he found himself assigned to a story on sewerage in Prince Georges County."[6]

A case in point was Wolfe's "Dispensable Guide" series. After less than a year on the *Post* staff, Wolfe contributed a 12-part series that provided a mock Michelin Guide to the cities President Eisenhower was visiting overseas. For example, "The way to make a fortune in Rome, it is said, is to open a dim restaurant and tell 10 ladies from Dubuque the tourists have never heard of it. By nightfall, the stampede will be on."[7] Of Greece, Wolfe wrote: "The great lover, poet and swimmer, Lord Byron, went to Greece in 1824 and drove himself to death in behalf of Greek independence from Turkey, and in Athens today, an Englishman can still cash a check on the good will he created."[8] And, of course, Wolfe took dead aim at the French: "One of the endearing things about the French is their belief that the world is divided into two manners of men: Parisians and peasants."[9]

Wolfe was also occasionally given a full page in a Sunday feature section for a long satirical piece illustrated with his drawings—remarkable for the newspaper in that time. The most impressive thing about the *Post* during Wolfe's years there was its ordinariness, yet Wolfe was sometimes given the license and the space to produce work whose appearance in a newspaper of that era was astonishing. It would be hard to find another American newspaper that would have published the "Dispensable

Guide" series or allowed a reporter to refer to the leader of the planet's largest nation as "Nicky" Khrushchev.[10]

Part of Wolfe's problem with the *Post* was that he did not hold the values traditionally shared by the other reporters. Covering a vital government meeting, making a foreign trip, these were seen by his colleagues as plum assignments. Wolfe seemed to enjoy turning ordinary stories into extraordinary features. At that time, a "feature" was on the lower rungs of the newspaper food chain. Writers were supposed to aspire to national stories on the front page. Even after an assignment in Cuba, Wolfe had not learned that lesson:

> [The city editor] sent me out to Oxon Hill because there was an escaped ape going down the phone wires hand over hand. Somebody in the neighborhood turned out to have a female ape to tempt it down with. It turned out there were people will all kinds of pets out there, apes, carnivorous fish . . . one family owned a tapir . . . a great ungainly thing. . . . I began to get fascinated with the bizarre things that cropped up with the new affluence. When I came back from Cuba, they asked me what I'd like to do next, and I said I'd like more ape stories.[11]

Instead of more ape stories, Wolfe was assigned to cover more mundane events. Wolfe might have flowered at the *Post*—his stylistic gestation might not have waited until after he left the newspaper—had the editors not thrown so many routine assignments his way. But having served up news stories of all varieties at the *Union*, Wolfe found that stories on the routine carnalities of city life (burglaries, house fires, assaults) did not hold his interest. Within ten days of the last installment in the "Dispensable Guide" series, Wolfe published a story headlined "Jaycees Tonight Pick 1959 Men of the Year."[12]

Chalmers Roberts speculates that, had Wolfe arrived at the newspaper a decade later, he would have been better understood by the editors. By that time, Ben Bradlee had become executive editor and collected a staff of all-stars, many of whom sought to emulate Wolfe's style. But the newspaper during Wolfe's tenure was, in Roberts's view, much too stuffy, serious, and old-fashioned to accept Wolfe's innovations. Although his talent was recognized, Roberts said, Wolfe was a "lonely rebel" at the newspaper.[13]

Though Wolfe's portfolio from the *Post* contains the usual assortment of reports on speeches, meetings, and random acts of violence, it also contains some splendid writing not often seen in newspapers of that era. Wolfe's features, as well as the sketches he convinced his bewildered editors to publish, show that the *Post* editors recognized his wit even if he was not always understood. His work at the *Post* also gave him a collection of articles that would later impress the editors of better newspapers.

Wolfe's tenure at the newspaper was not without note. He won Washington Newspaper Guild Awards in 1961 for foreign reporting and for humor, but they were apparently not enough to alter his decision to leave. Not long after Wolfe finally quit the *Post* in 1962, a friend from Springfield had earned a tryout at the paper. She wrote to Wolfe, asking what he thought of the place after his three-year stint. "The whole place is crackers," Wolfe wrote back.[14] Some of the puzzled *Post* staffers he left behind in Washington might have said similar things about their eccentrically dressed colleague.

The *New York Herald-Tribune*

After only a five-year apprenticeship at the *Union* and the *Post*, Wolfe realized he was fortunate to land, in 1962, in the city room of the nation's premier writer's paper, the *New York Herald-Tribune*. He was suddenly swimming in a talent pool that included some of the best and brightest journalists of his generation. Wolfe stood out at first for his dandified appearance, though he was not the first spiffy dresser to grace the halls of the *Herald-Tribune*. His newsroom contemporary Richard Kluger recalled: "The most exotic figure among the gifted newcomers to the *Tribune* city room was the trim, six-foot, white-suited frame of Thomas Kennerly Wolfe, Jr., whose modish like has not been seen there since the departure of the exquisitely got-up Lucius Beebe a dozen years earlier. . . . Wolfe was a certified intellectual."

He soon came to appreciate the freedom the *Herald-Tribune* offered. On his first assignment, Wolfe asked his supervising editor how long the story should be. The city editor—in Wolfe's description—looked at him as if he were crazy. "What do you mean how long do I want it?" the editor said. Wolfe elaborated: "Do you want six [para]graphs? Ten graphs?" The city editor snorted, "Just stop when it gets boring."[15]

Wolfe soon connected with Clay Felker, editor of the newspaper's Sunday magazine, *New York*, and it was an association that would greatly benefit both parties. Felker was from a journalism family. His father edited the *Sporting News* in St. Louis, the definitive journal of baseball. Felker had matriculated at Duke, then worked feverishly at *Esquire*. After losing out in a power struggle for editorial control of the magazine, he moved on to the *Herald-Tribune*. As redefined by Felker, the Sunday

New York supplement had an independence of design, content, and vision that created an identity that would outlast the ill-fated newspaper. Felker saw himself as a social geographer and wanted his publication to define the changing nature of popular culture. He gave his writers a broad license to go forth and "record it all."

It was a journalistic marriage made in heaven. Felker offered Wolfe the freedom he had lacked in the city rooms of traditional daily newspaper journalism, and Wolfe thrived. Felker encouraged experimentation; as Wolfe was fond of stating, "There are really no traditions in journalism worth observing."[16] Wolfe's stylistic breakthrough may have come in the pages of *Esquire*, but his refutation of journalistic conventions began with Felker's *New York*. As Wolfe described the "secret" of his writing style at that point, "I simply learned not to censor out the things that run through my mind as I write."[17]

Wolfe's *New York* breakthrough may have been his 1964 piece titled "The Girl of the Year" (collected in *The Kandy-Kolored Tangerine-Flake Streamline Baby*), an article devoted to "Baby" Jane Holzer, a socialite and underground film actress who was enjoying a season of celebrity. It was not a "story" in the old definition of journalism. It had no handle, no hook, in fact none of the usual accoutrements of the craft. Yet to Wolfe, who saw the world as a "weenie roast," the subject matter was fair game.[18]

Wolfe spent little time laboring as a traditional reporter at the *Herald-Tribune*. The newspaper recognized his abilities and granted him the license that previous newspapers, perhaps under the oppressive weight of deadlines and limited staffs, had been unable to give him. Though he was nominally still working for a newspaper—and would occasionally write articles especially for newspapers (often on the opinion pages)—his association with Felker and *New York* and his simultaneous pairing with the editor Harold Hayes and the managing editor Byron Dobell at *Esquire* signaled the end of his reporting days. From that point on, he would be a magazine writer and an author of books.

Tom Wolfe's influence was about to explode beyond the limited scope of the newspaper's readership and would make him a national figure. That was the period, Wolfe once said, when he believed he actually became what he had always wanted to be—a writer.[19] To his chagrin, Wolfe not only had become a writer but was seen as the leader of a whole new literary movement, a style to become known as the New Journalism.

Chapter Three

Pandemonium with a Big Grin

Tom Wolfe's arrival in New York journalism in 1962 was fortuitous. New York is historically one of the places where American craziness first takes root. (The other place, of course, is California—which also looms large in Wolfe's writing.) Wolfe's presence in New York during the craziest of twentieth-century decades is a sign of divine intervention. His record of that era—which he once described as "pandemonium with a big grin"—will give historians a more accurate picture of life in America during the 1960s than could ever be gleaned from the "totem" accounts of more traditional newspaper drudges. Recording the oddball nature of the era was a vital part of Wolfe's mission. "I was always just the humble chronicler, just the secretary taking notes," he has said.[1]

Totem is the word Wolfe employed to describe a journalism that does not illuminate or serve but merely exists. "A totem newspaper," Wolfe wrote, "is the kind of newspaper that people don't really buy to read, but just to *have*, physically, because they know it supports their own outlook on life."[2] Indeed, Tom Wolfe's innovative journalism may eventually have redefined the craft, but in his own eyes he was merely another laborer on a somnambulistic newspaper until he saw the work of Gay Talese.

Talese, a reporter for the *New York Times*, was also a frequent contributor to *Esquire*. After Wolfe read Talese's July 1962 profile of the boxer Joe Louis, he decided that he, too, would try something adventurous. Wolfe's whimsy, wordplay, and distinctive humor are sprinkled throughout his portfolio of writing for the *Union*, the *Post*, and the *Herald-Tribune*. Yet he alternately wrote the sort of journalism that H. L. Mencken called the "familiar series of rubber stamps instantly recognized by the generality of dolts, though not always understood."[3] Contained in Mencken's aside is the journalist's classic condescension toward and distrust of the reading public. Wolfe *could* rubber-stamp stories, providing fill-in-the-blank, cookie-cutter articles for the mouth-breathing masses.

Yet he chose not to underestimate his audience. Filled with admiration for Talese and bursting with a sort of missionary zeal, Wolfe decided to take readers along on a mission into uncharted journalistic territory. Although he always claimed he had nothing particularly radical in mind, he nevertheless used the bully pulpit of the *Herald-Tribune*—revered in American journalism as the "newspaper of the stars" (star writers, that is, who were allowed space and freedom to fertilize their prose)—to begin to carve out his unique vision of American life.

It was a "totem" assignment that led to his breakthrough. Wolfe wrote a rubber-stamp story about car customizers. Those engaged in debauching the American automobile were, to Wolfe, the sort of crazies that consumers of totem newspapers liked to read about, nutcakes who messed up those marvels of technology, kooks, loonies. Read a few paragraphs, chuckle, turn the page snorting, "I tell you, Martha, it's a crazy world." Yet when Wolfe went to cover the Hot Rod and Custom Car Show at a New York exhibition hall in 1962, he thought he was gazing into a new abyss of national culture. He turned out the requisite feature the newspaper expected but saw something larger as he spoke to the "kooks" about what they did. He provided readers with the examples they wanted of people on the fringe, yet he presented his subjects not as weirdos but as people busily redefining society. To him, the car show was not a freak parade, although he may have displayed it that way for the newspaper readers. He saw it as a harbinger of a changing culture. Wolfe said the *Herald-Tribune* was the only newspaper in town willing to break away from the totem formula, but he nonetheless gave the newspaper the stock story. He thought he needed even more freedom to do the sort of writing he had in mind.

So he decided to draw water from Talese's well. Wolfe talked to *Esquire*'s managing editor, Byron Dobell, about the phenomenon of custom cars, suggesting that it would write up into the sort of piece the magazine might like. Wolfe's sources had told him the real action in car customizing was in California. Dobell, who respected Wolfe's work on the *Herald-Tribune*, agreed to finance a mission to the Golden State and committed the magazine to a story on what Wolfe found there.

Writing the story, however, proved to be living hell for Wolfe. He expected a Breakthrough. He thought Absolute Truth would appear when he returned to New York and sat down at the typewriter. The magazine was ready to go. A two-page spread, with a spectacular color photograph, was laid out. The editors called to check on the progress of the story. It's coming, Wolfe told them, though the paper was blank. Days passed. Weeks. Finally, Wolfe confessed: he could not write the story.

Dobell controlled himself. Nothing would be gained by rage or a dressing-down. Fine. He told Wolfe to type up his notes and send them over. Someone else would write the piece. So that night, Wolfe sat down at the typewriter and began writing his memo. "Dear Byron," he started, followed by a moment-by-moment description of the time he spent in the California custom-car subculture. He recorded everything he could remember, paying little attention to style, since this memo was not for publication. But he wrote with frenzy and energy—there was deadline pressure after all, and some other writer was going to wallow in the *Esquire* byline glory that should have been his.

But after a while, Wolfe recognized that something was happening. He had begun his memo in the early evening, and by midnight he had written 20 single-spaced pages and was not slowing down. As he wrote, he listened to WABC—a 24-hour rock-and-roll station—and felt invigorated by the music's manic energy. He continued writing all night, finally finishing his memo a little after six in the morning. It ran 49 pages.

He dropped off the memo at *Esquire* and, although weary from his all-nighter, felt exultant as he went to work at the *Herald-Tribune*. Late in the afternoon, Byron Dobell called. He told Wolfe he had crossed out "Dear Byron" and was having the rest of the memo typeset for the next issue of *Esquire*, under Wolfe's byline. The byline read, in fact, "Thomas K. Wolfe," to distinguish him from the fabled, long-dead, required-reading-for-Lit-101 Thomas Wolfe. "That turned out to be an excess of caution on *Esquire*'s part," the magazine's editors wrote in a reminiscence. "The style of the piece established Wolfe as a unique presence in American journalism."[4]

The piece, titled "There Goes (Varoom! Varoom!) That Kandy-Kolored Tangerine-Flake Streamline Baby around the Bend" when it appeared in *Esquire* in 1963, was an immediate sensation. Reader reaction ranged from outraged (as Wolfe would say, "What inna namea christ is this?") to puzzled, to fascinated. The division between his readers was established from the start: Wolfe's admirers and Wolfe's detractors.

Over at the *Herald-Tribune* Sunday supplement, Clay Felker realized he needed to take advantage of his staff writer's newly recognized talent. Supported by the twin markets of *Esquire* and Felker's *New York*, as well as occasional assignments for the daily *Herald-Tribune*, Wolfe set to work chronicling American madness in the 1960s.

Wolfe may not have produced the definitive account of the Kennedy inauguration (though he did a number of preliminary stories for the *Washington Post*), and we do not have his pronouncements on the national mourning for the president. But many other events of American popular culture are preserved in stories by Wolfe. His subjects naturally included the new tastemakers, the beneficiaries of a growing leisure class and a culture that allowed young people a freedom previous generations could only have imagined. Wolfe was fascinated by this new breed of teenager. The arrival of the Beatles in New York in 1964 was a defining moment for a generation (bookending the tragedy of the president's assassination). Wolfe was at the newly named Kennedy International Airport for the arrival of the lovable mop-tops on 5 February 1964 and provided a front-page account for the *Herald-Tribune*.

Although the Beatles piece was not included in Wolfe's first book, it nonetheless had a long shelf life, and few books about the Beatles have resisted the temptation to quote from it. In the frenzy of the group's arrival, John Lennon, Paul McCartney, George Harrison, and Ringo Starr were seen by most other observers as interchangeable young men, with ridiculous hair and outrageous accents, whose primary function was to provide comic relief, so desperately needed after Kennedy's murder. Wolfe, however, sensed that this group was different and that their invasion of America signified a sea change in youth culture.

The Beatles story—devoted to the first 24 hours the group spent in America—employs some familiar Wolfe characterizations of youths (the phrase "transistors plugged into their skulls" recurs in many of his early 1960s pieces) and uses as its starting point the notion that the members of the band were lookalikes. But the article concentrates its frenetic energy on helping readers to know the differences between the mop-tops:

> The Beatles . . . are all short, slight kids from Liverpool who wear four-button coats, stovepipe pants, ankle-high black boots with Cuban heels. And droll looks on their faces. . . .
>
> A good-looking brunette, who said her name was Caroline Reynolds of New Canaan, Conn., and Wellesley College had paid a cab driver $10 to follow the [Beatle limousine] caravan all the way into town [from the airport]. She cruised by each Beatle, smiling faintly, and finally caught up with George Harrison's limousine at a light at Third Ave. and 63rd St.
>
> "How does one go about meeting a Beatle?" she said out the window.
>
> "One says hello," Harrison said out the window.[5]

Tom Wolfe's subject has always been popular culture ("with a capital *C*," as he once told an interviewer[6]), but forays into popular music allowed him to focus a good deal of his attention on youth. His article on Phil Spector—the young record producer who made the transatlantic crossing with the Beatles and presided over their final album release in 1970—was, for Wolfe, a significant breakthrough. The Spector piece, "The First Tycoon of Teen" (it appeared originally in the *Herald-Tribune* and was part of the *Kandy-Kolored Tangerine-Flake Streamline Baby* collection), marked Wolfe's first use of what would become one of his more controversial techniques.

As Wolfe recalled, "That piece I did on Phil Spector . . . was the first time I ever actually went inside of somebody else's mind. It is one thing to do an interior monologue in your own mind. It's something else to do one in someone else's mind."[7] It was dangerous territory for journalism. Wolfe witnessed Spector's paranoia in full bloom as the producer, terrified by an airplane's takeoff, forced the pilot to stop taxiing and let him off. Wolfe said he did not ask Spector what had been going through his mind as he fearfully worried about the possibilities of a plane crash. Wolfe frankly admitted he had projected himself into the situation.[8] Wolfe's critics jumped on the story as an example of his tendency to fabricate, but when they confronted Spector, he confirmed what Wolfe had written. The thoughts Wolfe had supplied for him in the story were essentially his own.

Phil Spector was, and is, one of rock and roll's more eccentric characters. In a field known for oddballs, Spector reigns supreme. During his marriage to the singer Veronica Bennett, for example, Spector would not allow her to leave the house alone unless there was an inflatable Phil doll on the car seat next to her, to ward off potential suitors. His antics in the recording studio were legendary. A deeply superstitious man, he "retired" first at age 26 when his masterpiece, Ike and Tina Turner's "River Deep, Mountain High," failed to reach number one on the charts.

The media largely mocked Spector for his weirdness, but Wolfe saw him as a representative of the new culture and those who would shape the future. Spector was a millionaire at 21, a successful record producer, a best-selling songwriter, and the owner of a recording company. To Wolfe, Spector was not merely an amusing young man, he was a Cecil B. DeMille for a new era.

In the Spector piece, Wolfe experimented with a number of devices. There is the opening interior monologue, as the young tycoon studies the world through the rain-streaked windows of a jet awaiting takeoff.

From that point, Wolfe launches into a long passage comprising mostly dialogue—showing that Wolfe understood Gay Talese's lesson about the power of dialogue to move a story along. Finally, there is the most conventional part of the matrix: standard, historical narration, not much different from the sort of workmanlike prose that might be found in any totem newspaper.

But the Spector piece was another step out onto the thin ice of journalistic innovation. For Wolfe, the mere fact that the critics' feathers were ruffled by the opening ramble through Spector's disjointed mind was reason enough to consider the piece a triumph. His rendering of the show-biz slang of Spector's entourage also showed that he had a talented ear for the slightest nuance of dialogue. He discovered that he could enliven even the historical narration that provides routine biographical background by inserting occasional exclamations: "Making money. Yes! At the age of seventeen, Phil wrote a rock and roll song called 'To Know Him Is to Love Him.' He took the title off his father's tombstone." He continues his summary of Spector's résumé: "Then he was going to UCLA, but he couldn't afford it and became a court reporter, one of the people who sit at the shorthand machine. . . . He decided to come to New York and get a job as an interpreter at the UN. . . . The night before the interview, he fell in with some musicians and never got there. . . . He wrote another hit that year, 'Spanish Harlem.' *There is a rose in Spanish Harlem.*"[9]

Wolfe followed the basic concept and structure of the totem form, yet at the same time he satirized it with his asides, exclamations, and insertions. It was as if he used the form only to rub the noses of totem-conditioned readers in it, to show new ways of covering the same terrain.

His profile of another pop music figure, the New York disk jockey Murray Kaufman (known on the air as "Murray the K"), allowed Wolfe to explore further the possibilities of dialogue. "The Fifth Beatle," like "The First Tycoon of Teen," appeared first in *New York*, which was now sharing Wolfe with *Esquire* and giving him major magazine–style freedom. Kaufman had, through a process Wolfe describes in near-scientific detail, ingratiated himself with the British group immediately upon their arrival in America. In the brutal world of New York radio, access to the Beatles meant everything. Wolfe showed how Murray the K got that access and maintained it, much to the irritation of other disk jockeys, the reporters trying unsuccessfully to get close to the group, and sometimes to the Beatles themselves. Nevertheless, Wolfe used the occasion to show how an opportunistic disk jockey could—literally overnight—make himself into one of the new elite of the crazy modern culture. In the old status system, Kaufman, the sort of character you did not shake hands with unless wearing gloves, would have been shunned. Yet under the new rules, Murray the K, by sheer force of his maddening will, could make himself into a cultural power broker.

A characteristic of Wolfe's early 1960s writing is apparent in the Spector and Kaufman profiles: like Talese, he is a genius at the examination of character and allows his subjects to reveal themselves through the words tumbling from their mouths. In the article, as the individual Beatles speak, Murray the K, responding like a one-man g(r)eek chorus, shouts the same refrain to each with the appropriate Beatle name substituted: "You're what's happening, Ringo!" "You're what's happening, Paul Baby!"[10] Kaufman assumes the role, in his own profile, of an instant hack phrasemaker.

Again Wolfe offers the exposition that is nearly antiexposition, inserting conspiratorial put-downs that draw the line between the old culture and the new. Immersed in the world of New York disk jockeys, Wolfe denigrates the music that was the rage a mere decade before: "Jazz, especially jazz as played by people like Miles Davis and Thelonious Monk, is considered a hopelessly bourgeois taste, the kind you might expect from a Williams College boy with a lie-down crewcut on a big weekend in New York."[11]

Before, a writer indulging in such a derogatory comment might have made a blanket reference to "squares." Wolfe's tactic, on the other hand, was to create a specific object of derision. It would become one of his trademarks. Here is another example, the target this time being the elderly patrons of a Las Vegas casino: "Some of [the women] pack their hummocky old shanks into Capri pants, but many of them just put on the old print dress, the same one day after day, and the old hob-heeled shoes, looking like they might be going out to buy eggs in Tupelo, Mississippi."[12] In his profile "The Girl of the Year," devoted to the socialite and underground film star "Baby" Jane Holzer, Wolfe describes the scene in a theater as the young-adult progeny of New York's old culture await the arrival of the Rolling Stones: "The little buds are batting around in the rococo gloom of the Academy of Arts Theater, trying to crash into good seats or just sit in the aisle near the stage, shrieking. And in the rear the Voice of Fifteen-year-old America cries out in a post-pubertal contralto, apropos of nothing, into the mouldering void: 'Yaaaagh! Yuh dirty fag!'"[13]

Wolfe fared best when chronicling characters—Phil Spector, Murray the K, the Beatles, Baby Jane Holzer—and less well when his concept was larger and more unfocused, such as Las Vegas. In the celebrated Las Vegas piece, one of Wolfe's early "hits," the most interesting character is an artist at defining this new culture: Benjamin "Bugsy" Siegel, the long-dead godfather of the Nevada town. Wolfe's piece offers many random snapshots of Vegas oddities, but he handles the historical background with great skill.

Another "place" article, Wolfe's account of his trip to the Peppermint Lounge, one of New York's famous night spots, falls flat. There are many brief encounters, but no focus. It is a story in search of a character. Wolfe seemed to know his greatest talent: following individuals around, recording their thoughts and actions, and watching others watch them. Spector and Kaufman were particularly good subjects.

The Kandy-Kolored Tangerine-Flake Streamline Baby contains many of Wolfe's early pieces: the profiles of Murray the K, Phil Spector, and Jane Holzer and some of his mood pieces, including the one on Las Vegas and another on the child-rearing habits of the rich and famous. There are a few sketches—an exercise in dialogue called "Voices of Village Square" and a short comic article titled "Why Doormen Hate Volkswagens." In addition to the 22 articles (a miscellany of profiles and mood pieces), the book provides a portfolio of Wolfe's drawings, some of which had first appeared in print back in his Springfield days. Wolfe compartmentalized the articles into sections with titles like "The New Culture-Makers" and "Status Strife and the High Life," and in his introduction he tied the pieces together with ruminations on the theme of status, a theme that came to him, he said, like a light bulb over the head of a cartoon character. As he madly typed his memo for that first *Esquire* assignment, he finally *saw* what he had *seen*:

> The details themselves, when I wrote them down, suddenly made me see what was happening. Here was this incredible combination of form plus money [at the custom-car show] in a place nobody ever thought about finding it, namely, among teen-agers. . . .
>
> Suddenly, classes of people whose styles of life had been practically invisible had the money to build monuments to their own styles.[14]

In the centerpiece of the book, "The Last American Hero," he returns to the automobile world that had started him on his frenzied tear through the world of America's new culture only 18 months before at the custom-car show, when his vision of change revealed itself to him. In "The Last American Hero," Wolfe is back on the East Coast, deep in the Carolina woods on a baked asphalt racetrack, immersed in the subculture of stock-car racing. Originally titled "Junior Johnson Is the Last American Hero. Yes!" when it appeared in *Esquire*, it is the most thoroughly realized work in the book.

Although not a rock-and-roll star or a national celebrity, the stock-car driver Junior Johnson was precisely the sort of prism Wolfe wanted through which to reveal his vision of the new culture. Wolfe adopts, even in the expository sections of the work, "the tone of the character"—in other words, the piece is written in Johnson's voice, even when he is not "speaking." The intricate details of the internal combustion engine, for example, are offered in a guttural Carolina drawl, punctuated with occasional snorts and laughs.

Of course, Wolfe had a larger purpose in "The Last American Hero" than merely chronicling the hero of the stock-car subculture. He used Johnson as a symbol of the drastic change the automobile had brought to American society since the end of World War II. "The car symbolized freedom, a slightly wild, careening emancipation from the old social order."[15] The new stock-car fans embodied a threat to the long-established American aristocracy because the car itself had served as an equalizing force for the class system. "Stock car racing was something welling up out of the lower orders."[16] As if to punctuate the message, Wolfe inserts a "Yes!" at appropriate moments in the story, serving, like "Amen!" in southern Baptist usage, as a sign of affirmation.

On the surface, "The Last American Hero" is an exciting tale of a moonshiner-turned-millionaire race-car driver. (In fact, this cinematic piece was made into a film in 1973.) But the Johnson story is also a vehicle of another sort: a view of the new order, a world upside down. As Wolfe said, the "disturbing message" to readers is that "Junior Johnson's racecar fortunes were more important than Lyndon Johnson's electoral fortunes," that "the aristocracy was finished," and that Americans cared not so much for the elite and the old social order as for "me and myself."[17]

The expression "good old boy," which Wolfe is credited with introducing into modern American parlance in the Junior Johnson story, was one he used to provide a glimpse into the relatively unexplored status structure that had been ignored by mainstream media:

> "Good old boy" is really a status denomination. It's a southern term. Good old boys are historically white males of a certain class—below the bachelor's-degree line in America—who share certain values that have built up in the South for the conduct of males. A good old boy is not try-

ing to get ahead or keep up with anybody next door. He just wants to be a good old boy. . . .

Maybe the height of the good old boy's aspiration might be the 12-gauge in the back window of the pickup truck, if you call that reaching high in the social "status-sphere."[18]

The two-part dissection of the *New Yorker* was written too late for inclusion in the book and is conspicuous by its absence in later collections. His article on the Beatles' arrival was probably seen as disposable at the time, though it has since become one of his most frequently cited pieces.

Although its contents are wide-ranging, Wolfe's first collection had a unifying theme: status. *The Kandy-Kolored Tangerine-Flake Streamline Baby* was to be the first in his series of explorations of that concept. When the book was published in June 1965, several critics were impressed by Wolfe's ability to make sense of the chaos he had so accurately recorded. As Kurt Vonnegut wrote, Wolfe "has a Ph.D. in American studies from Yale and he knows everything. I do not mean he *thinks* he knows everything. . . . He is loaded with facile junk." Vonnegut applauded Wolfe's decision to cast himself as a teenager in his appearances in the pieces and agreed with the author that teenage culture had become dominant. Vonnegut's influential review, which ran in the *New York Times Book Review*, was also extravagant in its praise. He called the book "excellent" and its author "a genius who will do anything to get attention."[19]

Newsweek's review was more concerned with Wolfe's method of chronicling the madness and focused on his explanatory preface and his account of the horrifying *Esquire* deadline, which had led him to leave the "system of ideas" and leap into the gaping void of pop culture, where he wallowed gloriously. The anonymous reviewer concluded that Wolfe belonged to "the old noble breed of poet-journalists, like Ben Hecht, and partly he belongs to a new breed of supereducated hip sensibilities like Jonathan Miller and Terry Southern, who see the complete human comedy in everything."[20]

Not all critics were so generous with their praise. Emile Capouya in the *Saturday Review* found Wolfe long-winded and his penchant for persistently punchy punctuation irritating. Capouya recognized "The Last American Hero" as the book's strongest piece but said it should have been cut by half. That Wolfe made the drawings in the "Metropolitan Sketchbook" was bad enough, Capouya wrote. That he *published* them in his book was salt in the literary wound. To Capouya, Wolfe had commit-

ted the ultimate sin of boring the reader. The review concluded: "One
wants to say to Mr. Wolfe: You're so clever, you can talk so well, tell us
something interesting."[21]

Critical reaction to Wolfe's first book was largely favorable, but a division was apparent: some reviewers deeply admired the book, others
found it immature and incomprehensible. That pattern would be repeat-
ed with the publication of many of Wolfe's later works: he divides the
camps. His work demands one extreme reaction or another. There has
been little middle ground in the reaction to the books of Tom Wolfe.

Chapter Four
The New Journalists

Whether he wanted to or not, Tom Wolfe served a dual role in the New Journalism movement of the 1960s: he was at once its most celebrated and prolific practitioner and its reluctant historian. Wolfe made no great claims for his experiments in prose when he began attracting notice in the early 1960s, and he certainly would not have professed to have originated anything—and if he had, he certainly wouldn't have called it *that*.

Wolfe recalled first hearing noises about something called "new journalism" around the middle of 1965, and he cringed when he heard the phrase. Anything tagged "new," he thought, was doomed to failure. Yet not only did the term catch on, it also became capitalized, and nearly a decade later, when Wolfe made an anthology of the hybrid form, he called it *The New Journalism* (1973).[1] As it turned out, Wolfe's scholarly training had not been for naught: he acquitted himself, as essayist and anthologist, with a book that is both a history of a literary movement and a selection of some of the best work in the genre. Unfortunately, Wolfe had no interest in updating what became a textbook,[2] and it was allowed to quietly go out of print in the 1980s, just as the phrase "New Journalism" itself became another discarded 1960s relic and was replaced by the less trendy "literary journalism."

To understand the impact of Wolfe and others in the 1960s, and to appreciate where Wolfe's early writing fits into the scheme of 1960s New Journalism, it is necessary to consider the other writers exploding on the scene at that time. The major characters, after Wolfe, are Gay Talese, Truman Capote, Norman Mailer, Joan Didion, and Hunter S. Thompson. Jimmy Breslin and George Plimpton also played a part. Although the New Journalism superstars were relatively few in number, there was little unanimity among them; they were no league of writers conspiring to commit journalistic revolution. Capote and Plimpton were bona fide members of the literary establishment—an establishment already inflamed over Wolfe and his "bastard form" and seething over his two-part series on the *New Yorker*, which *New York* published in the spring of 1965. Criticism rained down on Wolfe like burning debris that year, yet he was in the middle of a revolution in nonfiction writing. The

major players were not all associates, and some even professed extreme
dislike for others among them. Nevertheless, this small but disparate
group was redrawing the lines in the literary turf wars. To understand
Wolfe's role in the literary journalism revolution, it is necessary to discuss
these fellow revolutionaries.

Colleagues

In the essays in *The New Journalism* and in the introduction to *The Kandy-
Kolored Tangerine-Flake Streamline Baby*—as well as in his frequent speeches on the subject—Wolfe was not falsely modest when he described his
own role in shaking up both the journalism and literary establishments,
but he was also always lavish with praise of the other writers who experimented with the form. His anthology, published almost exactly ten
years after all the fuss began, was a way to draw more attention to others, and he included only two pieces of his own—excerpts from *The
Electric Kool-Aid Acid Test* and *Radical Chic and Mau-Mauing the Flak
Catchers*.

Wolfe turned journalism historian with the publication of articles on
the literary aspects of the craft in *New York* and *Esquire* in 1972. From
the pulpit of these four pieces, sewn together for his text in *The New
Journalism*, he railed against the fiction writers whose self-indulgence had
lost fiction its audience and forfeited its role as the preeminent form in
American letters. Although he cited many nineteenth-century examples
of what was mistakenly known as "new journalism," Wolfe said the form
came to the forefront in the 1960s because modern novelists had
eschewed realism in favor of an inner-circle contest to see who in the
pipe-puffing set could prove to be most literary.

Charles Dickens, James Boswell, Honoré de Balzac, and William
Makepeace Thackeray were among Wolfe's idols and provided models
for the foolishly named New Journalism. Wolfe was fond of citing
Dickens's *Sketches by Boz* (1836) as an example of a writer using fictional
techniques to tell true stories.[3] To Wolfe, there was nothing at all new
about New Journalism. These journalists, these proles, were merely
scooping up what the novelists had discarded, the tricks of the trade.

The four techniques were simple, road-tested devices available to any
writer willing to defy fashion.[4] The basic one, according to Wolfe, was
scene-by-scene construction. Rather than rely on historical narrative,
New Journalists told a story by moving from scene to scene. The con-
straints of daily journalism seldom allowed the intense periods of obser-

vation needed to construct such episodes. The historical literary model was, of course, James Boswell. He had observed Samuel Johnson at close hand for two decades in order to write the *Life of Samuel Johnson* (1791). Gay Talese's work was Wolfe's favorite example of this device. Talese was known for hanging out with his celebrity subjects rather than sitting down for formal interviews. He did not have the opportunity to hang out with anyone for 20 years, as Boswell had done, but he certainly employed the same device.

The master of the second device was Charles Dickens. The New Journalists realized that one of the brilliant methods Dickens and his contemporaries used to reveal character was extensive dialogue. Dickens showed readers the nature of Uriah Heep, the slimy, sneaky pariah of *David Copperfield* (1849–50), without putting much effort into physical description. With a finely tuned ear, Dickens conveyed much about Heep through reproducing his speech. This great tool adopted by the New Journalists was certainly reader-friendly as well: the frequent indentations for quotes surrounded the stories with a lot of easygoing white space and made the gray columns of type far less menacing.

The third device was third-person point of view. Novelists had the luxury of putting themselves inside the minds of their characters to show readers what they were thinking. This tool was not off-limits to New Journalists, Wolfe said. It simply required that writers ask better questions. Truman Capote did this in *In Cold Blood* by carefully reconstructing a murder through the eyes of two killers, then continually asking them what they were thinking as they committed their horrible crime. Critics lambasted New Journalists for using this technique, but Wolfe, Capote, and others suggested that careful reporting ensured its correct use.

The final device was what Wolfe called status-life details—the background colors, noises, tastes, and so on, that generations of newspaper copy editors had excised from writers' stories as superfluous. Not so, Wolfe claimed. The inclusion of details like hair styles, brand names, gestures, habits, and mannerisms gave stories the voice of authority. Too often journalism engaged readers on only one plane. This technique allowed writers to engage other senses (taste, smell, hearing), carefully selecting ambient particulars. Reviewers referred to the techniques Wolfe and the others used as "aural," that is, intended to enable readers to come as close as possible to experiencing events firsthand.

One of the more modern antecedents for the writing that exploded in the 1960s was John Hersey's 1946 book *Hiroshima*. Hersey, a Yale graduate and writer for the *Time* magazine machine, broke from the dictatorial confines of Henry Luce's publishing empire after the war when he visited the decimated Japanese city after the atomic bomb was dropped and wrote about the weapon's effects on eight residents of Hiroshima. Hersey did not even attempt to publish the piece in *Time*. To Henry Luce—and therefore to Time, Inc.—the bomb symbolized American superiority and technological genius. To Hersey, the bomb represented the most horrifying manifestation yet of technology's murderous potentialities. He wanted to take the abstract (faceless victims of the destruction) and make it concrete (eight people we come to know in the course of his book). Hersey, with the skills of a fine novelist, described what Toshiko Sasaki, a clerk in the East Asia Tin Works, was doing when the bomb was dropped:

> Just as she turned her head away from the windows, the room was filled with a blinding light. She was paralyzed by fear, fixed still in her chair for a long moment (the plant was 1,600 yards from the center [of the blast]).
> Everything fell, as Miss Sasaki lost consciousness. The ceiling dropped suddenly and the wooden floor above collapsed in splinters and the people up there came down and the roof above them gave way; but principally, and first of all, the bookcases right behind her swooped forward and the contents threw her down, with her left leg horribly twisted and breaking underneath her. There, in the tin factory, in the first moment of the atomic age, a human being was crushed by books.[5]

Hiroshima appeared first in the *New Yorker* and was, in fact, the entire editorial content of one issue. In book form, it became a perennial English-class text and steady seller. No one employed the term "new journalism" to describe it in 1946, but Hersey used all the techniques that were in vogue 20 years later; he wrote nonfiction as if it was fiction. Except for the fact that the scenes it describes were true, *Hiroshima* reads like a smartly done, darkly fascinating novella.

The *New Yorker* was a showplace for much of the writing that hindsight would characterize as New Journalism. In the 1960s *Esquire* became the premier showplace for innovative nonfiction. *New York* and, in the late 1960s and early 1970s, *Rolling Stone* played a part as well.

Gay Talese

So, there were many precedents before that momentous day in 1962 when Wolfe opened *Esquire* on his desk in the *Herald-Tribune* newsroom and beheld a story by Gay Talese, star reporter of the competing *New*

York Times, written about a real person as if he were a fictional character (see chapter 3). But Talese's role in inaugurating the New Journalism movement is never undervalued by Wolfe. Talese had the ability to transcend the confines of daily journalism and offer an original view of the world. For example:

> New York is a city of things unnoticed. . . . [It] is a city for eccentrics and a center for odd bits of information. New Yorkers blink 28 times a minute, but 40 when tense. Most popcorn chewers at Yankee Stadium stop chewing momentarily just before the pitch. Gum chewers on Macy's escalators stop chewing momentarily just before they get off—to concentrate on the last step. Coins, paper clips, ballpoint pens and little girls' pocketbooks are found by workmen when they clean the sea lions' pool at the Bronx Zoo.
>
> Each day New Yorkers guzzle 460,000 gallons of beer, swallow 3.5 million pounds of meat and pull 21 miles of dental floss through their teeth. Every day in New York about 250 people die, 460 are born and 150,000 walk through the city wearing eyes of glass or plastic.[6]

What Talese had learned to do with the standard totem feature article was to adopt the mood and tone of fiction. He offered the classic blueprint: he wrote nonfiction as if it were fiction. He advanced the story through a series of dramatic scenes, visualizing the piece as if he had created its characters, as if they were his to move about on a fictional stage. But his writing was not fiction. In the Joe Louis article and in a number of stunning and innovative *Esquire* profiles (of Joe DiMaggio, Frank Sinatra, and others), Talese showed an ability to adopt the fictional structure, using the timing and pacing of a good short-story writer. Talese, like any other ethical journalist, was bound by a commitment to truth. He could gather all of the information he needed only through hours upon hours of observation.

Talese was a model. His meticulousness was legendary in the field of journalism. He was known for creating a file folder for each interview he conducted. Even if he interviewed the same subject more than once, Talese created a folder for each session and included as much background as he could—notes about weather, clothing, food consumed—so that he could later re-create the experience more fully. He also eschewed pens and notebooks and would not even consider a tape recorder. He trained his mind so that he could produce stories rich in quotations so detailed that he was never challenged on points of accuracy. When he had finished a paragraph after agonizing over it for a day, Talese was known to post the manuscript page to a cork bulletin board and examine it through binoculars from across the room. His work habits were as distinctive as his prose.

Talese's *Esquire* profile of Frank Sinatra is perhaps the best example of his mastery of the New Journalism form.[7] He accumulated more than 200 neatly typed pages of notes, along with a $5,000 receipt for expenses.[8] The resulting article contained no interview with the singer, no one-on-one between Talese and the man known as "the Voice." Instead, Talese observed Sinatra as he tried to tape a television special while battling a cold, a disturbing set of circumstances for a singer. Readers learned more about Sinatra from the scenes related by Talese than they would have through an exchange of questions and answers, however, extensive. Talese made no judgments about the singer. He merely showed Sinatra, annoyed with his infirm voice, bullying those around him. Talese's literary idols were the brilliant *New Yorker* short-story writers John O'Hara and Irwin Shaw, and he tried to adapt their style to his personality profiles, keeping the narrator—himself—as invisible as his models had.[9]

Talese spent much of the 1960s crafting the magazine articles that embodied the best of New Journalism, and he later came to decry the decline in the quality of magazine journalism after he and Wolfe and the others began concentrating on longer projects. In Talese's case, he began studying American institutions—the *New York Times* in *The Kingdom and the Power* (1969), the Mafia in *Honor Thy Father* (1971), the sex industry in *Thy Neighbor's Wife* (1980), and the Italian-American experience in the nearly autobiographical *Unto the Sons* (1991)—and withdrew from the world of magazine article writing.[10] His works were painstakingly researched; never lapsing into the question-and-answer format, his interviews elicited the most intimate and richly detailed prose of all of the New Journalists. In *Thy Neighbor's Wife*, for example, he began with a recollection of a middle-aged man. The subject recalled, as a boy, buying a particular issue of a nudist magazine at a Chicago newsstand in the late 1940s. Through flashbacks of the boy's subterfuge at home to sneak the magazine up to his bedroom, the whole mosaic of his adolescent life is revealed. Finally, alone in bed with the magazine, he slowly masturbated to the image of a young woman reclining nude on a sand dune. In the subsequent chapter, Talese detailed the nude model's life, what had led her to that moment on the sand dune, posing in what was at the time a shocking picture. Talese's skill as a writer paralleled his ability to get his subjects—some of whom, like the *Playboy* magazine publisher Hugh

Hefner, were quite famous—to share the most intimate moments of their lives and tell about their first sexual experiences.

Talese inspired the great rush toward New Journalism in the early 1960s. Wolfe said Talese's *Esquire* articles were "so much better than what he was doing (or was allowed to do) for the *Times*."[11] Jimmy Breslin, Wolfe's colleague at the *Herald-Tribune*, was also experimenting with fiction techniques in the form of journalism. Breslin had labored facelessly in the vineyards of magazine freelancing until his book about the New York Mets' disastrous first season, *Can't Anybody Here Play This Game?*,[12] caught the eye of the *Herald-Tribune* publisher Jock Whitney. Whitney wanted to offset the "snoremongers" (Wolfe's term) on his newspaper's editorial page with a lively, more loosely defined column. In that era, the newspaper columnist was a character like Arthur Krock of the *Times* or Walter Lippmann of the *Herald-Tribune* who—in Wolfe's view—stepped back from doing the reporting that had given them stature and mulled over the reporting of other reporters, deciding "what it all meant." This sort of column made editorial pages a vast wasteland.

Breslin's column was different. It dealt, more often than not, with a news event. He worked with the city editor to find out what assignments were on the budget for reporters, and then he would go along with a reporter to the police station, the courthouse, the mayor's office—wherever the news was happening. Back at the office, the reporter would write a totem account of the event and Breslin would write one of his columns. He employed the techniques that Talese used on a larger scale in his *Esquire* pieces, often starting with a scene and allowing the dialogue to reveal character. In the space of a 500–600-word column, Breslin could speak volumes. The editors realized that his brilliance could easily be lost on the editorial pages, so Breslin's column often started on the front page.

Talese's experiments and the proximity of great talents such as Breslin and other *Herald-Tribune* writers (the sports reporter Dick Schaap and the author of *True Grit*, Charles Portis, among them) in the same newsroom inspired Wolfe to plunge into the game of being the best feature writer in town. Wolfe's frenetic style attracted a level of resentment to which Talese and Breslin appeared to be immune. Although Talese's writing rarely contained the verbal gymnastics Wolfe bounced through as a matter of course, the amount of detail in his articles and his rabid accumulation of raw material set Talese's work above that of the typical magazine writer. He worked well outside the conventions of everyday journalism.

Truman Capote

Despite the success of Wolfe and other practitioners of New Journalism, the literary establishment continued to disparage the style. Capote called his great work of journalism, *In Cold Blood*, a "nonfiction novel" so that the book would not be lumped in with Wolfe and company.[13] Other writers also attempted to keep their distance from the movement of which they were so obviously a part. The cumbersome subtitle of Norman Mailer's *The Armies of the Night* (1968) is *History as a Novel; The Novel as History*.[14] Mailer's *The Executioner's Song* was classified, at the author's request, as fiction, and the cover bears the legend "a true-life novel."[15] Despite the similarities of such works to New Journalism, the card-carrying literati were willing to call their nonfiction anything that did not include the term "journalism."

Capote's career with the *New Yorker* dated back to the 1940s, when he arrived in the city, a fresh-faced and precocious eccentric from New Orleans. Even though hired to run errands for the staff and open the mail, Capote soon insinuated himself into the role of de facto editor. While opening large manila envelopes of cartoons sent in by would-be contributors, Capote dropped the ones he didn't like down a narrow slot between his desk in the mailroom and the wall. He passed on to the editors only the cartoons of which he approved. Capote soon went on to acclaim as a writer with the publication of *Other Voices, Other Rooms* in 1948. For years cartoonists wrote irate letters to the magazine, inquiring about drawings that had never been returned. It was not until the mailroom desk was moved in the mid-1950s that the mystery of the disappearing cartoons was solved.[16]

By that time, Capote was a significant literary figure, known for his superb stories as well as for his short novels. But Capote's restlessness led him to nonfiction, and in 1955 he accepted an assignment from the *New Yorker* to accompany a troupe performing the Gershwin brothers' *Porgy and Bess*, with State Department sanction, behind the Iron Curtain. With a tremendous ear for unintentionally funny dialogue and a novelist's gift for selecting detail, Capote stayed out of the action and watched as the puzzled actors wondered why the great Gershwin tunes were getting no reaction from the Russian audiences. Finally, they realized the problem: since few in the audience spoke English, the performance was incomprehensible. Capote's account appeared first in the magazine and then in 1956 as the book *The Muses Are Heard*.[17]

The Muses Are Heard led him further away from his obvious career path toward a novelist's life. Capote's talent was too diverse and too restless to be confined. His *New Yorker* profile of the actor Marlon Brando ("The Duke in His Domain") showed his acute sense of personality. His slice-of-life pieces about the cities of his life, collected as *Local Color* (1950), showcased his powers of observation.[18] As the 1960s began, Capote found himself drawn to a story that would define the rest of his writing career and alter his life.

Four members of a Kansas farm family, the Clutters, were murdered in 1959, and the killers were still at large. To Capote and the *New Yorker* editor, William Shawn, the story of this multiple murder and its consequences provided the perfect vehicle for blending journalistic technique and literary style. "For several years," he wrote, "I had been increasingly drawn toward journalism as an art form in itself." The reason for Capote's attraction to journalism and his critique of modern letters sounded remarkably like Wolfe's:

> I had two reasons. First, it didn't seem to me that anything truly innovative had occurred in prose writing, or in writing generally, since the 1920s; second, journalism as an art was almost virgin terrain, for the simple reason that very few literary artists ever wrote narrative journalism, and when they did, it took the form of travel essays or autobiography. . . . I wanted to produce a journalistic novel, something on a large scale that would have the credibility of fact, the immediacy of film, the depth and freedom of prose, and the precision of poetry.[19]

With that lofty goal, Capote and two friends, Harper Lee (soon to become known for her novel *To Kill a Mockingbird* [1960])[20] and Jack Dunphy, journeyed to Holcomb, Kansas. They talked to the friends and neighbors of the Clutter family and insinuated themselves into the close circle of Kansas investigators trying to solve the crime. Capote's eccentricities were exacerbated by the resolute normality of the townspeople.

In rose-colored glasses and purple capes and with the odd and affected speaking voice he would display regularly on television talk shows, Capote was supremely out of place in a small, "resume speed" town on the west Kansas plains. To Capote, the townspeople were the oddballs, not him. "It was as strange as if I'd gone to Peking," he once said.

Harper Lee, a southern woman of tremendous graciousness and with a gregarious personality, helped open doors for her friend. She ingratiated herself, and then Capote, into the lives of the Holcomb residents, finally persuading them to open up. Although Lee and Dunphy aided in the reporting, the book's craft and clarity testify to Capote's prodigious talents. Feeling there were already plenty of barriers between himself and his interview subjects, Capote did not want to further distance himself by producing a pencil and paper or (God forbid) a tape recorder. He conducted his interviews as conversations, his subjects put at ease by Lee, and would commit all of their utterances to memory. At night, in his hotel room, Capote would type the interviews verbatim. Few other writers would have had the courage or the talent to pull it off.

Eventually, officials caught the murderers, two misfits named Dick Hickok and Perry Smith. They had murdered the Clutters thinking them rich, but they found in the farmhouse only enough money for two nights in a hotel room. Capote found communication with the pair— particularly Smith, the moody outcast—much easier than it had been with the townfolk. Smith shared his journals with Capote, and eventually, after the trial and as their execution date neared, even the more distrustful Hickok began to speak openly with Capote.

Capote delivered on many of the goals he had set out to accomplish. The book focused with photographic clarity on such moments as what the two killers did moments before the murders. They stopped at the edge of the town, and while Dick filled up the car's gas tank, Perry was in the filling station's restroom, contemplating what he was about to do:

> Dick dropped a dime in a vending machine, pulled the lever, and picked up a bag of jelly beans; munching, he wandered back to the car and lounged there watching the young attendant's efforts to rid the windshield of Kansas dust and the slime of battered insects. . . .
>
> The door to the men's room was still bolted. He banged on it: "For Christsake, Perry!"
>
> "In a minute."
>
> "What's the matter? You sick?"
>
> Perry gripped the edge of the washbasin and hauled himself to a standing position. His legs trembled; the pain in his knees made him perspire. He wiped his face with a paper towel. He unlocked the door and said, "O.K. Let's go."[21]

In Cold Blood was serialized in the *New Yorker* in 1965 and published in book form in 1966. Arriving when it did, it was part of the frenzy surrounding the New Journalism. Though it had been conceived back when Tom Wolfe was still an unknown drudge on a small daily newspaper, critics reacted as if Capote had been in collusion with the rest of the new breed. To create a distance, Capote invented a phrase to describe his "new art form": the nonfiction novel. It was New Journalism, of course. Wolfe was among those commenting on the book's brilliance. He applauded Capote's use of the parallel narrative—shifting between the killers on the run and the chaos left behind in Kansas, much like John Steinbeck had done in *The Grapes of Wrath* (1938).[22]

Unfortunately, *In Cold Blood* effectively ended Capote's fertile period. He became a celebrity, a fixture at major parties (and host of his own, the legendary black-and-white ball in late 1966). He took to the television talk-show circuit and, after a decade or so, was no longer famous for his brilliance as a writer. He was simply famous for being famous. He recycled and republished earlier works, collected his short journalism,[23] and offered quotations to reporters whenever they needed someone to comment on capital punishment. He attempted a return to fiction in the middle 1970s with a novel called *Answered Prayers* (1986), which disguised (albeit not too well) several of his wealthy society friends in fictional names and used the real names of others.[24] Excerpts in *Esquire* created a furor, and Capote found himself cut off from the social life he loved. His last work, *Music for Chameleons* (1980), he called his nonfiction short stories.[25] It was mostly a collection of memoirs and a long, true-crime story called "Handcarved Coffins," written in script form.

Capote died in 1983 after years of drug and alcohol abuse. Yet he had produced in *In Cold Blood*, the single best example, whether he liked it or not, of New Journalism.

Norman Mailer

When *In Cold Blood* appeared in 1966, several of Capote's contemporaries in noveldom decried his defection from the world of fiction. Norman Mailer bemoaned his colleague's new work, calling *In Cold Blood* a "failure of imagination," as if Capote had used reality as a last resort because his artistic faculties failed him. Ironically, within a year Mailer would join Capote in the ranks of New Journalism.

Mailer fulfilled the dreams of would-be writers of his generation by following the Ernest Hemingway model: going to war, followed by a career writing about war and the other manly arts. After Harvard, Mailer spent World War II in the Pacific, and almost immediately upon his return to America, he became a celebrated literary figure, a junior-varsity Papa Hemingway, with his novel *The Naked and the Dead*

(1948).[26] A few other novels followed, but they disappointed by comparison with the first, a riveting book. By the mid-1960s Mailer was still a novelist whose greatest promise was yet to be fulfilled. And then he suffered "a failure of imagination."

Mailer's celebrity involvement in an antiwar demonstration at the Pentagon (the protesters hoped to encircle the building, meditate, and cause the structure to rise off of its foundation) drew press attention. The author-turned-activist was arrested at the failed attempt at levitation. Angered at how he was treated in the press, Mailer sought to set the record straight. His articles about the event appeared first in *Harper's* (then under the editorship of Willie Morris) and later in his book *The Armies of the Night*. With the book's weighty subtitle—*History as a Novel; The Novel as History*—Mailer was apparently trying to distance himself from New Journalism, but nonfiction by any other name would still smell as sweet.

Mailer wrote of himself as "Mailer" and, on occasion, "The Beast." Propelling yourself into a book as a third-person creation was an old technique (it had worked for Henry Adams, why not for Mailer?), yet Mailer was able to revitalize it and study a character he knew well (presumably) rather than the disjointed creatures of his imagination (Rojack, for example, from Mailer's *An American Dream* [1965]) who had sleep-walked through his novels.[27]

Using the technique of intense scrutiny, Mailer was able to make the simple act of urination, for example, into compelling literature. At the theater where the protesters gathered before the Pentagon demonstration, and after consuming copious amounts of alcohol, Mailer found himself unable to control the urge to eliminate:

> Mailer was . . . in search of The Room, which, it developed was up on the balcony floor. Imbued with the importance of his first gig as Master of Ceremonies [and] . . . flush with his incandescence, happy in all the anticipations of liberty which this Gotterdammerung of urination was soon to provide, Mailer did not know, but he had already and unwitting to himself metamorphosized into the Beast.
>
> Taking a sip of bourbon from the mug he kept to keep all fires idling right, [he] stepped off into the darkness of the top balcony floor, went through a door into a pitch-black men's room, and was alone with his need. No chance to find the light switch for he had no matches, he did not smoke. It was therefore a matter of locating what's what with the probing of his toes. He found something finally which seemed appropriate, and pleased with the precision of these generally unused senses in his

feet, took aim between them at a point twelve inches ahead, and heard in the darkness the sound of his water striking the floor. Some damn mistake had been made.[28]

The Armies of the Night won the Pulitzer Prize and reestablished Mailer as a major literary figure, but in a new arena. He had written nonfiction before, of course, but now he was setting off on a nearly two-decade path as a New Journalist. He covered the Apollo 11 mission in *Of a Fire on the Moon* (1970), discoursed on the battle between men and women in *The Prisoner of Sex* (1971), and covered Muhammad Ali's bout with George Foreman in *The Fight* (1975).[29] Unfortunately, the technique that had worked so well in *The Armies of the Night* did not adapt well to these other books. Including himself as a character in that first New Journalism book made sense—he *was* a character. But what did he really have to do with the lunar mission? The astronauts Neil Armstrong, Buzz Aldrin, and Michael Collins were the only folks in the spacecraft. Why did Norman Mailer continue to intrude? As Wolfe wrote: "Mailer's autobiographical technique never succeeds in taking the reader inside the capsule, much less inside the points of view or central nervous systems of the astronauts themselves. This is a failure not only in technique but also in reporting. Mailer tends to be a very shy reporter, reluctant to abandon the safety of the Literary Gentleman in the Grandstand."[30]

These problems beset Mailer for several years. Ali and Foreman were in the ring, but *The Fight* was all about Mailer. What had been both a literary convenience and an intelligent storytelling device in *The Armies of the Night* seemed, in these later examples of New Journalism, but a monstrous ego in full flower.

These books made money, however, and publishers continued to queue up for Mailer's ruminations on the nature of stardom (the lavish picture-book-with-brow-furrowing-essay *Marilyn* [1973]), then his pontifications on street art, *The Faith of Graffiti* (1974).[31]

Yet Mailer had another great work of journalism in him. He insisted that it be classified as fiction, and its cover bore the legend "a true-life novel." Yet it was another example, like *In Cold Blood*, of the power of journalism mixed with the techniques of fiction: *The Executioner's Song*. The book's more than 1,000 pages tell the story of the career criminal Gary Gilmore, who, after being sentenced to death for a murder spree, called the state of Utah's bluff: he asked to be executed. No one had been executed in the United States in more than a decade, and the novelty of Gilmore's request attracted a lot of media attention. The killer even hired agents to handle the merchandising of his story. One such deal led to Mailer writing the book. If ever a book cried out for a character called Norman Mailer, *The Executioner's Song* was it. Yet Mailer restrained himself and never broke the proscenium. As Capote had, Mailer told in clinical detail how a murderer committed his detestable crimes. *The Executioner's Song* won the Pulitzer Prize—for fiction, of course—in 1980.

In a scene whose flat prose style was ideally matched to the inarticulate character of Gilmore, Mailer described one of the murders, committed to impress the criminal's girlfriend Nicole:

> Gilmore brought out the .22 Browning Automatic and told Jensen [the gas station attendant] to empty his pockets. So soon as Gilmore had pocketed the cash, he picked up the coin changer in his free hand and said, "Go to the bathroom." Right after they passed through the bathroom door, Gilmore said, "Get down." The floor was clean. Jensen must have cleaned it in the last fifteen minutes. He was trying to smile as he lay down on the floor. Gilmore said, "Put your arms under your body." Jensen got into position with his hands under his stomach. He was still trying to smile.
>
> It was a bathroom with green tiles that came to the height of your chest, and tan-painted walls. The floor, six feet by eight feet, was laid in dull gray tiles. A rack for paper towels had Towel Saver printed on it. The toilet had a split seat. An overhead light was in the wall.
>
> Gilmore brought the Automatic to Jensen's head. "This one is for me," he said, and fired.
>
> "This one is for Nicole," he said, and fired again. The body reacted each time.
>
> He stood up. There was a lot of blood. It spread across the floor at a surprising rate. Some of it got onto the bottom of his pants.[32]

Mailer occasionally practiced journalism again, but in the 1980s and 1990s he turned his energy back to fiction, writing an epic Egyptian novel, *Ancient Evenings* (1983), a throwback to earlier pulp fiction, *Tough Guys Don't Dance* (1984), and a massive tale of the Central Intelligence Agency, *Harlot's Ghost* (1991).[33] Each novel, in its way, was enriched by Mailer's labors in journalism.

Joan Didion

At times, the New Journalism explosion seemed like a boys' club. Indeed, many of the key works were contributed by male writers. But several women—Gloria Emerson, Gloria Steinem, Barbara Goldsmith, and others—were also key players. Perhaps the most important was Joan Didion, who served as a sort of anti-Mailer. Whereas Mailer's ego often obtruded, Didion could put herself into her nonfiction and remain inconspicuous. Whereas Wolfe, and especially Capote, made elaborate efforts to stay out of the story as a good omniscient novelist-narrator would, Didion nearly always showed up in her stories, but the device served mainly to provide a point of reference.

Didion, with her husband, John Gregory Dunne, wrote a 1960s column for the *Saturday Evening Post* called "Points West." They took turns offering views of the southern California madness they could easily view from their Los Angeles home. Although she simultaneously labored as a novelist, publishing *Run River* (1963), *Play It as It Lays* (1970), and *A Book of Common Prayer* (1977) while producing her highly regarded collections of journalism, Didion quickly distinguished herself as an observer of the American cultural spectacle.[34] In her profile of John Wayne, published just after the actor lost a lung to cancer and was making his first postoperative film, Didion's descriptions of the craft of moviemaking are wrapped up in her emotional attachment to the icon of her youth, an attachment she uses as a bridge to the masses of unknown readers:

> When John Wayne rode through my childhood, and perhaps through yours, he determined forever the shape of certain of our dreams. It did not seem possible that such a man could fall ill, could carry within him that most inexplicable and ungovernable of diseases. . . .
>
> "Hello, there," he said when he first saw the girl, in a construction camp or on a train or just standing around on the front porch waiting for somebody to ride up through the tall grass. When John Wayne spoke, there was no mistaking his intentions; he had a sexual authority so strong that even a child could perceive it. And in a world we understood early to be characterized by venality and doubt and paralyzing ambiguities, he suggested another world, one which may or may not have existed but in any case existed no more: a place where a man could move free, could make his own code and live by it; a world in which, if a man did what he had to do, he could one day take the girl and go riding through the draw and find himself . . . there at the bend in the bright river, the cottonwoods shimmering in the early morning sun.
>
> "Hello, there." Where did he come from, before the tall grass?[35]

Wolfe acknowledged Didion's self-confessed limitation that she considered herself too shy to be a good reporter, but he pointed out that "photographers she has worked with say her shyness sometimes makes her subjects so nervous they blurt out extraordinary things in their eagerness to fill up the conversational vacuum."[36] Her awe of John Wayne kept her at some distance in that piece, but it was early in her career (1964). Later on, in profiles of rock-and-roll musicians, actors, even her devastating look at a pre–White House Nancy Reagan, then California's First Lady, her unobtrusive presence did allow her, through her generally withdrawn reportorial technique, to craft some moments that touch the purest elements of the marriage of journalism and literary style. Didion accompanied a television news crew to the California governor's mansion and let them do the talking as they staged scenes of Nancy Reagan being herself:

> [The television reporter] suggested that we watch Nancy Reagan pick flowers in the garden. "That's something you might ordinarily do, isn't it?" he asked. "Indeed it is," Nancy Reagan said with spirit. Nancy Reagan says almost everything with spirit, perhaps because she was once an actress and has the beginning actress's habit of investing even the most casual lines with a good deal more dramatic emphasis than is ordinarily called for. . . .
>
> She smiled at each of us, and each of us smiled back. We had all been smiling quite a bit that morning. . . .
>
> We all smiled at one another again, and then Nancy Reagan walked resolutely into the garden. . . . "Fine," the newsman said, "Just fine. Now I'll ask a question, and if you could just be nipping a bud as you answer it . . ."
>
> "Nipping a bud," Nancy Reagan repeated, taking her place in front of the rhododendron bush.
>
> "Let's have a dry run," the cameraman said.
>
> The newsman looked at him. "In other words, by a dry run, you mean you want her to fake nipping the bud."
>
> "Fake the nip, yeah," the cameraman said. "Fake the nip."[37]

Although Didion's modesty about her reportorial abilities and her considerable skill as a novelist made her discount her abilities as a New Journalist, Wolfe said he believed she was a writer of the first rank in the hybrid form.[38] Other critics considered her modest intrusions into her stories merely convenient devices. "It's tempting to see Didion's timidity as a pose," wrote the critic James Atlas, "[as a] way of deflecting resentment, an apology for success. And there *is* a coyly self-dramatizing element in her work, a kind of relentless intensity."[39]

Didion's meditations on America in the 1960s and 1970s are collected in her journalistic anthologies, *Slouching Towards Bethlehem* (1968) and
The White Album (1979). Her later forays into nonfiction were extended
essays written for the *New York Review of Books*. Didion published *Salvador*
(1983), *Democracy* (1984), and *Miami* (1987) in the 1980s and compiled
another nonfiction anthology, *After Henry* (1992).[40] Although her presence in her work was a constant throughout her 30 years as a New
Journalist, Didion's appearances in her articles rarely approached the
level of encroachment practiced by a journalist who made his name and
his lucrative career as a literary creation in his own writing.

Hunter S. Thompson

Perhaps the most controversial of all of the New Journalists was Hunter
S. Thompson. He came from Louisville, where he began his road to fame
as a juvenile delinquent. He graduated to the service of his country in
the U.S. Air Force, and then, unable to hold a steady job in journalism,
the only profession that appealed to him, he headed to South America,
where he was able to land a gig as a roving correspondent for the
National Observer. That newspaper, conceived as a sort of Sunday edition
of the *Wall Street Journal* (even though the parent company, Dow Jones,
published it on Monday) allowed its weird correspondent to flourish.
Thompson's dispatches were filled with detail and sampled heavily from
such diverse influences as Hemingway and Graham Greene, yet always
with the reporter at the center of the story. Though he had had no formal schooling past high school, Thompson had given himself a crash
course in literature by retyping books he admired. From that simple act,
he said, he learned the structure and rhythm of writing.[41]

Proximity would, however, be Thompson's downfall. When he
returned to the States, the *Observer* editors met him at the airport. He
was a hero. But they wanted him at a desk in the editorial offices, and
such a position was revolting to the iconoclastic writer. Soon tensions
appeared that swelled into outright contempt. Thompson left the publication.

Like other writers of his generation, Thompson had assumed journalism was a day job until he found fame as the Great American Novelist.
He set to work on such a book but set it aside when a brief, bill-paying
magazine assignment for the *Nation* led to book contract offers stuffed in
his mailbox. The subject of the article was the outlaw motorcycle gang,

Hell's Angels. Thompson ended up riding with the pack for a year (in a
Buick, not on a Harley Davidson) and eventually was nearly killed when
the outlaws turned on him. The resulting book, *Hell's Angels*, was a triumph of participatory journalism. It made Thompson a name.

Thompson's work habits and lifestyle rendered him too erratic for
work on mainstream magazines, so he strung together freelance assignments from disparate and short-lived publications such as *Spider* and
Scanlan's Monthly. Thompson usually included himself in his articles, but
he took that technique to a new level with a piece for *Scanlan's* called
"The Kentucky Derby Is Decadent and Depraved." He was paired with
the English illustrator Ralph Steadman, whose first experience on
American soil would be the drunken debauchery of Derby Week in
Louisville. The assignment marked a homecoming for Thompson, who,
at the center of the story, tries to set the stage for the madness he wants
Steadman to see:

> "Just pretend you're visiting a huge outdoor loony bin," I said. . . .
> We had seats looking down on the finish line, color TV and a
> selection of passes that would take us anywhere from the clubhouse roof
> to the jockey room. . . .
> Now, looking down from the press box, I pointed to the huge out-
> door meadow enclosed by the track. "That whole thing," I said, "will be
> jammed with people; fifty thousand or so, and most of them staggering
> drunk. It's a fantastic scene—thousands of people fainting, crying, copulat-
> ing, trampling each other and fighting with broken whiskey bottles. . . ."
> "Is it safe out there? Will we ever come back?" [Ralph asked.]
> "Sure," I said. "We'll just have to be careful not to step on any-
> body's stomach and start a fight." I shrugged. "Hell, this clubhouse scene
> right below us will be almost as bad as the infield. Thousands of raving,
> stumbling drunks, getting angrier and angrier as they lose more and
> more money. By midafternoon, they'll be guzzling mint juleps and vom-
> iting on each other between races. The whole place will be jammed with
> bodies, shoulder to shoulder. It's hard to move around. The aisles will be
> slick with vomit; people falling down and grabbing at your legs to keep
> from being stomped. Drunks pissing on each other in the betting lines.
> Dropping handfuls of money and fighting to stoop over and pick it up."[42]

Thompson prepared Steadman for a look at The Face—the quintessential Derby fan, whose puffy, ravaged countenance would be the perfect illustration for Thompson's article. The Face finally appeared, of
course, when the hungover Thompson looked in his motel-room mirror
when the race was over.

Thompson's intrusion on his reporting was at the other end of the spectrum from Didion. She was nearly apologetic about her appearances in her articles, but Thompson was unabashedly the centerpiece of all his stories. Whatever the subject matter, the stories always ended up being about Thompson. Yet he was not an egoist, as Mailer was. Thompson dealt with himself in a self-deprecating manner, always using himself as his own foil. He portrayed himself as a burned-out loser, often too drunk or stoned to function well in society. Part of that image was based on fact. But Thompson himself admits that he exaggerated his abuses for literary effect, watering and manuring an image that made his lifestyle better known than his work.[43] It may have worked too well: Thompson found himself the victim of a notorious reputation that overshadowed his writing.

The Derby article provided Thompson with the breakthrough he needed. Under the magazine's severe deadline pressure, Thompson broke down, unable to provide traditional narration. He began teleporting his raw notes to the magazine, including dispatches describing his frustration in trying to gather information for the story. When he shut off the teleporter, he honestly believed that he would never get a decent magazine assignment again, but *Scanlan's* published the piece as Thompson had transmitted it, notes and all. When the piece appeared, it was hailed as a breakthrough. Bill Cardoso, then a reporter at the *Boston Globe*, wrote Thompson: "That was pure Gonzo Journalism."[44] Thompson's style had a name. A better name might have been "metajournalism," because Thompson then began a long series of pieces that made the process of gathering information into the subject of the story. He was always at the story's center—whether reporting a presidential campaign (*Fear and Loathing: On the Campaign Trail '72* [1973]), covering professional sports ("Fear and Loathing at the Super Bowl" [1974]), or frankly describing his failure to write two magazine assignments (*Fear and Loathing in Las Vegas* [1972]).[45] It was a technique that worked and also served to separate him from the other New Journalists. His Gonzo style formed a subgenre that could be practiced by no other writer. Gonzo Journalism was best defined as whatever Hunter Thompson wrote.

Tom Wolfe

Each of these characters—and many others, including Breslin, Plimpton, John McPhee, Joe Eszterhas, Michael Herr, and others—played a large part in the transformation of journalism from the labor of ink-stained wretches into a branch of the literary arts. But none of them besides Wolfe was willing to assume the responsibility of pontificating about just what it was they were up to. Wolfe, perhaps owing to his professorial training, sought to "package" and explain the movement. He assumed these duties by default. He cringed when the term "New Journalism" was applied to these articles and books but did not shrink from the service of his fellow writers. Eventually, of course, he collected several of these pieces, some of which (particularly the magazine articles that had never appeared in books) had been long lost to the trash cans. Embracing the very term he had once decried, Wolfe published *The New Journalism* in 1973. It includes his reminiscences of how he made his stylistic discoveries and sought to collect the experiences of his fellow innovators. With E. W. Johnson, Wolfe assembled an anthology that served as a primer of New Journalism's early years. In addition to the writers already mentioned, the book includes work by the film critic Rex Reed, *Rolling Stone*'s Joe Eszterhas, the black-humorist Terry Southern, and Michael Herr, who would achieve fame as the author of a celebrated book about Vietnam, *Dispatches* (1977). Supplemented by a number of other pieces by lesser-known practitioners of New Journalism, the book is a miniature history of the 1960s. The collection remains the best anthology of journalism in those years.

Truman Capote was often questioned with great resentment by critics and talk-show hosts about having it both ways, about calling his works both journalism and fiction. Even years after the mid-1960s explosion, it was obvious that the genre was difficult for many to grasp and certainly challenging to explain. Wolfe, despite his efforts at clarification and public relations, was waging a losing battle with the world of belles lettres in his quest to have New Journalism sanctioned as a respectable literary form. He suffered a serious handicap when it came to any negotiation with American literary lions. He had, after all, committed an unpardonable sin at the peak moment of New Journalism's emergence.

The literary community's distrust and resentment dated from Wolfe's two-part series on the *New Yorker*, published in April 1965.[46] The pieces were notorious even before they appeared, causing considerable consternation for Wolfe and not inconsiderable embarrassment. Attacking one of the leading vessels of American literature could not help but engender severe criticism.

Wolfe frankly admitted his frustration in trying to get those inside the magazine's closed circle to speak to him. He made his difficulties into the main theme of the pieces, foretelling the metajournalism practiced by Thompson. Rather than a convenient technique, metajournalism was really the only option left to Wolfe when the *New Yorker* staff clammed up.

Wolfe was roundly criticized for mocking the magazine's distinguished and beloved editor, William Shawn. To readers of Wolfe's article, Shawn was apparently guilty of being shy. Wolfe's prose mocked his quiet style and explored the varied and (one would believe) prolific neuroses of the staff members. Calling the magazine staff the "walking dead," with the editor as chief embalmer, seemed vicious. Shawn was a near-god to his colleagues, and scores of books by America's finest writers, noting his meticulous editorial eye, had been dedicated to him. But Wolfe looked past all that, apparently amused by the aging editor's idiosyncratic behavior. Wolfe even appeared to invent a past for the man. Shawn, as a schoolboy, lived in Chicago, and Wolfe somehow connected this fact with the notorious Leopold and Loeb murder of a young boy. Wolfe attributed the notion that Shawn had been the original intended victim to court records that never existed. This was pointed out in a public letter reprinted in the *Columbia Journalism Review* in which the *New Yorker*'s legendary fact checkers turned themselves loose on Wolfe's articles, finding a plethora of errors.[47]

Nearly every major writer associated with the *New Yorker* weighed in with one criticism or another. The reclusive J. D. Salinger, author of *The Catcher in the Rye* (1951), called Wolfe's pieces "unrelievedly poisonous." The celebrated reporter Richard H. Rovere said Wolfe's writing was "as irresponsible as anything I have ever come upon outside the gutter press," and Ved Mehta said the articles were a "blow against journalism."[48] But the most incisive and, thus, devastating criticisms came in the form of a letter to the *Herald-Tribune* publisher John Hay Whitney from a *New Yorker* legend, one of America's finest writers, E. B. White. White's letter was published in the newspaper on 25 April, and it remains a brief and brutal assessment of Wolfe's faults. Noting that Wolfe had violated every tenet of journalism White had known in his 50-year career, he characterized the *New Yorker* piece as a "sly, cruel and to a large extent undocumented" piece of work. "I can't imagine why you published it," White wrote Whitney. "The virtuosity of the writer makes it all the more contemptible. . . . The piece is not merely brutal, it sets some sort of record for journalistic delinquency." Wolfe's description of Shawn's physical appearance and mannerisms particularly outraged White. While recognizing the value of satire, parody, and other devices Wolfe used, White believed they had been perverted in the *New*

York article. Wolfe's writing was "not only below the belt, it is essentially wide of the mark," White wrote.[49]

Wolfe literally laughed off the criticism, using space in his introduction to *The New Journalism* to tell the literary community, in so many
words, to "lighten up"; in his view, the *New Yorker* articles had been a
convenient vehicle for threatened novelists to launch an attack on the
"bastard form."[50] The resentment would not, however, go away. As
Wolfe told a reporter a decade later:

> I ran into a *New Yorker* writer once at a party. He said to me, "I promised
> myself if I ever met you, I'd punch you in the nose." "And?" I replied,
> after sizing him up. "Well," he said, "I guess I'm just not the type."
>
> I may be tempting fate by saying this, but nobody in New York
> has ever gotten hurt in a literary fist fight, including Ernest
> Hemingway.[51]

Yet it was not the controversial *New Yorker* articles alone that brought
wrath upon Wolfe, it was also his strong, nearly baiting statements
about the New Journalism. "I had the feeling," he wrote, "that I was
doing something that no one had ever done before in journalism."
Proclaiming himself a prose pioneer did not endear himself to other
wordsmiths.

Despite Wolfe's lapses—and the *New Yorker* articles were breaches of
the highest order—Wolfe and other New Journalists survived. The
movement did not persevere, however, without drawing more criticism.
After a number of sins of fact had been committed under the aegis of
New Journalism, it fell to John Hersey to take the abusers to task in a
Yale Review essay.[52] The writer who had provided an early blueprint for
the merger of fact with literary style now decried the form. Hersey worried that the blending of fact and fiction in hybrid forms such as
Capote's "nonfiction novel" had not been good for the field of fiction (in
which he was a prolific practitioner)[53] and would perhaps sound the
death knell for true journalism. A novelist, Hersey noted, was given the
license to make up everything. A journalist had no such right. A journalist's license must bear the motto: "*None* of this was made up." But the
New Journalist, Hersey complained, carried another license, which read:
"This was not made up (except for the parts that were made up)."[54]
Having taken Capote and Mailer to brief task, Hersey concentrated his
efforts on Wolfe, a writer blessed with talent and style but devoid, in
Hersey's opinion, of reverence for fact. Fifteen years after the *New Yorker*

pieces, Hersey reiterated the factual errors and the outright fantasies in Wolfe's articles. In the halls of American literature, youthful sins were not forgiven.

Despite the eloquence of White and Hersey in attacking New Journalism, and the inescapable charges of falsity from which Wolfe could not shrink, New Journalism withstood censure and endured, and undoubtedly to the chagrin and consternation of others in the community of letters, Wolfe became a major figure in American literature of the late twentieth century.

Chapter Five
On the Bus

It was the perfect metaphor for the 1960s. Tom Wolfe, whose abilities as a creator of catchphrases should not be underestimated, came up with a beauty in *The Electric Kool-Aid Acid Test*: "Are you on the bus?" Are you with it? Are you hip? Are you cool? Or are you square? Are you part of the Establishment? Are you on the bus . . . or not? It was a decade that dealt in absolutes, and the answer to the simple question about the bus was critical.

Wolfe's metaphorical bus had a genuine, steel antecedent: a retired school bus painted in orgasms of wild, incongruous colors with a destination plate above the windshield that read "Furthur." The bus belonged to the novelist Ken Kesey and his fellow travelers, the Merry Pranksters. Their LSD-fueled cross-country trek in 1964 (along with its prelude and aftermath) was the subject of *The Electric Kool-Aid Acid Test*, Wolfe's second book, published in 1968.

For years, the book stood as Wolfe's Major Work, his attempt to carry off his New Journalism pyrotechnics at some length (413 pages to be exact). Since its publication, it has never been out of print and frequently is required reading for English courses in which undergraduates ponder the powers and principalities of lysergic acid diethylamide, the powerful hallucinogenic that fueled Kesey and his band of apprentice lunatics.

The book had its inception one day in 1966 when two letters written by Kesey made their way into Wolfe's hands. Kesey was the acclaimed young author of *One Flew over the Cuckoo's Nest* and *Sometimes a Great Notion*; he had gotten into some trouble with the California authorities and, when he wrote the letters, was on the lam in Mexico. The source of the letters was their recipient, yet another celebrated young novelist, Larry McMurtry, who had just published *The Last Picture Show* (1966) (*Lonesome Dove* [1985] was two decades in his future). He thought the letters told a fine yarn. Wolfe agreed, easily visualizing a piece entitled "Fugitive Novelist on the Run in Mexico." It looked like another wham-bam New Journalism exhibition for *Esquire* or *New York*. As Wolfe prepared to board a flight to Mexico City to search for Kesey, he learned that the police had gotten to him first and that the writer would soon be arriving at a San Francisco jail, back near his California home base.

Wolfe canceled the flight south of the border and instead journeyed to California. He met Kesey at the jail and briefly interviewed him. After the author was released on bail, Wolfe spent a month or so with him and the Merry Pranksters in the Bay Area. At first Wolfe conceived a lengthy article. But it soon became a three-part series for *New York* that he intended to revise, and perhaps lengthen, for inclusion in his next anthology (which would turn out to be *The Pump House Gang*). "I didn't intend to do a book on it," Wolfe told an interviewer. "Kesey and the Pranksters started out being a rather limited subject. . . . Gradually, the thing just got bigger and bigger in its scope because everything that Kesey ever tried went far beyond the whole question of drugs, to this whole matter of self-realization and what you're going to do with yourself on the frontier beyond catastrophe."[1]

Kesey was a writer of considerable talent. *One Flew over the Cuckoo's Nest*, published at the dawn of the 1960s, was in many ways a parable for the decade yawning ahead. It is the story of the quintessential rebel, a ruffian named Randle Patrick McMurphy, who seeks to avoid the rigors of chain-gang work by pretending to be a lunatic. Confined in a mental hospital, he inspires his languid fellow patients to rebel against authority, personified by their ward supervisor, Nurse Ratched. With the techniques and some of the language of the youth rebellion that was to follow, Kesey tells a story destined, despite moments of high comedy, to become a tragedy. His second book, *Sometimes a Great Notion*, is set in logging country, yet the rebellion in its narrative is against labor unions, earlier a bastion for liberal theocracy. Kesey, it appeared, was hard to predict. Wolfe was amused by his eccentric subject.

Wolfe eventually called his book editor (the legendary Henry Robbins of Farrar, Straus and Giroux) and said he wanted to ride the Prankster story for as long as he could. After hearing what Wolfe had found, Robbins agreed, and a contract was drafted.

Wolfe's fascination with Kesey and the Pranksters arose not merely from the salacious fact that they openly used LSD. It was what they did with the hallucinogenic drug that so intrigued Wolfe. "Kesey and the Pranksters did not use LSD to slide back into a passive . . . worldview," Wolfe wrote in an article about the book's genesis.[2] The Pranksters were a thoroughly American rabble seeking to confront the national conscience in their drugged state and to revel in their nation's excesses. No meditation, no Indian mysticism for this crew. They would take to the streets among the shiny black-shoe masses and shake things up a bit. There was also the matter of religion. Wolfe observed that the Pranksters took acid every Sunday, almost as if it were a sacrament. These "acid tests" were similar to early Christian ceremonies and also resembled Buddhist and Zoroastrian rituals. "All of the successful modern religions started out as religions of ecstatic experiences," Wolfe said. "First comes the ecstatic experience, then comes the theology. . . . Here I had a chance to look at a primary religion in its early stages, though this is not to put the experience of Kesey and the Pranksters on a par with that of Jesus or Buddha."[3]

Wolfe's monthlong stay with the Pranksters and his subsequent reporting of Kesey's early days and the epic coast-to-coast bus trip filled his notebooks. By September 1967 he needed to begin getting it all down on paper. In his description, Wolfe started writing frantically, just trying to register everything he had heard, seen, smelled, and tasted. He conceded that considerations of technique had him stalled at the writing stage, but he holed up in Virginia for three and a half months, away from the usual New York lunacy, turning out 10 to 20 pages a day. Eventually, he produced 1,100 manuscript pages. He claimed that there was "no revision at all" because of the book deadline and that he sent chapters off to Robbins as soon as he finished them. Only when the book galleys arrived did he make a few minor changes. The pressure worked well, he concluded. "Sometimes the greatest favor an editor can do a writer is trick him into yielding up the manuscript," Wolfe said of Robbins.[4]

He wrote scenes recounting in rich detail events he had witnessed. His aim was to stitch these scenes together after he had recorded everything he could. "The main thing was just to get it all down," he wrote.[5] This process of madly recording everything became the Wolfe technique—the frenzy of composition, it turned out, was perfectly suited to the frenzy of the events he was narrating. Gathering the material had taken a colossal amount of time. "The actual writing I do very fast," Wolfe told the interviewer Joe David Bellamy. He worked from an outline, which would become his standard practice. "By writing an outline, you really *are* writing in a way, because you are creating the structure of what you're going to do."[6] He had never written anything of such length before—his dissertation had been a mere 200 pages—so he decided to envision each chapter as a magazine article, since he was eminent in the shorter form and acquainted with the routine. He had secured a book contract, but the publisher's deadline was flexible, unlike a magazine's unflinching schedule. With no *Esquire* or *New York* breathing down his neck, he set up artificial deadlines. The pressure and the discipline would put him, he felt, in the right frame of mind.

To make these self-imposed deadlines, he sometimes stayed up all night, as if a magazine really were holding space for him. The prolific nature of his work for *Esquire* and *New York* had prepared him well, because it gave him focus. "If you're writing an article," he said, "as far as you're concerned that's the only thing you're ever going to write. You're writing *that* article and it absorbs your whole attention." After writing a few chapters under this regimen, however, Wolfe began to feel that it was taking a physical toll, and he substituted a daily quota of ten pages. Sometimes he made the goal in two hours. Other times it took a whole day. Shooting for ten pages of copy each day was more manageable, even if such a goal seemed at times a bit methodical. "Just like working in a factory," Wolfe said. "End of ten pages I'd close my lunch pail."[7] Near the end of the book, with light at the end of the tunnel, Wolfe upped his quota to 20 pages. When he finished, he thought it had not been as demanding as he had assumed it would be to write a big book under pressure. The publisher's deadline loomed, of course, but Wolfe also faced the cultural deadline. He had feared when he started the project that the psychedelic period and the widespread use of drugs—and particularly the interest in LSD—would dry up before his manuscript was published, making it "old news" as soon as it hit the bookstores.

Later he would be glad that he had imposed such pressure on himself, because he produced the book quickly, when it was still a part of its time, not an outdated artifact of an earlier era. It did, in fact, become a major cultural relic of the era it recorded. Battered paperback copies protruded from back pockets of faded denims, peeking from under tie-dyed shirt-tails. Wolfe perhaps assumed the book would be successful because of its immediacy and the closeness of its publication to the events it records. He certainly did not expect the book to have a long shelf life. As he said 20 years later, "I honestly thought it would stand up only until the highly educated people who were really involved—as I wasn't—in the psychedelic world wrote their big novels."[8] With no such novels forthcoming, Wolfe's book has remained the most vibrant literary chronicle of the era. Indeed, one critic asserted in the late 1980s that *The Electric Kool-Aid Acid Test* "remains the best book about 1960s America."[9]

The book commences with word of Kesey's imminent release from jail after his season on the run in Mexico, with Wolfe among the

Pranksters on the way to hail the freed hero. Readers immediately antic-
ipate the arrival of the book's protagonist, yet Wolfe fences with the
readers, stalling for several pages until the suitable point for the hero's
theatrical entrance into the narrative. The wait allows readers to see
Kesey through Wolfe's eyes, from the vantage point of the press, and to
comprehend the admiration, the nearly sacred regard, the Pranksters
held for their leader. Wolfe made himself a character, presumably feeling
that readers might want a point of reference, a more lucid pair of eyes
through which to witness the lunacy of the ensuing 400 pages. He is
hardly an Everyman, however, a point he makes in the book's first
drawn breath as he describes his outfit (silk jacket, high collar, expensive
footwear), as if to say, "I am as different from these people as they are
from you." Wolfe acknowledges his out-of-placeness by noting that the
oddball Pranksters regard *him* as the kook. (Defending his clothing tele-
pathically to a Prankster named Black Maria, he thinks, "Back in New
York City, Black Maria, I tell you, I am even known as something of a
dude.")[10]

Wolfe realized he did not have the ability or the desire to "fit in" with
the Pranksters. He arrived in his normal attire to work on the book and
never changed to the more casual kind of apparel the others wore. He
wanted to keep his distance—sartorially and metaphorically. "I quickly
realized that it would be folly to pretend for a moment to be 'on the bus'
with the Merry Pranksters," he said two decades later. "Once you pre-
tended to be or somehow assumed that you were a part of what was
going on, you were swept into the maelstrom!"[11]

Wolfe's clothing remained his badge of independence from the
Pranksters, yet his stubborn refusal to dress less nattily even while on
assignment cost Wolfe at least one outfit. Attired in one of his favorite
brown tweed suits, Wolfe was taking notes as he watched Kesey and one
of his friends attempt to move a sculpture. Kesey asked Wolfe to help.
As he helped to pick up the piece, Wolfe noted that it had recently been
painted and the paint was not yet dry. "I was berserk, I was confused,"
Wolfe said. He grabbed a can of turpentine and dumped it over the
stained parts of his jacket. Kesey smiled at Wolfe and said, "If you mess
around with shit some of it's going to rub off on you."[12]

Wolfe also knew that had he attempted to fit in, Kesey and his crew
would have put him down as a jackass. "There was a kind of creature
that Kesey and the Pranksters, practically everybody in the psychedelic
world, detested more than anything else, and that was the so-called
weekend hipster . . . somebody who was hip on the weekends but went

back to the straight job during the week." Wolfe said Kesey had a test for weekend hipsters: he would suggest to the assembled Pranksters and hangers-on that they all hop on motorcycles and ride naked up the highway. They would do it too, Wolfe said, and that was usually the point at which the weekend hipster—a lawyer, say, with a fear of an indecent exposure charge—would back off.[13]

Like Hunter S. Thompson, Wolfe chose to make the process of getting the story into the story itself. He frankly admitted that he went into the telling of the Kesey saga with a preconceived headline idea ("Young Novelist Is Real-Life Fugitive"), and he described his difficulty in simply finding the writer.

Wolfe fills the early passages of the book with extreme detail, flattening out each moment like a marijuana smoker's unplugged sense of time. He meticulously sets the stage for Kesey's arrival. Even the elevator ride up to the visiting room in the jail is included in the minutiae, and Kesey's arrival, in "tight blond curls boiling up around his head," is played for all its dramatic effect.[14]

It was after the first chapters of prologue that Wolfe faced his most rigorous task: re-creating the bus excursion of nearly three years before and evoking for readers the sensation of being "on the bus." He profited from historical serendipity: the whole trip had been filmed and diaries had been kept. Pranksters had evidently committed every microsecond to memory. Squirreled away in his Virginia hermitage with these artifacts of the trip, Wolfe felt certain that he could convincingly report the trip's experiences and, after extended interviews and chats with the Merry Pranksters, that he could also share the feel of the trip.

To do this, Wolfe discerned that he would have to dive "inside the subjective reality" of Kesey and the Pranksters. His goal was to "get completely inside Kesey's mind, based on interviews, tapes that he made, or letters that he wrote, diaries and so on."[15] Of course, it was a questionable technique, but Wolfe felt it was the only way to tell the story. Employing the standard totem reportorial technique would have distanced him too far away from the story, and he would not have been able to provide the level of perspicacity made possible by the inside-the-subject's-mind technique. It was a necessity that he get inside Kesey's mind to tell the story, Wolfe said, because the drug-addled writer was so different from himself and his experiences were so alien. "I'm attracted to things I don't know about," Wolfe said.[16]

It was fortuitous that Kesey had surrounded himself with a couple of writers whose heightened observations would augment Wolfe's knowledge of Kesey's outlaw period in Mexico as well as the whole Prankster experience. McMurtry's observations were vital, as were those of Robert Stone, another Kesey cohort who went on to publish the highly regarded *Dog Soldiers* (1974) and *A Flag for Sunrise* (1982). At first, he worked against Wolfe. Stone was writing a piece on Kesey for *Esquire*, while Wolfe intended his work for *New York*. Stone became aware of Wolfe's project during Kesey's hiding-out days in Mexico and told Kesey's associates not to reveal his whereabouts to Wolfe. Stone was saving Kesey for himself, but when *Esquire* rejected his article, Stone generously passed all of his notes, with the attendant insights drawn by one within the Kesey camp, to Wolfe. He also agreed to an interview with Wolfe, whose questioning skills he came to respect highly. "He's a dangerous kind of interviewer," Stone said, "because he really does put you at your ease."[17] Wolfe perceived that many readers would glory in the lurid aspects of the book: sex, drugs, and rock and roll. That was something, Wolfe wrote, over which he would have no control. "I do hope," Wolfe said, "that some [readers] will see [the Pranksters'] adventure as I do, as a forerunner of an Acid Test almost everyone will be facing in the years ahead."[18] It was Kesey's ordinariness that made him such an ideal subject, Wolfe said. Here is a good old boy (in one sense very much like Junior Johnson) from a farm family, good American stock, who makes all of the right moves: to college, to athletic glory as a wrestler, to academic honors, to young American novelist. When this character turns out to be the leader of a drug-based religious group, Wolfe reasoned, it says something about changes in the national psyche that might be unavoidable for everyone else in America. Kesey was the perfect microcosm. As Wolfe said in 1987: "The changes in him are on the heroic scale, in the literary sense and they're the heroic version of changes that were going to affect a lot of children over the succeeding twenty years."[19]

Wolfe begins the story at the end, with Kesey's return from Mexico. He then re-creates Kesey's transformation from "the hick with intellectual yearnings"[20] to potential guru of a new drug-based religion. The epic bus trip forms the book's centerpiece, and Wolfe so insinuates himself into the early scenes that he writes with the seeming authority of one of the passengers, sitting alongside Cool Breeze or Stark Naked or Zonk or any of the other characters, as they roll through the Southwest, through the heart of America, straight to the capital of craziness, New York City.

The beatnik hero Neal Cassady, of course, assumes a major role, offering stoned monologues whether an audience is present or not. Among

Cassady's apparent addictions was conversation. As Wolfe describes him: "He will answer all questions, although not exactly in that order, because we can't stop here, next rest area 40 miles, you understand, spinning off memories, metaphors, literary, Oriental, hip allusions, all punctuated by the unlikely expression, 'you understand——.'"[21]

Along the way, Kesey and crew encounter the Old America and some representatives of the New: the Hell's Angels, the writer Hunter Thompson, the Beatles, and a youth culture on the verge of exploding from the confines of the old manners and morals. Despite the promise inherent in being avatars of a new order, the Pranksters by the end of the book are chanting not a mantra, or the name of a new guru, but instead a phrase that encapsulates their missed opportunity: "We blew it! We blew it!"[22] What had been so full of promise has become a wake.

The inevitable question in any discussion of Wolfe's technique in *The Electric Kool-Aid Acid Test* again reeks of sensationalism: how could he write so evocatively of the experience of hallucinogenic drugs unless he had taken them? He freely admitted that he had. He had a friend who was able to obtain LSD. Wolfe took 125 milligrams and immediately began suffering what he was certain was a fatal heart attack. "I had a terrible time the first three hours," he recalled. "I thought my heart was larger than my body." As his body absorbed the shock of the drug, he began to feel that he was becoming part of the shabby carpet in his friend's apartment. It was, in his recollection, a "wretched" carpet too. The indignity! If one has to become floor covering, why not something grander? "I was in a room with a nubbly twist rug, with the little tips sticking up," Wolfe said, "and the afternoon sun was shining off the tips. I began to feel I had merged with them, and somehow through that I'd learned all about the common people of America. I'd almost merged with them, too."[23] At the time, the carpet-melding took on near-religious significance for Wolfe. Later he said the incident did not mean "a goddam thing."[24] He felt it was nearly his duty to take the drug or risk being unable to convey the altered state of his protagonists. It was something he never wanted to do again, he told the president's son Ron Reagan, who interviewed him years later. "It was like tying yourself to the railroad track and seeing how big the train is, which is rather big," he said. "The drug is so powerful."[25]

Many critics complimented Wolfe on his fairness in telling the story of a group that was so foreign to his experience. He offers excruciating insight into the drug culture and yet refrains from making judgments. He is, in fact, so circumspect that when Kesey's band slips LSD into the

Kool-Aid at a southern California gathering billed as the Los Angeles "Acid Test," Wolfe makes no moral pronouncement about the irresponsibility of that act. Although Wolfe found himself in basic agreement with Kesey on a major point—that many people could use a little mind expansion—Kesey's open-checkbook solution of drug use as the path to deeper consciousness did not wash well with Wolfe. Although he does not condemn Kesey, Wolfe also presents an undoctored portrait of the lives of habitual drug users.

Without overstating the message, Wolfe ultimately offers a verdict on Kesey: he insinuates that the young writer—in the language of the era—most assuredly did blow it. The cross-country trek had begun as a frivolous adventure; it ended as not much more, and perhaps no real harm was done. But the greater good that Kesey had envisioned as the result of his hallucinogenic pilgrimage did not come to pass. The story of Kesey and the Pranksters was, in a way, the whole story of the 1960s in a nutshell: the ultimately doomed search for a guru.

C. D. B. Bryan, in the *New York Times Book Review*, called the book "astonishing" and claimed that Wolfe was "precisely the right author" to show Kesey's transformation from promising young writer to cult leader. Wolfe's participation in the story made the book's flaws inevitable, but it was, in Bryan's view, worth the risk. Occasionally, Bryan wrote, Wolfe's technique got in the way ("he piles elaboration upon elaboration until reality is buried under illusions of evaluation"), but this "weakness" turned out to be the book's major strength: "It is Wolfe's enthusiasm, and literary fireworks that make it difficult for the reader to remain detached. He does not hesitate to tell us what to think, how to react, even what to wear as he wings us along with Ken Kesey and his band of Merry Pranksters in a brightly painted, Ampex-loaded cross-country bus."[26]

Joel Lieber, writing in the *Nation*, complimented Wolfe on his ability to re-create the psychedelic experience in words. Relating an essentially nonverbal experience in words was a daunting task, Lieber wrote, but Wolfe accomplished it magnificently. Although he chastised Wolfe for revealing little below the surface of Kesey, Lieber called the book "a genuine feat and a landmark in reporting style."[27]

Karl Shapiro, in the *Washington Post*, was effusive in his praise for the book's achievement:

> Tom Wolfe is more than brilliant. . . . He is more than urbane, suave, trenchant and all of those book review adjectives. He really understands

his subjects, is really compassionate (when possible), really involved with what he says and is clearly responsible to his judgments. Tom Wolfe is a goddam joy. Also, not to insult him, he writes like a master.[28]

For years, at campus speaking engagements, Wolfe was asked about Kesey and the Pranksters and what they were up to, as if he were another member of that entourage. Wolfe told the student audiences that he had been doing a job—writing about Kesey—and that, though there was no coldness between them, he and the chief Merry Prankster were not intimate friends. Still, students wanted to know about the lifestyle the *Acid Test* had so meticulously described. "I began to see I was perceived as a medium who could put them in touch with the other world," Wolfe said. "And all these people were patiently listening [to my speech], *just* to get to the question period, or to get me alone to ask, 'What's Kesey doing now? What's he really like? Where can I find a commune?' I could have started a column like 'Dr. Hip Pocrates, Advice for Heads.'"[29]

For his part, Kesey had gone from Creator of Characters to Being a Character—in a best-selling book, no less. Kesey had no major criticisms of Wolfe's book other than that the author "tried to be nice" by not revealing some of the seamier aspects of the Pranksters' experience with a group of rowdy Hell's Angels. Wolfe's genteel nature had led him to pull back and not offer clinical details of that assault. Wolfe agreed with Kesey that the scene had been the book's weak point.[30]

Kesey got around to telling his version of the Pranksters saga in 1991, when he published *The Further Inquiry*.[31] Twenty-five years older than the precocious author who had boarded the multicolored school bus with Neal Cassady and their friends in early 1964, he was also 25 years away from the auspicious start of that promising young man. When Kesey got off the bus—literally, later that year, figuratively, not for a decade—he was a burnout, apparently another casualty of the 1960s.

Admirers of the *Acid Test* did not learn a lot from *The Further Inquiry*. Kesey tells his story in irritating screenplay form, with a generous assortment of color photographs, many of them drawn from the filmed record of the trip, printed on paper with blue-sky-with-clouds backgrounds. The book also includes a mini-movie: when you flip through the pages quickly, a dance by Cassady appears in the lower righthand corner. The book is a visual feast, but a literary famine.

Kesey centers his book on Cassady, cult hero and muse to so many important writers of that era: Kesey, Wolfe, Thompson, and Kerouac.

Cassady's charm was considerable, but Kesey fails to do justice to the man, as earlier writers succeeded in doing. Unlike Wolfe, Kesey was too close to Cassady. Cassady's genius—if he had one—was as what would later be termed a "performance artist." Despite the skills of his many writer friends, Cassady too often comes across in print as merely a drunken lech. Kesey's book presents a heavenly trial for Cassady, who died in the late 1960s. The divine courtroom allows Kesey to dwell on the character of his subject, but he ultimately does not reveal any more about the man than Wolfe and others did. For some reason, Kesey apparently felt Cassady was in need of exoneration—that his was a great mind that was a terrible thing to waste.

Like most of his books after the early 1960s, *The Further Inquiry* was greeted with a shrug by much of the literary establishment. Many critics noted that the story had been told before—and more ably—by Tom Wolfe.

Chapter Six
Other People's Parties

The success of *The Electric Kool-Aid Acid Test* was the beginning of the end for Wolfe's career as primarily a magazine writer. He began talking about longer projects. Indeed, in the early 1970s he had discussed writing the novel that came out near the end of the next decade—and would absorb him for most of that decade—*The Bonfire of the Vanities*. In the interim, he produced a lot of other work, including his masterwork of journalism, *The Right Stuff*, his large project of the 1970s.

He continued to contribute to magazines, of course, but often these articles were excerpts from books, rough drafts of material he hoped to craft into long book chapters, or only secondarily for the magazine market—that is, material he was trying out on an audience before polishing it for hardcover appearance.

So the books published in the late 1960s up through the mid-1970s constitute the last collections of his prolific contributions to magazines (primarily to *Esquire* and *New York*): *The Pump House Gang* (1968), *Radical Chic and Mau-Mauing the Flak Catchers* (1970), and *Mauve Gloves and Madmen, Clutter and Vine* (1976). It would be time-consuming and perhaps even counterproductive to go through these anthologies article by article; instead, I will discuss the major pieces in each collection. Wolfe is supremely gifted as both an observer and explainer of popular culture, and he is a unique literary stylist as well. These anthologies provide evidence of all of these talents. His skill as an observer and his steadfast desire to remain one—to not subject himself to the potential embarrassment of participating in the cultural spectacle—render him something of a note-taking wallflower at the cultural orgy on the extremes.[1] That image of Wolfe at other people's parties, drawn from his observations in the "Radical Chic" piece, is the residue of his magazine-writing period: the outsider looking in, seeing all.

The Pump House Gang

The Pump House Gang was overshadowed by *The Electric Kool-Aid Acid Test*, since most critics tied the books together in reviews. *The Pump House*

Gang had been ready to go some months before, but the stunt of releasing two books in one day was irresistible to the publisher. As a result, the collection suffered short shrift in the reviews.

In fact, Wolfe's interest in the Bauhaus school of design—the subject of a book more than a decade in his future—shows up in *The Pump House Gang*. In a way, the book is something like "Son of *Kandy-Kolored*": a miscellany of pieces, profiles of subjects ranging from the silicon-enhanced stripper Carol Doda to the *Playboy* publisher Hugh Hefner, to the media scholar Marshall McLuhan. By design, the collection includes few celebrity profiles. "I always tried to avoid writing about famous people," he said. "I was afraid that readers would like the pieces for their subjects, not for my writing."[2] Despite the disparate nature of the selections, Wolfe was able to draw these pieces together as more than mere assemblages of journalism-for-hire (have reporter's notebook, will travel). With the title piece as a starting point, Wolfe used *The Pump House Gang* as a tableau of American style in all its diverse forms.

"The Pump House Gang" is quite similar to *The Electric Kool-Aid Acid Test*, concerned as it is with the young populace of what was just beginning to be called the "counterculture." The "gang" is a bunch of lethargic midteens who hang out on the beach in La Jolla, California, and mock anything having to do with beings older than 25. Without being puritanical or judgmental to any extreme degree, Wolfe describes the gaggle of young hedonists and their nonrelationship with the outside world, as represented by innocent visitors to the beach:

> But exactly! This beach *is* verboten for people practically 50 years old. This is a segregated beach. They can look down on Windansea Beach and see nothing but lean tan kids. It is posted "no swimming" (for safety reasons), meaning surfing only. In effect, it is segregated by age. From Los Angeles on down the California coast, this is an era of age segregation.
>   . . . In California today surfers, not to mention rock'n'roll kids and the hot rodders or Hair Boys, named for their fanciful pompadours—all sorts of sets of kids—they don't merely hang around together. They establish whole little societies for themselves.[3]

Wolfe's point of entry to the story is a confrontation between an old couple—a swimsuited old gent with hairless legs encased in black nylon socks, his wife with a "shaking Jello smile"—and the surfer gang. There is no violence, except for the hatred and revulsion in the thoughts of the younger set. Wolfe discards the old couple as they set up their camp on the beach with folding chairs, newspapers, and tanning ointment and immerses himself in the doings of the young, towheaded rabble. At first glorying in the wonder of surferspeak, Wolfe soon emerges from his brief foray into the beach branch of youth culture with a depressing and frightening evaluation: these kids are going nowhere. They are disconnected. They are "beached whales." What could have been a purely enjoyable observational piece about yet another strain of *kookus Californius* turns into a somewhat melancholy deliberation on lives without vision and void of hope. Comedy becomes, by the last paragraphs of the article, a prelude to a tragedy Wolfe feels is inevitable.

The story did not sit well with members of the gang. Portrayed as future losers, the young surfer dudes and dudettes said they were betrayed by the Ice Cream Man, that guy in the white suit. "Most of us thought he was a geek," one of them said. "Some people thought he was a narc because of the oddball way he dressed. . . . Back then, nobody had ever heard of Tom Wolfe." Indeed, the image of the natty Wolfe, notebook at the ready, chatting with a monosyllabic, tanned beach boy is irresistible. Nevertheless, the crowd opened up to him. Afterward, they felt betrayed, and graffiti scrawled on the pump house wall read, "Tom Wolfe is a dork."[4]

Twenty-five years after the publication of "The New Life out There" (the original title of the article) in *New York*, the *Los Angeles Times* sent a writer down to the beach to find out what had happened to the original rabble. Wolfe's prediction had come true in part. Some had eschewed the beach life and grown up to be responsible and contributing members of society. Yet some had followed the career path Wolfe had outlined: drugs, jail, dead. Others just disappeared. Those who survived to make the transition to mainstream life insisted that they had not "sold out" by doing so. They were not the outsiders they had scorned so viciously on the beach a quarter-century before. They certainly were not the beached whales of Wolfe's prediction. Members of the pump house gang came to criticize Wolfe's methods. His article claims intimacy with their private lives, and yet, they reported, he never followed them home. He stayed at the beach and asked them questions. They also accused him of some outright fabrications. The parents who were offstage characters in Wolfe's story were very real and concerned about their children, the pumphousers recalled years later.

Despite these complaints, some of the gang said that what Wolfe wrote was the truth in spirit, if not in letter. As one of the prominent characters in the 1966 article, Liz Derks, recalled in 1991: "I sometimes stop and think, 'Yeah, maybe we did do all those strange things.' And I still think it's wild that some famous writer made a big deal out of our group. Or else nobody would even be talking about us today. The way I look at it, Tom Wolfe put us on the map."[5]

Of the other pieces in the book, "The King of the Status Dropouts," Wolfe's profile of Hugh Hefner, serves perhaps as a keystone for his understanding of the new culture he was so deftly chronicling. As he wrote in the introduction to the collection, Hefner was a sort of Jay Gatsby in real life. Shut out from legitimate Chicago society because of his somewhat humble social origin and the fact that he published—no matter how glossy and homogenized—what upper-crust society deemed a "girlie magazine," Hefner was persona non grata among the ruling elite of Chicago. He had, therefore, created his own world. Hefner, Wolfe was informed in casual conversation, never left his home, the famous Playboy Mansion. In fact, he rarely left his bedroom. He never dressed but nearly always padded about the mansion in silk housecoat and pajamas, puffing on his pipe, guzzling prolific amounts of Pepsi, and ruling as master of a very controlled universe. Gatsby tries to buy his way into society. Hefner created his own—a society not defined by geography but by attitude. And he ruled over this domain from his great revolving bed. To say this fascinated Wolfe is to belittle his contemplation of Mr. Playboy. Wolfe's story was pure hyperventilation:

> Thirty-nine years old! A recluse! Bonafide! Doesn't go out, doesn't see the light of day, doesn't put his hide out in God's own unconditioned Chicago air for months on end; *years*. Right this minute, one supposes, he is somewhere there in the innards of those forty-eight rooms, under layers and layers of white wall-to-wall, crimson wall-to-wall, Count-Basie lounge leather, muffled, baffled, swaddled, shrouded, closed in, blacked out. . . . He's down there, the living Hugh Hefner, 150 pounds, like the tender-tympany green heart of an artichoke.[6]

Hefner was proof, if we still needed any, that American society had undergone a revolution since the beginning of the century. Jay Gatsby has a hope of buying his way into the old order. Despite his wealth and accomplishments, Hefner did not because of how he had made his money: preying on lust. As Wolfe wrote: "So he has gone them one better. He has started his own league. He has created his own world, in his own palace. He has created his own statusphere."[7]

Carol Doda, an exotic dancer, did the same to a lesser, yet at the same time more extreme, degree. She had her average-size breasts injected with silicon until her chest was large enough to give her a new career. Her 44-

inch bustline drew thousands of patrons to San Francisco's Condor Club and served for three decades as one (or rather two) of the city's most notable tourist attractions. Silicon status. Doda recognized the nature of this bit of invention. Throughout Wolfe's profile, she refers to herself in the first person, but her breasts in the third ("When a man asks me out," she told Wolfe, "I never know if he is interested in me or *them*.")[8]

Another profile subject, Marshall McLuhan, was going one step further: he was not merely redefining society but redefining civilization. A prophet of the media explosion, McLuhan first sounded the alarms that still echo through modern society. Another piece, "Bob and Spike," examines a new cultural couple who, in the Gatsby tradition, bought their way into New York City's artistic community. All around him, Wolfe easily found examples of the new status: Elvis Presley and the Beatles, for instance, the biggest stars the music industry had produced, came from low-rent backgrounds. Such a background became so much the vogue that those from more conventional and comfortable homes began to invent a working-class history for themselves in order to qualify according to the new cultural rules.

Yet not all of the pieces in the book deal with the celebrity strain of status. Visits to London and an outright delineation of the new rules of behavior ("Tom Wolfe's New Book of Etiquette") fill in the gaps in the picture of the decade's cultural changes. Recording these changes had to be done outside of the cocoon of the New York media axis, Wolfe said.

The isolation of the city prevented many of the nation's premier writers, who had been drawn to New York because of its concentration of intellectual power, from witnessing the changes that had begun and taken root elsewhere. What appeared as startling insights to the editors of *New York* and, thus, the readers, was actually old stuff. As Wolfe told an interviewer when *The Pump House Gang* was published:

> It seems that a lot of people made a great discovery in other parts of the country, which was that you could take all of this money that had been coming after the war, and the free time that people suddenly had, and do something else instead of trying to compete in the old way for status in a community system. . . . A lot of the people outside New York found out that they could form their own little status groups, set their own rules, like surfers, kids who were living by themselves for much of the summer, in garages and things like that.[9]

The critic Lawrence Dietz said *The Pump House Gang* was essential for anyone who hoped to understand the psychic changes befalling America in the last half of the twentieth century. Furthermore, Dietz wrote, the age had found its perfect stylist: "Wolfe's elliptical, ellipses-filled style is perfectly suited to describe this America."[10] Jack Kroll of *Newsweek* was even more effusive in his praise. In a dual review of *The Pump House Gang* and *The Electric Kool-Aid Acid Test* (virtually all of the critics paired them), Kroll gushed: "Tom Wolfe is some kind of great writer. . . . Among journalists, Wolfe is a genuine poet. . . . In a way, Wolfe is in the line of the great journalizing American fictionists from Stephen Crane to Ring Lardner to Hemingway to John O'Hara to Mailer."[11] Jack Richardson, in the *New Republic*, likened Wolfe's effervescent prose style to the rambunctious rhetoric of a Baptist preacher:

> [Wolfe] is a word-spinner wondering at the creation of the Lord, the creation, mind you, not the Lord himself, for Wolfe is a journalist and his sermon, well-tuned to the demands of the faithful, rejoices over what is simply happening, what the new thing is for today. Never mind if the new things are trivial or pathetic (these are archaic categories anyway), faith and exuberance will redeem all. Just listen to the language, hear the onomatopoeia and the conglomerate adjectives and all the old prejudices about significance will be washed away.[12]

The Pump House Gang continued some of the general themes of *The Kandy-Kolored Tangerine-Flake Streamline Baby* and served Wolfe as a more focused pulpit from which to delineate his vision of America and to note the decline of the altruism of the past and the self-obsession that had begun to rise in the 1960s and would continue during the years he continued writing for magazines.

Radical Chic and Mau-Mauing the Flak Catchers

Throughout his career, Wolfe has been a brilliant phrasemaker. Rarely was he more on-target than with "radical chic," his acidic description of how white liberals suffused with guilt embraced those who claimed to be dedicated to hating them. Actually, the term "radical chic" was coined by the journalist Seymour Krim in a 1962 *New Yorker* article; it had been published in a book collection just prior to Wolfe's attendance at the infamous party.[13] Wolfe was mainly responsible for popularizing the phrase.

Radical Chic and Mau-Mauing the Flak Catchers, an exercise in coast-to-coast culture-watching, was different from Wolfe's earlier books. A slim volume, it contains only two pieces; the first, written for *New York* and the more celebrated of the two, is "Radical Chic." It is a cautionary tale bearing the moral: "Do not invite Tom Wolfe to your parties. He will *see* you." In fact, Leonard and Felicia Bernstein did not invite Tom Wolfe to their defense party for the Black Panthers in their Manhattan townhouse in 1970; they invited David Halberstam. Wolfe saw the invitation on the desk of his Pulitzer Prize–winning *New York* colleague and, since Halberstam was not around, called the R.S.V.P. number, identified himself, and asked if he could come. Sure, a voice told him. Wolfe arrived with a reporter's notebook and a Bic pen, introduced himself to the Bernsteins, and openly took notes all evening. He made no attempt to hide what he was doing. Then he watched the spectacle unfold.

Here was the higher echelon of New York's upper-crust arts and intellectual community wining and dining the militant members of the Black Panther party, a group rebelling against the very things the high-society members represented. Many of the partygoers squirmed in paroxysms of white liberal guilt as they tried to ingratiate themselves with the grim-faced, combat-garbed Panthers. It was as if Wolfe were witnessing, at that party, the dawn of Political Correctness. Wealthy white members of the power structure, suffused with anguish about the material wealth they had accumulated, were trying to deny it all so that they could be like their less fortunate, disenfranchised brethren. The disenfranchised, of course, wanted more than tea, crumpets, and sympathy. They wanted to be included in the mainstream of society and have opportunities to become part of the power structure.

Merely entertaining the radicals, having them up to the house, introducing them to their wealthy friends—that appeared to be all the Bernsteins intended by hosting the party. Yet the Panthers, with whom Wolfe seems genuinely sympathetic, called the bluff of the white liberals. Beginning with a supposed vision of Leonard Bernstein's from years before—a black man rising from the depths of a grand piano to challenge the great maestro, who always saw himself as a friend of the oppressed—Wolfe then simply reports the goings-on. The partygoers coo over the hors d'oeuvres, admire the furnishings, and compliment one another on their love beads, turtlenecks, and other desperate attempts at youthful hipness. The Panthers are reserved, partners with Wolfe in observation.

Wolfe offers occasional hilarious asides about some of those in attendance. For example, Carter and Amanda Burden, a young and beautiful New York society couple, are revealed to be in apparent competition with other trendies in becoming hipper than thou. In asides that convey the tone of a conspiratorial whisper (the speakers for the Panther fund-raiser had begun), Wolfe allows as how the Burdens were the first couple to adopt a totally radical-chic lifestyle and mentions that, as *Vogue* had pointed out, "Mrs. Burden, with the help of a maid, is learning how to keep house."[14]

As the speakers begin, the self-congratulatory serenity expires. The Panthers want to talk about educational programs and before-school breakfasts for disadvantaged youth. They want to talk about the injustice that oppresses millions of black Americans, and they want to describe their attempts to seize control of the power structure. But the partygoers have another agenda. One tuxedo-sporting, slick-haired dandy shouts toward the speakers, in pure Southhampton lockjaw, "Who do you call to give a party?"[15] The Panthers are both amused and enraged by the hypocrisies of the Park Avenue set, who see identification with social justice as simply that year's fashion. Leonard and Felicia Bernstein, Carter and Amanda Burden, and other party guests (among them, the journalist Barbara Walters and the film directors Otto Preminger and Sidney Lumet) do not escape unscathed from Wolfe's eye.

The silliness of the disconnected lifestyle of the superbly wealthy comes through in what Wolfe terms the "great recurrent emotion" of radical chic, which he attributes to a Park Avenue matron swooning over the brothers in their combat gear: "These are no civil-rights *Negroes* wearing gray suits three sizes too big—these are *real men!*"[16] The foolish statements and behavior of Bernstein and his friends make them ripe for the picking. As Wolfe said later, his "uncharitable instincts" were aroused by the blindness of people who portrayed themselves as know-it-alls. If written with care and accuracy, such scenes can be telling in the extreme. "For example," Wolfe said, "it never occurred to Leonard Bernstein that there could be anything humorous about the spectacle of the Black Panthers outlining their ten-point revolutionary program in his 13-room duplex on Park Avenue."[17] It was not the leftist political slant of most of the partygoers that Wolfe found so compelling, even if those so inclined tended to take political umbrage at Wolfe's article. "I have never been very much interested in politics," Wolfe told an interviewer. "I'm much more interested in intellectual fashion. . . . When I got to New York [after graduate school], I found there are so many people who totally accept what is current intellectual fashion and then pat themselves on the back for being nonconformists."[18]

Wolfe was not the only reporter at the party. Charlotte Curtis of the *New York Times* was also present; her story aroused much anger when it appeared, not only in the New York newspaper but also, via the New York Times News Service, in papers all over the country. But the coup de grâce occurred a few months later when "Those Radical Chic Evenings" appeared in *New York*. Wolfe became even more of a pariah. The doors that had been closed to him after "Tiny Mummies!" was published were nothing compared with the slamming doors that the report of the Bernstein party inspired. What he had done seemed so *impolite* to members of society. He had been a guest at the party—it just wasn't good form to write about it. Wolfe believed there was a larger reason for the anger over his piece: "It was laughter in church. . . . I was a heretic for saying there was something amusing about Mr. and Mrs. Leonard Bernstein giving a party for the Black Panthers . . . at which the Panthers were invited to rise up and tell all assembled exactly what horrible things would happen to them the day the Black Panthers had their way."[19]

Wolfe was offered a dressing-down by the great maestro's sister, who wrote Wolfe a letter offering a litany of the many lapses in good conduct he had committed at the Bernsteins' home that night, not the least of which was concealing a tape recorder in his clothing and recording the partygoers without their knowledge. "I knew then I was right on course," Wolfe said. "Kind of a left-handed compliment. Actually, I knew that if I hadn't been accurate, that would have been the first cry."[20] Wolfe attributed his accuracy to "the oldest and most orthodox" of techniques: he took notes.[21]

From the other side of the aisle came further damnation. A reporter from *Time* asked one of the Black Panther ministers for a reaction to Wolfe's account. The reply: "You mean that dirty, blatant, lying, racist dog who wrote that fascist disgusting thing in *New York* magazine?"[22]

The other part of the book, "Mau-Mauing the Flak Catchers," is a related story of activity on the other coast. A kind of primer on dealing with minority issues, its subject is the bureaucracy that allegedly serves the poor. Wolfe, well versed in the works of the sociologist Max Weber, could see how principles and intentions often do not work when they are applied. "Mau-Mauing the Flak Catchers" is a perfect companion piece to "Radical Chic," both in terms of geography and in subject: they trace parallel journeys into high and low society.

A far shorter piece, "Mau-Mauing the Flak Catchers" concerns slum life in San Francisco. For it, Wolfe adopts the language of the ghetto. "Mau-mauing," for example, is a ghetto term. As Wolfe's downstage narrator explains, a civil rights demonstration is but a vague threat. It shows whitey general resentment. But mau-mauing is in-person, in-

your-face resentment intended to strike fear into the bureaucracy. It
works.

The two pieces in the book are excellent examples of Wolfe's technique of including status-life details. As the mau-mauing brigade heads
downtown to the welfare office, they run into the chief flak catcher.
Wolfe stops the story for a paragraph to describe the low-life civil servant
from head to toe:

> All you have to do is look at him and you get the picture. The man's a
> lifer. He's stone civil service. He has it all down from the wheatcolor
> Hush Puppies to the wash'n'dry semi-tab-collar shortsleeves white shirt.
> Those wheatcolor Hush Puppies must be like some kind of fraternal garb
> among the civil-service employees because they all wear them. They cost
> about $4.99 and the second time you move your toes, the seams split and
> the tops come away from the soles. But they all wear them. The man's
> shirt looks like he bought it at the August end-of-summer sale at the
> White Front. It is one of those shirts with pockets on both sides. Sticking
> out of the pockets and running across his chest he has a lineup of ball-
> point pens, felt nibs, lead pencils, wax markers, such as you wouldn't
> believe, Paper-mates, Pentels, Scriptos, Eberhard Fabel Mongol 482's,
> Dri-Marks, Bic PM-29's, everything. They are lined up across his chest
> like campaign ribbons.[23]

The flak catcher exists to insulate the serious decision-making
bureaucrats from the people they are supposed to be helping. The mau-
mauers ask the flak catcher questions that he cannot answer and then
fume while he takes a long time giving them a nonanswer. Then ensues
the staged threats of violence, all committed with utter seriousness.
Going inside the mind of a mau-mauer allows Wolfe to explore the
process from within. As one review summarized it, here were the "finer
techniques" of the art: "First, aspect: 'You go down there with your hair
stickin' out!' Second, mien: 'Don't say nothing. You just glare.' Then,
tactics—which include bringing along some ringer Samoans who all
look ten feet tall."[24]

In the end, the mau-mauers show the flak catcher the power of intim-
idation, they have the pleasurable satisfaction of a good mau-mauing
(like a fine meal), and Wolfe records the spectacle. The flak catcher is
frightened out of his mind, but the mau-mauers are only having good
sport. But beyond sport, mau-mauing is, for the black man, "a beautiful
trip," Wolfe writes. "It energized your masculinity."[25]   There is, of

course, no danger to the flak catcher or anyone else in the episode Wolfe sociologically observes and describes.

Some critics preferred this second, shorter, and less notorious story to the flashier, celebrity-filled "Radical Chic." Citing the piece's "ethical sense" and "genuine humor," the critic Peter Michelson said, "'Mau-Mauing the Flak Catchers' [is] much closer to Wolfe's good work. Here he dismounts his hobby horse."[26] Other critics complimented Wolfe on his eye for the ludicrous, which they saw as part of a larger design: "Poverty. Racism. Eldridge Cleaver. Is nothing sacred to Mr. Wolfe? Of course not. His instinct is for comedy and he reduces everything to the ridiculous. . . . 'He doesn't care,' the Wolfe critics cry. . . . Partly true, no doubt. But to leave Mr. Wolfe there—pat and a touch cruel—is to ignore his passion. Beyond his mere knowingness he has a deeper urge to know."[27]

Joseph Epstein wrote in *Commentary* that in planning their splendid benefit for the Panthers, the Bernsteins overlooked one major detail: "Keeping the journalist Tom Wolfe the hell out of their Park Avenue duplex. . . . The Bernsteins' evening with the Panthers is a subject Tom Wolfe might almost be said to have been born to write about."[28] The *New York Times Book Review* was less kind. Characterizing the inclusion of status-life details as reflective of Wolfe's inability to "keep his hands off" of seemingly superfluous information, the critic concluded that the fun of Wolfe's writing had worn thin.[29]

Wolfe has said that he has a special affection for *Radical Chic and Mau-Mauing the Flak Catchers*. "As a piece of sheer writing, it's my favorite book," he said in 1987.[30] The slim volume may be the most convenient example of how Wolfe employs his techniques—recording dialogue, including status-life details, and using scenes rather than exposition—in crafting New Journalism pieces.

Mauve Gloves and Madmen, Clutter and Vine

Wolfe's last real collection (other than *The Purple Decades*, an anthology drawn from his earlier collections) does not have the unity of *The Kandy-Kolored Tangerine-Flake Streamline Baby*, *The Pump House Gang*, or *Radical Chic and Mau-Mauing the Flak Catchers*. He had written introductions to the first two books to establish a context for readers. The two stories in *Radical Chic* were also obviously related. Although the pieces in *Mauve Gloves and Madmen* echo Wolfe's usual concerns with status, the collection also serves as an introduction to his later magazine writing. In most of the pieces in the earlier collections, Wolfe is an observer. In his two books on art, *The Painted Word* and *From Bauhaus to Our House*, and in half of the pieces in *Mauve Gloves and Madmen*, Wolfe is an essayist.

He was concentrating on longer works. He conceived his novel *The Bonfire of the Vanities* even before attending Leonard Bernstein's party in 1970. Then came the all-consuming assignment on the space program, which ate up much of that decade for him. When he did write for magazines after the early 1970s, his writing took the form of longer, chin-scratching articles (such as the pieces on art for *Harper's*) or adaptations of parts of his books.

So *Mauve Gloves and Madmen, Clutter and Vine* has something of a schizophrenic quality. Some pieces carry the stamp of Wolfe the Reporter, but more of them are the work of Wolfe the Social Philosopher. It was in this second guise that Wolfe, in 1976, in one of his seminal magazine pieces, coined a phrase that will no doubt figure prominently in his obituary: "the Me Decade." Unlike "radical chic," this phrase was completely original with Wolfe.

Although ostensibly tied to the rise of Jimmy Carter as a presidential candidate in 1976, Wolfe's original *New York* article, "The 'Me' Decade and the Third Great Awakening,"[31] transcends the "feel good about yourself and while you're at it think good thoughts about America" nature of the Carter message and looks to the "considerable narcissism" that was endemic in 1970s America. Well within his new role as an essayist (but unlike the man he had dubbed a "snoremonger," Walter Lippmann), Wolfe surveys the landscape of self-indulgence, including brief journalistic stops at EST sessions (Erhard Seminars Training, founded and run by Werner Erhard), the Esalan Institute (whose specialty was "lube jobs for the personality"), and other encounter groups.[32] He offers the famous hair-dye advertising slogan as the rallying cry for the Me Decade: "If I've only one life, let me live it as a blonde!" All this leads away from the basic American value of altruism:

> The husband and wife who sacrifice their own ambitions and their material assets in order to provide a "better future" for their children . . . the soldier who risks his life, or perhaps consciously sacrifices it, in battle . . . the man who devotes his life to some struggle for "his people" that cannot possibly be won in his lifetime. . . . Most people, historically, have *not* lived their lives as if thinking, "I have only one life to live." Instead they have lived as if they are living their ancestors' lives and their offspring's lives and perhaps their neighbors' lives as well. They have seen themselves

as inseparable from the great tide of chromosomes of which they are created and which they pass on.[33]

Yet the narcissistic interpretation of Wolfe's essay limited the scope of readers' understanding, in the author's view. The flip side of the self-preoccupation he describes was a recognition of the new masses, whose lives of quiet desperation were suddenly perceived as more important; in being so recognized, the daily drudgery of life was elevated in status. The simple fact of gender assumed a tremendous importance. The women's movement of the 1970s is the perfect example. As Wolfe wrote four years after "The Me Decade and the Third Great Awakening" appeared: "One's existence *as a woman* . . . as *Me* . . . became something all the world analyzed, agonized over, drew consciousness from or, in any event, took seriously. . . . Out of such intense concentration upon the self . . . came a feeling that was decidedly religious, binding one beaming righteous soul to the other in the name of the cause."[34]

The prevailing preoccupation with self naturally led to the new frontiers of sexuality, where concerns about the quantity and quality of orgasms became fixations. The reporting had essentially been done. Wolfe may have taken a few bites from self-help seminars, but the material was ripe for collating. The "Me Decade" was a phrase in search of coinage. Wolfe did it. Although proud of concocting it, Wolfe said it was an obvious label just waiting to be put into words. "When I called the 1970s the Me Decade, I was smart enough to wait until 1976 before I opened my mouth," he said.[35]

The rest of the *Mauve Gloves* miscellany includes one of Wolfe's favorite pieces, "The Truest Sport: Jousting with Sam and Charlie," a story of two Vietnam fighter jocks that, with its pilot lingo, prefigures *The Right Stuff*. For this piece, Wolfe was back in his reporter mode, expertly describing the inarticulate coolness of two brave pilots. "The Commercial" was Wolfe's first published fiction since college, an interior monologue that comes from the skull of a famous black athlete manipulating the white power brokers during the making of a television advertisement. Back in the essay mode, his thoughts on the pornography of violence lead to his recurring theme of status: "Violence is the simple, ultimate solution for the problems of status competition, just as gambling is the simple, ultimate solution for economic competition."[36] His first piece for *Rolling Stone*, an extension of radicalism into fashion, "Funky Chic," had appeared in the magazine in 1973. By 1976, when the book was published, it was nearly outdated by the trend toward disco clothing. The article offers another pulpit from which to rail against the Park Avenue pretensions detailed in *Radical Chic*: suddenly, poverty was *in*, but as Wolfe notes, "Everybody had sworn off fashion, but somehow nobody moved to Cincinnati to work among the poor."[37] A series of Wolfe's vicious, satirical drawings fills out the book.

His move into the role of social critic suited Wolfe well and was the logical extension of his career. As he concentrated on larger works after the mid-1970s, the shoes of a mordant observer seemed to fit and provided him with a graceful transition from his earlier incarnation as a newspaper and magazine reporter. As he assumed this mantle, he began an association with another magazine, one that was more at home with the social criticism he now espoused: *Harper's*.

Chapter Seven
The World of Art

Of the many objects on the American landscape that Tom Wolfe has chosen to study, he frequently returns to the world of art. He has often illustrated his works with his original drawings, which are not the usual crude scrawls with which some authors have littered their books. On the contrary, his artistic style displays the same cutting, satirical grace of his prose. One of his books, *In Our Time* (1980), is almost exclusively devoted to his drawings, although it includes some of his funniest and most brilliant writing.

In his more traditional role as an essayist and social observer, Wolfe has produced two works devoted to branches of American art. One of his first major magazine articles, "The Courts Must Curb Culture" (1966), noted that modern art had become the new religion of the American elite.[1] He enlarged on that theme nearly two decades later in a *Harper's* essay called "The Worship of Art," in which he noted that art had utterly replaced any notion of spirituality in many aspects of modern life.[2] *The Painted Word* (1975) is an extended attack on the bankruptcy of modern art. *From Bauhaus to Our House* (1981) is a similar assault on the architectural community. Both books inspired violent reactions from those he derided, though few could argue with Wolfe's interpretation of the varied histories of the disciplines. He had done his homework. Both books were freckled with examples and illustrations that backed up his assertions. The two books on art had done precisely what he wanted them to do: ruffle feathers.

The Painted Word

Helen Hughes Wolfe must have read her son "The Emperor's New Clothes" when he was a child. The story of the boy who sees through sham and deceit makes a good analogy for Wolfe and the way he has looked at the world of art. In Wolfe's view, it was blatantly obvious: the art world was perpetrating a hoax. The highly regarded works of "art" of the modern era were nothing more than carefully crafted mockeries.

Wolfe sounded the alarm in his books, as if to say, "We're being sold a bill of goods. The emperor has no clothes!"

In *The Painted Word*, Wolfe stepped firmly away from his position as a "mere" magazine writer and became the essayist of the later part of his career. It was a logical and necessary development. Removed from the day-to-day grind of newspaper or magazine work, Wolfe was able to adjust the rhythm of his work. With more time for research, he also had more time for contemplation. And the editors were asking him to go beyond the approach of "recording it all" to expounding on "what it all means."

The primary assertion of the extended essay is that the New York school of painting was a creation of self-serving art critics and that the whole modern art movement was a hoax perpetuated on an unsuspecting public by artists of meager talent. The book was Wolfe's primer on twentieth-century art and showed him comfortably adapting to his role of social critic, even if his transition was not greeted with universal praise. The commentator William F. Buckley, Jr., characterized the book as "a moustache painted in broad daylight on the *Mona Lisa*."[3] The extreme critical scorn that greeted the book generally cited Wolfe's status as an outsider in the modern art world, something that came as a relief to the author. Although the book certainly contains stinging criticism, Wolfe was also encountering once again, as he had with the "Radical Chic" essay, the thin skin of those who bowed to intellectual fashion. Those in the ranks of the outraged were primarily art critics or defenders of the art critics. How ironic, Wolfe said: "If you even make *gentle* fun of people who inhabit the world that you and I live in or the world of the arts, or anything having to do with expression, they *scream like murder*. And of course they have the equipment to fight back."[4]

And fight they did. *The Painted Word* set off a frenzy that made the uproar occasioned by *Radical Chic and Mau-Mauing the Flak Catchers* look mild by comparison. One of the most outrageous of criticisms came from the *New Republic*, in an essay that charged the conservative establishment with having prepared Wolfe at Yale in the 1950s as some sort of "secret weapon" to destroy the Left and all of its institutions (the modern art community being one of those institutions, of course). Wolfe was a cultural kamikaze in the service of this conspiracy, functioning much like the character played by Laurence Harvey in the classic film of paranoia, *The Manchurian Candidate* (1962). "I loved that," Wolfe said. "And he's talking about Yale. When I was at Yale, William Buckley was writing *God and Man at Yale*, saying that it had been taken over by the Left and that the Left was pouring all of this poison into the innocent vessels of the young."[5]

The Painted Word took as its starting point Wolfe's encounter with the Sunday *New York Times* arts section, in which the critic Hilton Kramer asserted, in an article about an exhibition of paintings at Yale: "Realism does not lack its partisans, but it does rather conspicuously lack a persuasive theory. And given the nature of our intellectual commerce with works of art, to lack a persuasive theory is to lack something crucial—the means by which our experience of individual works is joined to our understanding of the values they signify."[6]

Wolfe was startled by the passage. It meant, to him, that the visceral enjoyment of a work of art was fraudulent and that modern art was now a *literary* experience. As Wolfe noted: "In short: frankly, these days, without a theory to go with it, I can't *see* a painting."[7] In the (art) world according to Wolfe—described in the remainder of the profusely illustrated book—the tale of the twentieth century unfolds in a series of vignettes about the major critics and artists of the modernist movement. The self-perpetuating critics had put themselves in roles that validated their self-importance to the innocent audience, making the explanation of the painting, in Wolfe's words, as important as the painting itself. This exercise all turned on the performance of the artist in what Wolfe called "the BoHo Dance": "The artist feels he must first come to lower Manhattan. He could do the same paintings in Albuquerque but he is not going to be noticed unless he gets involved in the lower Manhattan art world . . . [which involves] no more than three thousand people, and they practically all live in New York City."[8]

In Wolfe's tale, artists often appeared to be tools of the major critics, Clement Greenberg and Harold Rosenberg. Patrons and critics, according to Wolfe, controlled the destinies of such artists as Jackson Pollock. Greenberg, denying the three-dimensional effects of painting and extolling the "flatness" of much of modern art, saw Pollock's work as a suitable vessel for him to use in expounding his views. As Wolfe wrote of Greenberg, "he used Pollock's certified success to put over Flatness as *the* theory—the theoretical breakthrough of Einstein-scale authority—of the entire new wave of the Tenth Street *cenacle des cenacles*."[9]

Charges such as these were inflammatory in the self-congratulatory community of critics. Since Hilton Kramer would have had a conflict of interest in reviewing *The Painted Word* for the *New York Times*, his colleague John Russell did the deed. Russell said there was nothing at all "silly" about Kramer's original assertion in the *Times* article that had

inspired Wolfe's attack. Russell's prominently displayed piece savaged
Wolfe, stating that the author was a gadfly ill equipped to write about
something of which he had no understanding: "It is dismal to read a
book by a reputedly very clever man in which virtually every single sen-
tence goes off the rails and has to be lifted back on by an effort of good
will. Mr. Wolfe is a fellow of infinite jest, as all know, and when he
knows what he is talking about he can be very droll indeed. . . . But
most of the time in "The Painted Word," he does not know what he is
talking about."[10]

However, at least one of Wolfe's assertions was later confirmed by
biographers of Jackson Pollock. Wolfe had claimed that Pollock was a
tool not only of Greenberg and Rosenberg but also of his art dealer,
Peggy Guggenheim. The biographers concluded that, however disturbing his comments were to the arts community, Wolfe was on the
right trail and his description of Pollock's self-destructive habits was
on-target.[11]

The virulent attacks on the book substantiated one of his major
points, Wolfe said. There were a number of political attacks as well,
including the *New Republic* article declaring Wolfe a fascist. Some
attacked his mental competence, claiming that Wolfe was known to be
insane and *Harper's* was irresponsible for publishing the original piece.
And there were what Wolfe called "the X-rated insults." Not long after
the book's publication, Wolfe said, a "well-known abstract-expression
painter" said, at a dinner party, that Wolfe was like a young child at a
pornographic movie: he could follow the basic action of the film but
could not understand the nuances ("I loved the notion that there was
someone in this day and age who professes to find *nuances* in a *pornographic movie*," Wolfe said). Soon, *Time* magazine's art critic, Robert
Hughes, wrote that Wolfe was bereft of understanding of the art world,
like an 11-year-old at a pornographic film.[12] Russell's review in the *New
York Times Book Review* used a similar image: "If someone who is tone-
deaf goes to Carnegie Hall every night of the year he is, of course, entitled to his opinion of what he has listened to, just as a eunuch is entitled
to his opinion of sex."[13]

To Wolfe, the use of these related (and faulty) metaphors became
"indirect proof of a point I was making in *The Painted Word*—just how
small a world the art world is. As far as I know, neither of those men
[Hughes and Russell] were at the dinner party. But this conceit, this
metaphor, quickly passed around to the 3,000 souls who make up the
entire New York art world."[14]

Not all of the critical community chose to vilify Wolfe. Ruth Berenson, writing in *National Review*, said the book "will delight those who have long harbored dark suspicions that modern art beginning with Picasso is a put-on, a gigantic hoax perpetrated on a gullible public by a mysterious cabal of artists, critics, dealers and collectors aided and abetted by *Time* and *Newsweek*. Those who take modern art somewhat more seriously will be disappointed."[15]

Wolfe considered the drubbing to be the price of being outspoken. "Every time I go into the intellectual arena, the reaction is outrage in the extreme," he told an interviewer four years after *The Painted Word* was published. Members of the intelligentsia, Wolfe noted, liked to see themselves as social critics, firing off sharply worded commentaries to the *Times* impugning the government and other institutions. Wolfe said when the tables were turned and the criticism was directed toward intellectuals, they showed tremendous bite: "They can do a lot more than the government to hurt you. What risk is there in attacking the government? There are people who make full-time livings attacking the CIA and the FBI, and nothing ever happens to them. But the intellectuals bite back, and they can write bad things about you."[16]

From Bauhaus to Our House

The critical bludgeoning that followed *The Painted Word* did not dissuade Wolfe from further missions into enemy territory. Although he originally intended his second book of art criticism to be wide-ranging, covering architecture, serious music, dance, and philosophy,[17] the book centered only on architecture. With *From Bauhaus to Our House*, the operative literary reference once again was to "The Emperor's New Clothes," and the theme of a hoodwinked public, threading the essays together, reappeared as well. The essays were originally published in consecutive issues of *Harper's*, to which Wolfe had become a monthly contributor.

Again, in architecture Wolfe saw a triumph of criticism over sense and—since these artists had a direct effect on domiciles and workplaces—comfort. The architectural community, like the art world, had immersed itself in a self-congratulatory and self-perpetuating pool presided over by a handful of critics. Wolfe's book is unabashedly biased by his taste in buildings, which favors almost anything built before 1920. Yet since that time, the architectural community had been under the control of a few semidictatorial theoreticians. As Wolfe told an interviewer, "I learned that in order to achieve a first-rank reputation in

architecture, you must enter the academic sphere. It is now more important to have academic architectural concepts and do architectural drawings of unbuilt buildings than to build buildings."[18]

The villain in this piece was Walter Gropius, "the silver prince" (as
Wolfe called him), founder of the Bauhaus School of Design in the
Weimar Republic of post–World War I Germany. Gropius indoctrinated
his students with his beliefs and even controlled their diets, feeding them
mush and raw vegetables, with a little garlic for flavor. This bad-
breathed army of disciples spread Gropius's design concepts throughout
the world, until nearly all public buildings began to resemble what
Wolfe called a "duplicating-machine replacement-parts wholesale distri-
bution warehouse."[19] Gropius's troops, holed up at American centers of
learning, indoctrinated susceptible students, who then went forth to celebrate blandness and call it clever.

Wolfe saw a delightful irony in the fact that American capitalism
enthroned itself in corporate headquarters that had roots in something
far outside the national experience. Surveying the buildings that housed
CBS, Exxon, J. C. Penney, and other giants of free enterprise, Wolfe
noted that they were tributes to the vision of architects from socialist
societies. The towers and blocks of steel and glass were, in Wolfe's view,
totally un-American in origin and style. The appeal of the Bauhaus style
was its "Europeanness." It was avant-garde, and therefore, Wolfe wrote,
it was irresistible to the American architectural community, which
embraced the style with a warmth that would be lacking in the buildings they constructed.

The Bauhaus students and *their* students created a long line of academic progeny who controlled the prevailing thought of the architectural
community, making it difficult for a designer to gain any stature outside
of the closed circle. Wolfe recalled an encounter after he had published
an article that commented favorably on the work of Eero Saarinen, who
had designed airport terminals—including Kennedy International and
Washington's Dulles—that gracefully resembled birds' wings. The article merely complimented Saarinen's work and suggested he was worth
reconsideration as an artist. An architect at a party pointed out to Wolfe
that Saarinen's basic problem was that he was not a member of the
(Bauhaus) club. If you use Saarinen as an example, the man told Wolfe,
people won't take you seriously. As Wolfe wrote:

> I wish there was some way I could convey the look on his face. It was a
> cross between a sneer and a shrug that the French are so good at, the look

that says the subject is so *outre*, so *infra dig*, so *de la boue*, one can't even spend time analyzing it without having some of the rubbish rub off.

The principle illustrated by the Saarinen case was: no architect could achieve a major reputation outside the compounds, which were now centered in the universities. The architect who insisted on going his own way stood no chance of being hailed as a pioneer of some important new direction.[20]

What infuriated Wolfe perhaps the most was that the academicization of architecture had led to a denial of some of the basic American characteristics that had previously been celebrated in this country's buildings. Now buildings were constructed not to pay homage to human qualities or ideals, but merely to celebrate modern architecture. It was, in Wolfe's view, morally and aesthetically bankrupt.

The fertile ground for this intellectual tyranny in the architectural community, Wolfe felt, was America's lingering inferiority complex. He used architecture as a vehicle to explain a larger problem. "My interest in writing *From Bauhaus to Our House*," he said, "was not to express aesthetic preferences in architecture but to present an intellectual history of how ideas take hold in the United States, which is still a little colony of Europe when it comes to ideas."[21] Wolfe elaborated on this idea in characteristically hyperbolic fashion in a television interview:

> This is the American century, so-called. Our people are so wealthy and so full of animal energy that every 43-year-old cablevision lineman's out on the disco floor with his red eyes beaming through his walnut-shell eyelids, dancing with his third wife or his new cookie until the onset of dawn or saline depletion. And in *this* century, the robust, full-blooded American century, what do we have in the way of architecture? A European style that prohibits any display of animal energy, grandeur, wealth, power, or any of the rest of it. And rather supinely, the most influential people in America—not the little people—have very willingly gone along with this, because it's *European*.[22]

From Bauhaus to Our House at times has a shrillness that *The Painted Word* avoids, but it is nonetheless a deeply entertaining book, and it attracted a great deal of attention. It followed Wolfe's best-selling *The Right Stuff* by only two years, and the ponderousness of the topic was deflated by Wolfe's deftness as a writer.

The book also served a cathartic function for Wolfe, who had used the two excursions into the arts to exorcise some of the demons that, as a full-fledged social critic, he was not obliged to exorcise. Looking back on the two volumes, he said, "If these books have served no other useful purpose within these worlds [the orbits of modern art and architecture] than to make the soup bubble a little faster, they are worth it," he said. "I do think my books have been of benefit to these worlds, but I will get, and will expect, no thanks."[23]

In Our Time

By default, Wolfe's 1980 near-coffee-table book, *In Our Time*, belongs, for the purposes of this discussion, among his art books. It is, in fact, an example of Wolfe's art: it includes his drawings, ventures into verse, and short, uncollected prose pieces. The book attracted little attention upon its publication, but it is important as a showcase of his abilities as a caricaturist and social critic with a sketch pencil.

The book serves primarily as a collection of Wolfe's drawings, some from as far back as his *Washington Post* days, and includes most of the memorable works from his earlier books: brutal drawings of Sen. Edward Kennedy, the artist Andy Warhol, and the *Playboy* publisher Hugh Hefner, as well as Wolfe's story-in-pictures "The Man Who Peaked Too Soon." The bulk of the book, as well as its title, comes from Wolfe's late-1970s monthly feature in *Harper's*, "In Our Time," a one-page drawing with text on some aspect of modern culture. Perhaps the most successful of these works is "The Jogger's Prayer." Wolfe's joggers are a supercilious elderly couple who beseech the Lord for the largesse to not feel *too* superior as they pad through the neighborhood, past their neighbors' "chuck-roast lives and their necrotic cardio-vascular systems and rusting hips and slipped disks and desiccated lungs, past their implacable inertia . . . past their Cruisomatic cars and upholstered lawn mowers and their gummy-sweet children already at work like little fat factories producing arterial plaque, the more quickly to join their parents in their joyless bucket-seat landau ride toward the grave."[24]

The two sections that were primarily text show Wolfe in a rather cranky mood on the plague of the 1970s, the disposable marriage. In "Stifled Giblets," which originally appeared in *Life* magazine, Wolfe looks back at the Me Decade and does not like much of what he sees. He observes the marital situations around him: men wallowing in middle age, casting aside their wives for young "cookies." Wolfe was outraged (he was finally entering the world of matrimony himself after a goodly wait) but treated the issue with his usual comedy. "The New Cookie,"

Wolfe wrote, was the girl in her twenties for whom the American male now *"customarily* shucks his wife of two to four decades when the electrolysis gullies appeared above her upper lip."[25]

In the other text section, "Entr'actes and Canapes," Wolfe railed against a variety of 1970s phenomena, including disco (the creation of "the male-homosexual netherworld"), punk rock ("a concept that had vitality only as a gob of spit"), George McGovern ("so boring he made your skull feel as if it were imploding"), the film of *The Great Gatsby* ("the Fitzgerald novel as reinterpreted by the garment industry"), and the dead king, Elvis ("Valentino for poor whites").[26]

Brother Wolfe pounded his pulpit over the sins of the decade he had named yet did so with a nod and a wink. Without all of these excesses and disgusting elements, of course, social critics would be making heavy weather of it. *In Our Time*, because it recycles much earlier material— and because it followed by one year *The Right Stuff*—did not attract a lot of attention as a "major book." Yet it contains, in one lavish volume, some of Wolfe's best work on the carnalities of modern history.

Chapter Eight
The Brotherhood

It began with a question: What do you do *after* you've walked on the moon? What is left to achieve? You have utilized all of the technology humans have devised since Neanderthal man first used tools, and you have boldly gone where no one has ever gone before, to the moon. What next? Is there any excitement left on earth? Would going to Kmart on a Saturday afternoon suddenly lose its thrill?

It was that question, a corollary of Fitzgerald's aphorism about there being no second acts in American life, that led Wolfe to investigate what he came to call "post-orbital remorse," the feeling of depression shared by members of a very small club: those who had walked on the moon. The astronaut Edwin "Buzz" Aldrin from the first lunar-landing mission and the later moon-walker Edgar Mitchell were among those who returned to earth seemingly a little shaken up by the whole experience. (Not all of the astronauts appeared to have trouble coping: for instance, Neil Armstrong, the first human on the moon, settled into a career as an academic on the University of Cincinnati faculty.) The question intrigued Wolfe, and he decided to investigate.

Wolfe entered the world of the astronauts with a simple "I was there and this is what I saw" assignment: he would cover the launch of the final moon mission, Apollo 17, in 1972. The *Rolling Stone* editor, Jann Wenner, wanted Wolfe merely to record the spectacle of the launch. If there were rock-and-roll groupies, the editor theorized, surely there were astronaut groupies. Wenner talked a good line to the writer he introduced to magazine staff members as "the *great* Tom Wolfe": "He said everybody would be there," Wolfe recalled. "A 136-year-old slave, New York café socialites, King Hussein, Governor [George] Wallace, everybody. And it was going to be a regular reunion for all the astronauts who'd gone before."[1]

What Wolfe assumed would be a single magazine assignment soon grew into a four-part series, which appeared over the first three months of 1973. He wrote the articles in a voice he called the "Astronauts' Collective Unspoken." Wolfe had quickly noted the brotherhood of the astronauts; the language they shared seemed to erect an invisible wall between themselves and mere mortals such as Wolfe. The tight circle was what he eventually came to call the Brotherhood of the Most Righteous Possessors of the Right Stuff, but at first it seemed like no more than a small fraternity of comrades, or a club whose hazing ritual was being catapulted into outer space. The first article began: "Heeeee-yuh-yuh-yuh-yuh-yuh-yuh-yuh we're not laughing at you, Tom. It's just that the question you're asking always used to be such a joke to us." The question he had asked, of course, was, "What was it really like?" The Astronauts' Collective Unspoken answered somewhat derisively, not because it was inarticulate, but because it was impossible to explain to someone who was not part of the club, not part of the Brotherhood.

Wolfe soon realized this was more than a magazine series. The issue of bravery fascinated Wolfe. "I was interested in who do you get to sit on top of these enormous rockets, on top of really enormous amounts of liquid oxygen. Highly volatile stuff. The Saturn 5, as I remember, was 36 stories high. You just light a match and *varoom!* it goes up. My God, I wondered, how do they just sit there?"[2] It was too great a story *not* to tell. Wolfe did his part by *Rolling Stone* and then embarked on a project that would take up much of his professional time during the 1970s. He set aside plans to write the Big Novel of New York, his long-talked-about *Vanity Fair* for a modern era. For more than six years, he researched the space program, going back to the days of the anonymous test pilots in the high desert of California in the late 1940s. Eventually, he wrote—quickly and furiously, by his account—and the result, in 1979, was *The Right Stuff*, a masterpiece of journalism.

Big Daddy of the Skies

The series attracted a great deal of attention. The fact that Wenner had lured Wolfe to *Rolling Stone* was itself a news story. The early 1970s was an extremely fertile period for the magazine, which was then based in the former offices of a bankrupt brewery in San Francisco. *Rolling Stone* had given Hunter S. Thompson nearly free rein in its pages, and it employed other gifted writers, such as Grover Lewis, Joe Eszterhas, and Chris Hodenfield. Tom Wolfe launched the "little rock-and-roll magazine" (Wenner's mock-humble reference to his publication) into the journalistic stratosphere.

Wolfe hooked into the depression that Aldrin and Mitchell felt upon their return from the moon. These two men shared their feelings of anticlimax after realizing, with a certainty that few earthbound humans could appreciate, the fact that their lives had peaked.

Having taken these first steps into the orbit of the astronaut club, Wolfe was not willing to back away into contracts for other magazine assignments, leaving this subculture (with its exclusive membership) behind. There was something about the character of these men that made Wolfe want to go deeper into the story. His research began assuming a life of its own. His three weeks of work at Cape Kennedy (as Cape Canaveral was known for a decade or so after the president's assassination) had introduced him not only to parts of the astronauts' tight circle but also to the unspoken code the men followed and the various hierarchies within the circle. Some groups could not be penetrated. Alan Shepard, the first American in space, complained about Wolfe's research methods. "I think it was unfortunate that Tom Wolfe didn't talk directly to any of the original group when he wrote the book," Shepard said. "He never interviewed any of us for the book. . . . Basically, the story line was OK, but the descriptions of the personalities and characters were definitely off the mark."[3] (Shepard, who coauthored a memoir with another Mercury astronaut, Donald "Deke" Slayton, wanted to call their book *The Real Stuff*. Their publisher convinced them to name it *Moon Shot* [1994].) Wolfe said that Shepard had told him he would cooperate only with writers of scientific works, not sociological ones. Wolfe claimed that he interviewed many of the other astronauts and that they were quite willing to tell their stories, especially those who had left the military or experienced the strict image control exercised by *Life* magazine in the early 1960s, when it had paid the pilots handsomely for the exclusive rights to their life stories. John Glenn, who had retired from the military for a failed run at the U.S. Senate in 1964, allowed Wolfe to accompany him on another campaign a decade later; the author said that despite political commitments and enormous demands on his time, the former astronaut was "pretty generous" in making room for Wolfe in his schedule. Contrary to Shepard's claim, Wolfe said he spoke to all of the Mercury astronauts who were still alive. (Gus Grissom had died in the fire that destroyed Apollo 1 on 27 January 1967, a catastrophe that also killed two other astronauts, Edward White and Roger Chafee.)[4]

As Wolfe's research led him further into the history of the Apollo program, he learned the reverence those astronauts had for the ones who had gone before and on whose "backs" they stood: the original Mercury astronauts. As Wolfe immersed himself in their world, he learned that they too looked backward, to the faceless and unknown test pilots whose courage and sacrifice had made space travel possible. Those test pilots, in turn, revered one character in particular, "the most righteous possessor of all the possessors of the right stuff."[5]

The subject was too large, Wolfe believed, to confine to a magazine series, and he himself was much too interested to let that amount of coverage suffice. In addition to being able to relay dramatic tales and fascinating anecdotal information about the adventures in space travel, Wolfe had serious literary reasons to pursue the story. Writing about these characters would provide him with another opportunity to go against the grain and snub his nose at the literati. Writing about such fearless characters and unapologetically calling them "heroes" would certainly annoy the literary world, and Wolfe loved to annoy the literary world. Especially during the Vietnam War era, the military was a convenient villain. In the 1970s any work that gave favorable treatment to this monster class would be outrageous, so, of course, Wolfe decided to pursue the story. "It was a vacant lot in literature," Wolfe told an interviewer. "After World War I, there was a definite block against portraying military men in anything like a heroic light. You just couldn't write 'The Charge of the Light Brigade' any more and be taken seriously."[6]

Despite frequent interruptions in the 1970s (Wolfe published *The New Journalism*, *The Painted Word*, and *Mauve Gloves and Madmen, Clutter and Vine* while working on "the astronaut book," as it was known), Wolfe was able to devote most of his time to research. He wrote the manuscript itself rather quickly: he sat down with his stacks of notes in late 1977 and presided over the book's publication less than two years later. Wolfe had originally intended to take the story from the days of the test pilots up through the Skylab program, which dominated America's space program in the 1970s. But after 450 manuscript pages—at which point Wolfe had taken the story from 1947 through the last Mercury (that is, the last single-astronaut) mission in 1963, he decided he had a book and ended the tale.

The Right Stuff shows Wolfe as a mature New Journalist, still traveling in the hyperbole that was his stock-in-trade yet using the pyrotechnics more wisely, spinning terrific tales of the lives spent on the threshold of space. The test pilots and astronauts who fly through the book's pages are heroes. They are not without flaws, but Wolfe revels in their flaws; his admiration not only makes the characters more sympathetic but magnifies their heroism.

Case in point: the most righteous possessor of all possessors of the right stuff. When, in his research, Wolfe was led back to the test-pilot subculture of the late 1940s, he discovered that the test pilots looked back to one man who was the best that their breed could offer: Chuck Yeager, the fearless pilot who served as the Rosetta stone for space travel. Yeager was virtually unknown outside of the circle of pilots, an anonymity that was apparently fine with him. Yet Yeager was the man who had broken the sound barrier, the first to fly a plane past the speed of Mach 1. No one had flown that fast before. Engineers had theorized that anyone who attempted to fly that fast would vaporize in the atmosphere. Yet Yeager did it, with two broken ribs no less, suffered when he was thrown from a horse after tossing back a few drinks at a bar. Though in pain, Yeager did not want to be scrubbed from the flight of the experimental X-1 aircraft that would test the limits of Mach 1. So, on 14 October 1947, Yeager gamely smiled through the excruciating bite in his midsection and, with a nearly immobile right arm, set off to make aviation history. A straight-arrow, lantern-jawed hero who never drank or suffered a mishap with a horse would have bored readers. Yeager's nonchalance rendered him Mount Rushmore material.

Top of the Pyramid

The book begins with the essential irony of the test-pilot trade: these men lived cheek by jowl with death, yet they never talked about it. Journalists rarely found themselves at such risk, so naturally Wolfe was attracted to the courage these men had to exhibit merely to show up for work. As he once told an interviewer:

> My obsession was really with the psychology of the pilot. An Apollo astronaut told me that he realized there were thousands of ways you could die in space. He said he had told himself beforehand: "Well, the odds are probably 9 to 1 that I'm going to die. So I have to decide whether it's worth it." He thought that over, and he decided: "Well, yes it is. This is the point to which my whole career has led me." He said that once he had worked that out in his mind, everything else was fairly easy. That's the kind of thing that fascinated me.[7]

Immersing himself in the military subculture, Wolfe explored the domestic madness of a life in the service. These families lived on pennies, in wretched quarters provided by the government, and never spoke of the horrifying reality that when the wife bade good-bye to her husband each morning, she stood a good chance of never seeing him again. This existence was played out in key places scattered around the nation—

Patuxent River in Maryland, Cecil Field in Florida, and Muroc Field (later known as Edwards Air Force Base) in the high desert of California. Wolfe centered most of the action in California, where pilots who had truly made it were stationed. Flying, as it turned out, was only part of the drill of test-pilot life, which also included drinking and driving and horseback riding.

The watering hole for these fearless pilots was Pancho's Fly Inn, a saloon housed in a desert shack and presided over by Pancho Barnes, a woman whose own career as a pilot was marked by considerable achievements. (She had broken Amelia Earhart's airspeed record for women, then barnstormed around the nation with "Pancho Barnes' Mystery Circus of the Air.") The walls of her saloon were festooned with portraits of pilots, members of a club no one wanted to join: to earn a spot on the wall, one had to have died in the line of duty and been "burned beyond recognition."

Part of the training at Edwards Air Force Base was to play for the fighter jocks the tapes of the conversations between the air traffic control tower and the doomed pilots to try to figure out what had gone wrong. With his plane locked in a fatal tailspin, the pilot was still possessed enough of his wits to ask the tower what course of action he should pursue. As Wolfe wrote of these listening sessions:

> And everybody around the table would look at one another and nod ever so slightly, and the unspoken message was: Too bad! There was a man with the right stuff. There was no national mourning in such cases, of course. Nobody outside of Edwards knew the man's name. . . . He was probably a junior officer doing all this for four or five thousand a year. He owned perhaps two suits, only one of which he dared wear around people he didn't know. But none of that mattered!—not at Edwards—not in the Brotherhood.[8]

The pilots in the Brotherhood were climbing a pyramid, and at the top, waiting to be knocked off, was the reigning fighter jock of the time, usually Chuck Yeager. If a hotshot came along and knocked Yeager off the top of the pyramid, Yeager would take his plane out again, fly faster than anyone had ever flown before, and resume his place. In writing about Yeager, Wolfe betrays none of his patented cynicism. Wolfe's anti-sentimentalist style allows him to write about an "almost unmentionable" subject ("manliness," one reviewer termed it) without becoming mired in the maudlin or mundane.[9]

In the drawling, fearless Yeager, the author had found a pure and genuinely heroic character to tower over his book, which was itself a testament to the bravery of hundreds of other heroes. Yeager's voice, pure West Virginia laconicism, nearly becomes a separate character in the book. In the gripping scenes leading up to the breaking of the sound barrier in 1947, Wolfe uses the voice to convey Yeager's bravery. The test was set for Tuesday, 14 October. On the night of Sunday, 12 October, Yeager and his wife, Glennis (whom he honored on his World War II fighter plane, as well as on his experimental crafts, by painting "Glamorous Glennis" on the side), were at Pancho's, knocking back a few at the bar, consistent with the fighter-jock tradition of drinking and flying. Late in the evening, the Yeagers decided to mount a couple of Pancho's horses and ride like hell through the desert in the dark. All part of the tradition. But a low-hanging branch from a Joshua tree interfered with Yeager's plan as he chased his wife through the sagebrush. Without even knowing what hit him, Yeager was knocked from the horse to the hard floor of the desert, knocked senseless, with a couple of broken ribs thrown in for good measure. Yeager chose not to see a military doctor. Word would get around and he would be scrubbed from Tuesday's flight. On Monday morning, he hopped on one of Pancho's old motorcycles and rode to a nearby town, where a civilian doctor confirmed that he had broken two ribs. The doctor taped up Yeager and told him not to move his right arm for two weeks and to avoid any physical exertion. Not telling the doctor that he would disobey the order because he planned to make history the next day, Yeager promised to take care of himself.

On Tuesday, the pain was still excruciating. Yeager felt he needed a confederate, so he informed his fellow pilot, Jack Ridley, who was to serve as flight engineer for the test and would ride in the B-29 that took the X-1 aloft and then "dropped" it into the stratosphere for the test. Wolfe passes along the cadence of the two men's speech (Yeager from West Virginia, Ridley from Oklahoma) as he tells how they solved Yeager's little "problem":

> Out in the hangar Yeager makes a few test shoves on the sly, and the pain is so incredible he realizes that there is no way a man with two broken wings is going to get the door [of the X-1] closed. It is time to confide in somebody. . . . Ridley . . . will understand about Flying & Drinking and Drinking & Driving through the goddamned Joshua trees. So Yeager takes Ridley off to the side in the tin hangar and says: Jack, I got me a little ol' problem here. Over at Pancho's the other night I sorta

... dinged my goddamned ribs. Ridley says, Whattya mean . . . *dinged*? Yeager says, Well, I guess you might say I damned near like to . . . *broke* a coupla the sonsabitches.[10]

Ridley solved the problem by sawing off a broom handle and, at 26,000 feet, with Yeager cradled in the experimental craft, showing him how to reach across with his good hand to use the broom handle to "whang" the door locked.

Finally aloft, disengaged from the guide plane, and invisible to the observers on the ground, Ridley in the B-29 and Yeager in the X-1 carry on their "good old boys" conversation over the intercom, broadcast on the flight line. Yeager drawls anything of note: "Had a mild buffet there . . . jes the usual instability." As the X-1 reaches .96 Mach, near the dreaded speed at which some planes had disintegrated, the point at which, folklore had it, the demon in the sky consumes aircraft and pilots alike, Yeager is still cool ("Say Ridley . . . make a note here, will ya?") as he reports that the instability decreased as he passed .96. And then, as those on the ground fear for Yeager's life even if he does not, they hear that drawl from heaven: "Say Ridley . . . make another note, will ya? . . . there's something wrong with this old machometer . . . it's gone kind of screwy on me." And then it comes: an explosion that shakes the desert. The next sound those on the ground hear is Ridley's reply to Yeager: "If it is, Chuck, we'll fix it. Personally, I think you're seeing things."[11]

It was all a code, of course, in case their radio frequencies were monitored by agents of communism. Yeager's casual comment that the machometer had "gone screwy" was his way of letting the ground flight engineers know that he had passed Mach 1—as if the thundering sonic boom had not been enough to clue them in. As an engineer had theorized years before, Mach 1 was the speed of sound, and the distorted sonic waves would, at that speed, react with a reverberating fury.

Yeager took the machine to Mach 1.05 and felt the sensation of shooting through the top of the sky. Out of the atmosphere, he glimpsed the enveloping blackness of the cosmos and its stars at mid-day, the moon and the sun at the same time, day and night simultaneously. Yeager was poised on the threshold of space.

It was a great day and a triumph for Yeager, but the pilot was not to revel in the glory that came with such an achievement. His achievement was kept secret by the military, and it was not until years later—after several other achievements in the skies that seemed to dwarf Yeager's initial giant step—that the military acknowledged Yeager's break-through. By that time, the public consciousness was more concerned with rockets and space travel, and the exploits that had made that area of interest possible just were not relevant anymore. Furthermore, the public mind was confused. The British had produced a film, *Breaking the Sound Barrier* (1951), that seemed to indicate that *they* had made the big breakthrough. Invited to the American premier of the film, Yeager saw on the screen pure movie hokum and said so at a press conference after-ward. It was not just the lack of any mention of his own role that annoyed Yeager, it was the extreme inaccuracy of the flying as it was portrayed in the film. If a real-life pilot had done what the pilot in the film does, he would have died. To Yeager's chagrin, many of the stories about the film and his comments identified him as "the first *American* to break the sound barrier."

Yeager remained a hero within the Brotherhood, whose members generally dismissed the ignorance and values of the outside world any-way. Yeager, the great pioneer, was rewarded within the air force (even-tually being promoted to general), and he became legendary among pilots. His voice was as influential as the man himself. Wolfe introduces Yeager's voice—its studied laconicism, its maundering accent—as the voice of all airline pilots who calmly tell passengers and air traffic control (in their best imitation of Yeager's West Virginia cadence) that things are all right.

Yet Yeager was denied access, by military protocol, to the space he had been the first to glimpse. Wolfe's book, when it appeared over 30 years after Yeager broke the sound barrier, made the pilot a national hero. He became a commercial spokesman, published two best-selling volumes of reminiscences, and even played a small part in the film ver-sion of *The Right Stuff*. National recognition was late in arriving, but it finally came, thanks to Wolfe.

Star Voyagers

The character of Yeager, established so forcefully early in *The Right Stuff*, bestrides the rest of the book as a Colossus by which all possessors of the right stuff will be measured. Wolfe explores—at times with great come-dy—the race to beat the Russians into space that followed the achieve-ments of Yeager and the other test pilots. A whole generation of fighter jocks in the early 1950s wanted to knock Yeager off the top of the pyra-mid, and as they climbed, the rules suddenly changed.

The Russians changed the rules with the launch of the *Sputnik* satellite in 1957. The space race cast the pilot brigade in the role of Cold Warriors and abrogated the need for a philosophy of space exploration, something Wolfe said was lacking in the first decades of America's adventures in the heavens. "All that was required was—and this seemed like a big *all*—was to catch up with the Soviets in space. It seemed a problem of . . . [an] absolutely crucial nature for this country. So you didn't need to have a reason to go into space. The idea of keeping up with the Russians continued."[12]

Nevertheless, the Russian entry into space launched another—and critical—offensive in the cold war. Aerospace pioneers like Yeager had served their purpose, but the symbolic value of control of space travel was the new priority. There was new urgency in the lives of the fighter jocks. Being the new Yeager at the top of the pyramid was not as vital as becoming the human occupant of a space capsule. Test pilots began queuing up to become astronauts (literally "star voyagers") in spacecraft that required relatively little piloting or flying ability. Yeager and the other great pilots were left behind, partly by their own choice (Yeager wanted no part of a piece of machinery rocketing out of his control) and partly by design (as a high school graduate, he did not fit the astronaut college-boy profile). The irony of the world's best test pilot not being suitable for his country's space program was staggering.

Wolfe then shifts the terrain from the milieu of the fearless pilots in the California desert to the series of low-rent locales from which the astronaut pool was drawn: navy, marine, and air force pilots competed in a series of mind-numbing, body-torturing tests to become the first of a new breed of pilot. The seven who survived the program—Scott Carpenter, Gordon Cooper, John Glenn, Gus Grissom, Alan Shepard, Walter Schirra, and Deke Slayton—dominate the second half of the book, but the figure of Yeager remains just offstage, occasionally brought forth by Wolfe to offer commentary on the astronauts' adventures. Despite being left by the wayside of the space program, Yeager remains an important character. At first, he seems to mock the misadventures of the space program, particularly the notion that chimpanzees could occupy the spacecraft as effectively as astronauts. Eventually, however, Yeager makes a point of lauding the astronauts for heroism, blessing them with the respect they deserved from other members of the flying corps.

The astronauts rose from the anonymity and occasional squalor of military life (the housing frequently left much to be desired) to the pinnacle of American fame. Without having flown a single mission into space, the seven star voyagers became, thanks to the media, the finest pilots humanity had ever known. At home, their wives and families waited dutifully for the payoff that would surely follow the low-rent existence they had suffered and the long and agonizing testing to see if their husbands had the right stuff for the astronaut corps. Wolfe shows a clear understanding of the mind-set of the military spouse:

> Betty [Grissom] was not as upset about her husband's protracted absence as a lot of the other wives would have been. . . . Few wives seemed to believe as firmly as Betty did in the unofficial Military Wife's Compact. It was a compact not so much between husband and wife as between the two of them and the military. . . . The wife began her marriage—to her husband and to the military—by making certain heavy sacrifices. She knew the pay would be miserably low. They would have to move frequently and live in depressing, exhausted houses. . . . If her husband happened to be a fighter pilot, she would have to live with the fact that any day, in peace or war, there was an astonishingly good chance that her husband might be killed, *just like that*. In which case, the code added: *Please omit tears, for the sake of those still living.*[13]

The payoff came in the form of promotions: when the husband was promoted, the wife was also promoted—in status. Moving into the astronaut corps was a step into the elite of the elite. With one press conference, the one at which the seven astronauts of the Mercury program were introduced to the public, the men and their wives became national celebrities. The payoff came. Their military salaries remained miserable—less than $10,000 a year—but Henry R. Luce of the Time-Life empire appeared offering an unheard-of amount of money: $25,000 a year to each family for exclusive rights to the privilege of ghostwriting their "personal stories."

Of course, these personal stories were slick, varnished accounts of what astronaut life *should* have been like. The magazine staff members who ghostwrote the stories for the pilots and their wives were told to serve up hero stuff to satisfy the readers' need for such material. Wolfe portrays the press covering the space race as a monolithic Victorian gentleman. He wrote:

> It was as if the press in America, for all of its vaunted independence, were a great colonial animal. . . . The animal seemed determined that in all matters of national importance the *proper emotion*, the *seemly sentiment*, the

fitting moral tone should be established and should prevail; and all information that muddied the tone and weakened the feeling should simply be thrown down the memory hole. . . .

The public, the populace, the citizenry must be provided with *the correct feelings!* One might regard this animal as the consummate hypocritical Victorian gent. Sentiments that one scarcely gives a second thought to in one's private life are nevertheless insisted upon in all public utterance.[14]

Wolfe had noted the Victorian gent years earlier while working at the *New York Herald-Tribune.* In the aftermath of President Kennedy's assassination, Wolfe had been sent out with a platoon of reporters to get "man on the street" reactions to the murder. What Wolfe found was a number of ethnic groups eagerly blaming other ethnic groups for conspiring to kill the president. Wolfe dutifully typed up his notes. When it fell to him to collate the "man on the street" piece that night, Wolfe discovered that his notes were not among those the editor passed on to him. He typed his quotes into the story, but in the next morning's newspaper, he saw that his material had again been removed. "Then I realized that, without anybody establishing a policy, one and all had decided that this was the proper moral tone for the president's assassination. It was to be grief, horror, confusion, shock and sadness, but it was not supposed to be the occasion for any petty bickering. The press assumed the moral tone of a Victorian gentleman."[15] He used the image because such characters had different codes of conduct for private and public lives.

Wolfe meticulously tells of the astronaut training and the government's paranoia about the Soviet Union gaining a foothold in the stars and having to sleep at night under the light of a communist moon. Yet a key factor daunted the American program: U.S. rockets kept exploding. Several tests ended the same way: with an inferno on the launch pad. Within the elite community of the astronauts, however, the immediate concern was not about death on the launch pad but about who would be the first to have the chance to risk their lives. John Glenn, as the oldest of the astronauts, pushed himself relentlessly to be in better physical condition than the others. He and Scott Carpenter sought to enhance their already squeaky-clean images, in the hope of moving up in the flight order.

In the end, the navy pilot Alan Shepard became the first American in space. (The Russian Yuri Gagarin went first.) Wolfe recounts each flight in detail: the horrors of the second flight when Gus Grissom's capsule sank on splashdown; the weird "fireflies" that daunted John Glenn's orbital mission, and the frightening moment when they feared his reentry shield had come loose; Scott Carpenter's experience with his furiously shaking capsule; and the last Mercury flight, when Gordon Cooper was the last American to fly alone into space.

Wolfe deals with the popular culture of the 1960s and the role the astronauts played in the decade. With a frankness missing from the official *Life* magazine accounts of the astronauts, Wolfe describes the "groupies" who followed the seven pilots around as they trained in Cocoa Beach, Florida, far from their families. In one of his pure sociological "solos," Wolfe hones in on Gus Grissom and Deke Slayton:

> As soon as Gus arrived at the Cape, he would put on clothes that were Low Rent even by Cocoa Beach standards. Gus and Deke both wore these outfits. You could see them tooling around the Strip in Cocoa Beach in their Ban-Lon shirts and baggy pants. The atmosphere was casual at Cocoa Beach, but Gus and Deke knew how to squeeze casual until it screamed for mercy. They reminded you, in a way, of those fellows who everyone growing up in America had seen at one time or another, those fellows from the neighborhood who wear sports shirts designed in weird blooms and streaks of tubercular blue and runny-egg yellow hanging out over pants the color of a fifteen-cent cigar, with balloon seats and pleats and narrow cuffs that stop three or four inches above the ground, the better to reveal their olive-green GI socks and black bulb-toed bluchers, as they head off to the Republic Auto Parts store for a set of shock absorber pads so they can prop up the 1953 Hudson Hornet on some cinderblocks and spend Saturday and Sunday underneath it beefing up the suspensions. Gus and Deke made a perfect pair, even down to their names. Not even the sight of the boys in their . . . Ban-Lon could turn off the girls to the presence of the astronauts.
>
> There were juicy little girls going around saying, "Well, four down, three to go!" or whatever—the figures varied—and laughing like mad. Everybody knew what they meant but only halfway believed them.[16]

At the book's end, following the litany of American achievements in space, Wolfe brings Yeager back to center stage. The pilot was back at Edwards Air Force Base. It was 1963, the year of Cooper's flight, the last in the Mercury program. Yeager was nearly 40, no longer the young fighter jock he had been 16 years before when he shattered the sound barrier. But Yeager was still experimenting with new planes. He had taken the NF-104 up three times before; Wolfe describes Yeager's brush with death on his fourth flight in the final chapter, "The High Desert."

At 104,000 feet, 20 miles up in the sky, the NF-104 began to buffet and disintegrate. Throughout the book, Wolfe allows himself to be driven by the strong narrative of the story he has framed and does not indulge in the many devices he had used in the 1960s, in the first rush of New Journalism. But at this moment, as the aircraft begins to come apart, Wolfe takes readers inside Yeager's brain to describe the fall to earth and Yeager's desperate effort to eject from the doomed plane:

> He's falling 150 feet a second . . . 9,000 feet a minute . . . *And what do I do next? . . .*
> He's down to 12,000 feet . . . 8,000 feet above the farm. . . . There's not a goddamned thing left in the manual or the bag of tricks or the righteousness of twenty years of military flying. . . .
> Yeager hasn't bailed out of an airplane since the day he was shot down over Germany when he was twenty. . . . He hunches himself into a ball, just as it says in the manual, and reaches under the seat for the cinch rung and pulls. . . . He's exploded out of the cockpit with such force it's like a concussion. . . . He can't see. . . . *Wham* a jolt in the back. . . . It's the seat separating from him and the parachute rig. . . . He's suspended in midair . . . weightless. . . . The ship had been falling at about 100 miles an hour and the ejection rocket had propelled him up at 90 miles an hour. For one thick adrenal moment he's weightless in midair, 7,000 feet above the desert. . . . In that very instant *the lava* [from the rocket propellant]—it smashes into the visor of his helmet. . . . Something slices through his left eye . . . he's knocked silly. . . . He can't see a goddamned thing. . . . His left eye is gushing blood. . . . He's burning! . . . There's rocket lava inside the helmet. . . . He's choking . . . blinded. . . . The left side of his head is on fire. . . . He brings up his left hand. . . . His index finger is burning up. . . . His goddamned finger is burning! . . . The desert, the mesquite, the motherless Joshua trees are rising slowly toward him. . . . He can't open his left eye. . . . He can make out the terrain. . . . Over there is the highway, 466, and there's Route 6 crossing it. . . . Nearly down. . . . He gets ready. . . . Right out of the manual. . . . A terrific wallop. . . . He's down on the mesquite, looking across the desert, one eyed. . . . He stands up. . . . Hell! He's in one piece![17]

With a minimum of moralizing, Wolfe concludes the book with a note on the nature of fleeting flame. After the Mercury program was finished, the space program was expanded and a series of two- and three-man flights planned, with a lunar landing as the eventual goal. The fame the early astronauts had experienced passed. They were no longer the

Original Seven, and no longer were they Cold Warriors. They joined Chuck Yeager in the wings as they watched others take the stage.

The title of the book became one of the clichés of the era. Scores of magazine profiles about Wolfe (or about any other writer, for that matter) were titled "The Write Stuff." In interviews, Wolfe was frequently asked to state what "the right stuff" meant. "It has a very narrow definition," he said, "and there's no way anybody can learn that particular code without becoming a military pilot. It's being willing to enter a profession in which the risk of death is very high. Your ability to deal with that risk is what separates you from other people and from your fellows."[18] To Wolfe, "the right stuff" was a "status sphere" that allowed him to enlarge upon his notions of the role of status in modern life—in this instance, as it related to a particular, somewhat small subculture, the American astronaut corps.[19]

The Critical Reception

Published in the fall of 1979, *The Right Stuff* became Wolfe's best-selling book to that date. The style was less hyperbolic than in his earlier work, and he showed himself to be totally absorbed in the subject. He brought phrases from the test-pilot fraternity into common parlance: for example, a pilot testing the limits of his plane and himself was "pushing the outside of the envelope." A pilot who made a mistake (and some theorized that Grissom had erred when his capsule was lost at sea) was said to have "screwed the pooch."

Of his style, Wolfe said he never thought about a "Tom Wolfe style" until he read that he had one. It began to make him self-conscious. His style was feral and exaggerated because he was writing, in the 1960s, about rather wild times. Readers typecast him in that hyperventilated mode. *The Right Stuff*, Wolfe said, appeared to be a major departure, but in fact he was modifying his style to the language of the astronauts. "Many people thought my style had changed," Wolfe said. "In my mind, I was simply adjusting my style to the tenor of pilots at the world that they inhabit. I wasn't changing. I was just dealing with different material."[20]

In an age that had celebrated cynicism and seemed, sadly, without heroes, Wolfe established the pilots and astronauts as figures worthy of intense admiration. Rather than employing the *Life* magazine technique, Wolfe freely presented his characters with all their flaws intact. This made the pilots and astronauts more human and, therefore, even more heroic.

The Economist called the book "an epic poem about courage" and lauded Wolfe for showing the literary courage to deal with a subject that was
so often derided—heroism. Another critic cast Wolfe in the role of the
"campfire tale-spinner"; by his count, the book's 400-plus pages contain
"probably a couple of years' worth of campfire tales."[21] Noting that
Wolfe had done time as a pop sociologist in the 1960s, one critic specu-
lated that the author of *The Right Stuff* may very well have taken the
next leap and invented a new field: pop history.[22] C. D. B. Bryan, in the
New York Times Book Review, said the book was "Tom Wolfe at his very
best" and unleashed a litany of adjectives to describe it: "technically
accurate, learned, cheeky, risky, touching, tough, compassionate, nostal-
gic, worshipful, jingoistic—it is superb."[23] R. Z. Sheppard, in *Time*,
noted that "even the creakiest practitioner of the inverted-pyramid style
of journalism will have to agree that behind the mannered realism of *The
Right Stuff* thumps the heart of a traditionalist. The organizing principle
of the book is an old-fashioned fascination with, and admiration for, the
test pilots and fighter jocks of the U.S.'s first astronaut team."[24]

Critics were almost universally enamored of the book. Looking over
his notices, Wolfe could not help but exult. "I could hardly ask for a better reception," he said. "Just about the time you think the world has it in
for you, suddenly you're buried in orchids and things even up."[25] Some
reviewers stated that they believed Wolfe had mocked John Glenn with
his goody-two-shoes portrayal of the popular astronaut. Wolfe was startled by the reaction. "In my mind, he was not a negative. He was a
moral zealot. That's rare today; they usually cover it up. I felt I understood him. He was a Presbyterian. I was raised a Presbyterian. In the
Presbyterian scheme of things, there's no problem being both moral and
extremely ambitious—no problem at all. But many reviewers considered
him a prig, a prude, and I must acknowledge that to most readers he
does come off that way."[26]

Peter S. Prescott, in *Newsweek*, saw the book as a fulfillment of what
Wolfe had set out to do nearly two decades before with the New
Journalism:

> The satirist, amused by the men, admires what they accomplished. In his
> imperial manner, Wolfe occupies the heads of the astronauts as they
> undertake their most dangerous ordeals, imposing his own metaphors on
> their experience to make the drama more comprehensible, more coherent.
>   Wolfe helped to invent this kind of smart-ass, exclamatory journal-
> ism; his witty prose alone is evidence of what the writer's right stuff is.[27]

Another critic had a special perspective on Wolfe's work. Michael Collins was a member of the second generation of America's astronaut corps, and he was part of the 1969 lunar-landing mission (although he stayed airborne in the command module while his comrades Armstrong and Aldrin romped on the moon). Collins credited Wolfe's achievement and detected wistfulness between the lines: "Wolfe has captured the essence of the astronauts—the 'right stuff'—but they have captured him too. I think the problem is that he wants to be one."[28]

Nevertheless, some reviewers thought Wolfe had fallen short of the mark. Thomas Powers, in *Commonweal*, said that Wolfe did not have a likable persona, and therefore *The Right Stuff* was not a likable book. "There is not an ounce of kindness, sympathy or generosity in it," Powers wrote. "Wolfe's book is not a history; it is far too thin on dates, facts and source citations to serve any such purpose."[29] John Romano, in the *Nation*, decried Wolfe's interest in subcultures. "Wolfe seems to see society as a sort of quilt of them, overlapping but discrete," Romano wrote. "But there is nevertheless an underlying structure to society. . . . Where *The Right Stuff* falls short . . . is precisely in failing to bring out the connections between the world of the fighter-jocks, the subsequent astronaut period and the broader society of which they are a part."[30]

The Right Stuff won both the American Book Award and the National Book Critics Circle Award in 1980.

Celluloid Heroes

Wolfe's work had inspired filmmakers before. *The Last American Hero*, starring Jeff Bridges, was made from Wolfe's profile of Junior Johnson. Hollywood had not chosen to produce any other pictures from Wolfe's work, but the long-awaited astronaut book had great cinematic potential, even if the story, because of its subject, dictated a huge budget.

The book was purchased by Irwin Chartoff and Robert Winkler, two producers who had supplied the Academy Award winner for Best Picture of 1976, the boxing film *Rocky*, and both of whom were associates of Wolfe's from his days at the *Herald-Tribune* in the 1960s. They managed to outbid Universal Pictures for the rights to the book. Rumor had it that the studio saw *The Right Stuff* as a great vehicle for the comic actors John Belushi and Dan Ackroyd.

Chartoff and Winkler first hired the screenwriter William Goldman to turn Wolfe's 500-page book into a screenplay. Goldman, best known for *Butch Cassidy and the Sundance Kid* (1969), loved the parts about the astronauts but thought the book had been oddly constructed. Wolfe introduces Yeager but virtually drops him for most of the book as he writes about the Mercury program. Then he resurrects Yeager for the dramatic scene at the end. With the producers' permission, Goldman decided to leave Yeager out of the story altogether.

The producers hired Philip Kaufman to direct the film. At that point, Kaufman was known primarily for *Invasion of the Body Snatchers*, a 1978 glossy update of the 1956 paranoid thriller. Kaufman read Goldman's draft and decided that he did not want to make a movie with no Yeager in it. Kaufman rewrote the script and received sole credit on the screen. Kaufman valiantly tried to follow the structure of the book, even though doing so violated sound moviemaking principles. Yeager's story was vital to Kaufman's version of the tale, and he used the character much the way Wolfe does: as a one-man Greek chorus. After Yeager achieved ascendancy in the heavens, the others came to test themselves against his standard. In the critical role of Yeager, Kaufman cast the Pulitzer Prize–winning playwright Sam Shepard, an occasional actor, opposite another novice actor, the rock-and-roll star Levon Helm (drummer and vocalist for the Band), as his companion Ridley. Their dialogues helped Kaufman offer commentary on the transitory nature of heroism, a major theme in Wolfe's book that, handled incorrectly in the film, could have been heavy-handed. Helm is also the film's narrator, a twanging voice of God that intones some of Wolfe's key phrases.

As the Mercury astronauts, Kaufman put together an impressive ensemble cast and focused his narrative energies on four of the seven: Scott Glenn as Alan Shepard, Fred Ward as Gus Grissom, Ed Harris as John Glenn, and Dennis Quaid as Gordon Cooper. The companion domestic stories of their wives were given full treatment, including the marital troubles in the Cooper household. With a great deal of humor, flawless acting, breathtaking flying scenes, and the tone of an epic cinematic adventure, *The Right Stuff* was released to great acclaim in the fall of 1983. The popular critics Gene Siskel and Roger Ebert agreed that it was the best picture of the year. Although it was nominated for an Academy Award in the best picture category, it won only three technical Oscars and another statue for the composer Bill Conti's uplifting score.

Wolfe said he was "shocked" by the film. After his third screening, he figured out why. "What was on the screen was not my book," he said. "It was something else. It was something else pretty good."[31] Out of respect for his producer pals Chartoff and Winkler, Wolfe demurred when asked to criticize the film.

Yet the film itself was overshadowed by something over which Wolfe, Kaufman, and the producers had no control: American politics. As the film hit screens around the country, the astronaut John Glenn, now Senator John Glenn of Ohio, was campaigning for the 1984 Democratic presidential nomination. The film earned a lot of publicity from that coincidence, and the actor Ed Harris, cast as John Glenn, made the cover of *Newsweek*. Glenn's unflagging patriotism in the film was seen by some as subliminal campaigning. Although Glenn tried to distance himself from the film, and the producers downplayed any political significance to their work (at the same time glorying in the publicity), *The Right Stuff* was seen as a political film. Appearing on a television news program, Wolfe tried to separate his book and the film from any political inferences: "When I wrote the book *The Right Stuff*, I meant the book to be a study of courage, and particularly the courage of the military pilot. . . . It is not a book that dwells on John Glenn."[32]

Wolfe became so identified with *The Right Stuff* and the astronauts that he assumed a status as an elder statesman of the space program. When race and gender lines were finally crossed in space travel, ending the astronaut corps' days as a white men's club, reporters usually called Wolfe for comment. When the space shuttle *Challenger* exploded on 29 January 1986, killing all of the astronauts aboard, television talk shows booked Wolfe to discuss the psychological makeup of those who possessed the right stuff. What the *Challenger* tragedy added to the epic of American space exploration was the arm of calamity reaching beyond the military world, where the pilots were schooled to risk death daily, and into the civilian world. Among those killed in the explosion was Christa McAuliffe, a schoolteacher who would represent the beginning of a new era: civilian space travel. As Wolfe noted in a discussion with the television journalist David Brinkley:

> I think we have to realize that Christa McAuliffe was to represent a complete crossover in the space program from the era of the man of steel, people like Alan Shepard and John Glenn, and to an era in which space was going to be for the public. And that's what Christa McAuliffe represented. She was a woman who taught social studies in a high school in New Hampshire. . . . This young woman found herself, whether she knew it or not or wanted to be there or not, out on the edge of a still-raw technology.[33]

Of Wolfe's nonfiction, *The Right Stuff* stands as perhaps his most important book. He uses the techniques of the novelist to unfold a sweeping tale of pioneers and heroism. Although it bears some of the techniques and stylistic pyrotechnics for which he was known, it is narrative force that drives this book. With the skills he had admired in Dickens and Zola, Wolfe crafted a nonfiction novel of his own. That massive, absorbing task complete, Wolfe turned his attention to the project he had been plotting—and delaying—for so long. It was time to write his novel.

Chapter Nine
The Novelist

Having often pronounced the novel dead in his role as a historian-essayist on the subject of the New Journalism, Tom Wolfe set about in the early 1980s to exhume it. He had no intention of joining the ranks of those American writers who had turned the novel into a mere exercise in style to impress other writers. Wolfe the novelist used the same inspiration as Wolfe the journalist. In large part, his conception of the novel was drawn from the works of Charles Dickens, whom he often cited as a model in his pronouncements on the New Journalism. He also included Honoré de Balzac, Émile Zola, and William Makepeace Thackeray. These novelists had employed a style of reporting not far removed from that of modern journalism, and it infused their novels with a vigor and bite that resonated through the centuries. Their novels had a richness that Wolfe found tragically lacking in late-twentieth-century fiction. That dearth left the field of fiction open to relatively new players such as himself.

Wolfe had always recognized the importance of fiction as historical chronicle. He said that he assumed his book about Ken Kesey, *The Electric Kool-Aid Acid Test*, would have a short shelf life, that it would last only until the literary figures of that era produced the great novels of psychedelia. He felt the same about *Radical Chic*, which he also thought would be disposable after a brief time. The endurance of both books surprised their creator. He was further surprised by the literary community's apparent lack of interest in producing fiction to encapsulate the era, the way Dickens and Zola did in their work. Engaging in such an effort in the last part of the twentieth century, Wolfe came to realize, would go against the grain of intellectual fashion. Writing a "big novel," a novel that dealt realistically with the issues and styles of a particular time, would earn a writer no recognition. Literary fashion dictated that writers undertake more self-conscious pursuits: the absurdist novel, metafiction, or whatever. "You had to move in an arcane direction to gain recognition," Wolfe said.[1]

Wolfe began talking about writing the great novel of New York as far back as the late 1960s. Other, perhaps less forbidding assignments intervened: *Radical Chic* came along in 1970, then the astronaut stories for *Rolling Stone* and the ensuing years lost to research on the space program. Throughout this period, however, he spoke of writing a big novel and was quite frank with interviewers, often talking about what he had in mind. Having eviscerated the modern novel in countless speeches and in the introduction to *The New Journalism*, Wolfe was at first hesitant about declaring himself a would-be novelist. In 1974 he told the interviewer Joe David Bellamy:

> I think the only future for the novel is reporting, which means there's not going to be *much* difference between the best novels and the best nonfiction. . . . I'm having this battle with myself right now on this *Vanity Fair* book. . . . I want to do a book that performs something of the same function of Thackeray's *Vanity Fair*, and I'm weighing whether this should be fiction or nonfiction, because everything is going to be based on a journalistic reality. Now, the question is to me a completely technical one. Once I reach that decision, the rest is purely technical.[2]

There were other reasons to write a novel, among them, the self-imposed threat that it was time to put up or shut up. He had bashed fiction writers so relentlessly that he felt he had to walk in their literary shoes to retain credibility. He was also curious about his talent: could he indeed write a novel? It looked easy, but was it really? Although he realized he might fail as a novelist, he did not want to regret never having tried. "I didn't want to reach the end of my career and look back and say, after all this theorizing about fiction and nonfiction, 'What would have happened if I had tried a novel myself? What if this theorizing was an elaborate screen I've constructed so I don't have to face the challenge?'"[3] Wolfe admitted that he suspected he had made such an issue about the poor quality of modern fiction because he thought subconsciously that he could not write a novel. He had to prove something—to himself as well as the literary community.[4] In short, did he have the right stuff to be a novelist?

New York's "High" and "Low"

The Right Stuff and the sale of the film rights to movie producers gave Wolfe enough financial security to take the time he would need to write the book. After finishing *From Bauhaus to Our House* in 1981, Wolfe had cleared the decks of book commitments and also ended his run as a monthly contributor to *Harper's*. Blank pages awaited his novel. By his own description, Wolfe worked diligently for months and got nothing done. "It was frightening in this stage of my career to be doing a novel," he said. "I was really under a lot of pressure. I knew I could expect no mercy, after all the things I've said about contemporary fiction."[5]

Many writers might approach work on a novel by first creating characters, choosing a theme, or constructing a strong plot. Wolfe began only with the notion that he wanted to write a novel of New York. He began, therefore, with the setting. Then he awaited characters to step onstage from his subconscious. They did not arrive. He was greatly influenced by *Vanity Fair*, but he realized that if he just followed the model of Thackeray's novel, he would omit the "underclass" of New York. Once he made the determination that his novel would include both the "high" and "low" of New York, he thought that settling into a comfortable routine as a reporter would lead him in the direction he needed to go if he hoped to ever complete his novel.

After months of work with little to show for his efforts, Wolfe returned to reporting to jump-start his ambitious book. Dressed in conventional suits (he eschewed his customary white clothing), he showed up at the Manhattan Criminal Court Building and watched the parade of members of New York's "low" society appear before the judges. The judicial system was an equalizer, Wolfe felt, the one place where the high and the low intersected. One of Wolfe's acquaintances was a judge named Burton Roberts, who allowed the writer to observe several of his cases and even sit next to him on the bench during one hearing. Another friend of Wolfe's, Edward Hayes, had served as an assistant district attorney in the Bronx. Hayes informed Wolfe that the Manhattan courts, brutal as they may have seemed to a judicial novice, were nothing compared to life in the Bronx. Finally, after two years of research and roughing out characters, Wolfe took a journey to the Bronx. The cruelties of life in that borough contrasted superbly with the lives of New York's "high." Ideas began to form and disparate notions began to come together. Wolfe had not written any substantive scenes because he had no outline for the book, and he was a firm believer in outlines. His experiences in the Bronx gave him the idea of how New York's high and low could intersect on his fictional stage.

By this point, Wolfe had invested three years in the book but had not written any usable scenes. All he could show for his efforts were his considerable notes from his courtroom visits and an outline. He needed pressure to force himself to write the book. Something akin to the ferocious deadline pressure of a newspaper would do, he reasoned. Again he considered his literary models: Dickens, Balzac, Zola. They had written some of their books on deadline, serializing them in newspapers of the day. A chapter or two would appear each week in the newspaper. The results had been fabulous, in Wolfe's view. He reasoned that he could risk his reputation with such an experiment.

Weekly deadlines might be a bit much, so Wolfe approached Jann Wenner of the biweekly *Rolling Stone* with his idea. With a 100-page outline and chapter summaries to go on, as well as his deep affection for Wolfe, Wenner agreed to the project. He offered the writer an unprecedented amount of space and a $200,000 contract. Then Wolfe began writing, under the gun.

Having invested so much time in researching the area where he knew the scattered characters would intersect, the courts, Wolfe did not have the patience to invest a lot of time in his protagonist. For the serialized version of the novel, he made Sherman McCoy a writer. This choice turned out to be the most troubling part of what Wolfe referred to as his public first draft. He had not done any research about writers. "I thought I knew it all, and I didn't," he said. "I hadn't even thought of myself in the role of the writer."[6] Early in the serialization, Wolfe realized the enormity of this mistake as a career choice: he had no interest in showing Sherman at work. A character sitting at a typewriter is rather dull, so he wrote no scenes with Sherman actually working. He had committed himself to Sherman being a writer in *Rolling Stone*'s pages, but before the first few installments appeared, Wolfe made a critical decision that would affect the shape of the finished version of the story, the book. He had heard a number of stories about the frenetic Wall Street world, and he spent a day in a bond-trading firm. He saw the disease he came to diagnose as "money fever" and decided that it had to become a large part of his book if he truly wanted it to reflect New York City in the 1980s.

This realization magnified, in his mind, the enormity of his error in making Sherman McCoy a writer. Nevertheless, Wolfe was a professional, and he pressed on with the serial, storing away changes, new plot developments, and other improvements for the rewrite stage of what he had titled *The Bonfire of the Vanities*. The reference was to the fifteenth-century Italian monk Savonarola, a reformer eventually burned at the stake for heresy in 1498. As Wolfe noted:

It wasn't a perfect analogy. In the real "bonfire of the vanities," Savonarola sent his "Red Guard" units into people's homes to drag out their vanities—which were anything from false eyelashes to paintings with nudes in them, including Botticellis. This bonfire [in the novel] is more the fire created by the vain people themselves, under the pressure of the city of New York. . . . People are always writing about the energy of New York. What they really mean is the status ambitions of people in New York. That's the motor in this town. That's what makes it exciting—and it's also what makes it awful many times.[7]

Before he could make any improvements on his tale, however, he had to deal with the matter at hand: the killing biweekly deadline pressure he had put himself under. As Wolfe lamented to one interviewer: "These deadlines were coming . . . like waves . . . one after another after another every two weeks. I couldn't sleep. I'd go to bed and then 2½ hours later my eyes would open up like . . . umbrellas. Like a pair of umbrellas! I couldn't get them closed again!"[8] The magazine had ballyhooed Wolfe's great experiment when the serialization began. Soon, however, it was being presented only dutifully, as if it were a feature the editors could barely tolerate. Though Wenner never wavered in his support—which Wolfe was appreciative enough to recognize in the book version ("Grateful acknowledgment is made of the daring of *Jann Wenner*, who published an early version of this book serially, chapter by chapter, as it was being written, without a safety net, in *Rolling Stone* magazine")—others at the magazine resented the enormous amount of space given to the tale with the wavering story line. Wolfe could not hold himself back from tinkering with the story, incorporating features that he had intended to hold onto until he was doing the book rewrite. He began, by his own admission, tampering with events he had recorded earlier, creating narrative chaos. He hoped the fickle *Rolling Stone* readers would not notice. He was aware that he was getting off track and making numerous mistakes. He was also aware that his prose was not being greeted with great acclaim, that the readers were not "thronging the docks" to snap up the next issue of *Rolling Stone*, as readers had done a century earlier for new installments from Dickens. "No one was rude enough to say, 'This isn't the hottest thing in history,'" Wolfe said, "but I was beginning to feel that's what the verdict was."[9] Wolfe questioned his sanity in pursuing the project instead of something safer, like a project he had already planned, a sequel to *The Right Stuff* telling the history of the space program up through the Skylab project.

The serialized version of the novel lumbered to a close in 1985 (Wenner had trumpeted the installments on 21 covers during 1984 and 1985), and Wolfe immediately began the work of expanding his story and completely rewriting the tale. Casting Sherman McCoy as a bond salesman was the critical move. It allowed the protagonist to serve as a prism through which to view the "greed is good" mentality of America in the 1980s. That feature was one of the many delights of the book that would serve as the quintessential American novel of the era.

A Novel without a Hero

Vanity Fair, Wolfe's model, bears the subtitle *A Novel without a Hero*. Sherman McCoy, although introduced first in Wolfe's epic, is not a heroic character; nor are the many other figures who traipse across the *Bonfire of the Vanities* stage. Readers are likely to identify with Sherman, though he has many offensive characteristics. Wolfe responded to the criticism that few of his characters are sympathetic: "I think that's one of the most truthful things about the book," Wolfe said. "How many Chuck Yeagers are flying around?"[10]

The importance of *The Bonfire of the Vanities* and its scope require a detailed synopsis. The novel begins with a brief and foreboding prologue of racial tension. New York's Jewish mayor is heckled when he ventures up to Harlem to make a placating appearance before a crowd of angry black residents. Racial and ethnic insults fly, along with a half-consumed jar of Hellman's mayonnaise hurled at the mayor's head.

Quickly, Wolfe moves his story to the lavish $1.6 million apartment of the bond salesman Sherman McCoy, his wife Judy, daughter Campbell, and assorted servants. Although it is a rainy evening, Sherman is unveiled in his foyer as he prepares to take his unwilling dog for a walk. He is not very devoted to his pet; he merely wants to get out of the house to call his mistress, Maria Ruskin. However, Sherman accidentally dials his own phone number and, before realizing his mistake, asks to speak to Maria. Judy recognizes her husband's voice, and Sherman hangs up in horror. Sherman reaches Maria, who is married to a wealthy businessman named Arthur Ruskin, and arranges to meet her at an apartment she keeps for such liaisons. He tells her about the phone call but soon forgets as he and Maria passionately make love. Back home, he denies all knowledge of the mistaken phone call and stonewalls his wife on the issue. Feeling invulnerable as a Wall Street bond salesman whose phone calls control the flow of millions of dollars on the planet, he is, in his mind, a true "master of the universe," an earthbound realization of the action figures his little daughter plays with.

Up north, in the Bronx, Wolfe introduces another sort of world: Gibraltar. That is the name of the fortresslike Bronx County Office Building. Larry Kramer is a young assistant district attorney. Mired in an unexciting marriage and a runty apartment, he trudges daily into this fortress of law in the outlaw nation of the South Bronx. Another dweller in the massive building is Judge Myron Kovitsky, who, when heckled relentlessly by a manacled prisoner in a police van, spits on the inmate:

> Kovitsky . . . took a deep breath, and there was a tremendous snuffling sound in his nose and a deep rumbling in his chest and throat. It seemed incredible that such a volcanic sound could come from out of such a small thin body. And then he *spit*. He propelled a prodigious gob of spit toward the window of the van. It hit the wire mesh and hung there, a huge runny yellow oyster, part of which began to sag like some hideous virulent strand of gum or taffy with a glob on the bottom of it.[11]

Kramer's boss is the Bronx County district attorney, Abraham Weiss, who has his eye on the mayor's office. Nearly 90 percent of all cases prosecuted in his jurisdiction are black and Hispanic. If Weiss wants the mayor's job, he has to have a high-profile case taking on the white establishment, and he has enlisted his subordinates in a search for such a case. To Weiss, Kramer is just another drudge in the office, but Kramer wants to make himself known, to become indispensable to his boss.

Several miles south, on Wall Street, Sherman is in full flower. His indiscretion of the night before already forgotten, he strides confidently between the rows of desks with their computer terminals at Pierce and Pierce, the huge brokerage firm for which he sells bonds. Sherman is portrayed as part of a generation of young men who absorbed the world of arts and letters at major universities, but unlike the altruistic earlier generations that produced Jefferson, Thoreau, Frederick Jackson Turner, and the like, they have left their alma maters to take over Wall Street. Within five years of graduation, the inheritors of the American educational tradition are pulling down a quarter-million a year and clearing at least a cool million by the time they turn 30. As a complicated transatlantic sale of French bonds nears completion, Sherman congratulates himself on his financial genius and his acumen as a master of the universe.

A week passes, and Sherman's mistress Maria has made a quick trip to Europe. Having played the dutiful husband for a full week—despite a chilly reception from his wife—Sherman takes the night off from domesticity to pick up his mistress at the airport, with postflight sex at her love nest on the agenda. But Maria's passion in Sherman's Mercedes roadster distracts him, and he misses the turnoff to Manhattan. Soon the couple find themselves in the South Bronx. The streets are nightmarish, crowded with the sort of people Sherman's lifestyle has allowed him to insulate himself from: the poor, the underclass, blacks and Hispanics. The rabble is in the street, all around the car, *touching* the car. Maria is horrified and shrieking. Negotiating his Mercedes through the crowd, Sherman sees what he thinks is an arrow, perhaps leading to a ramp back to the highway. He turns, finally away from the crowd, and finds that the ramp to the highway is blocked by a discarded tire. He gets out of the car and is removing the tire when he is approached by two young black men. Their intent is unclear, but Sherman thinks they plan to rob him. He tosses the tire at them, then leaps in the car, which Maria is now driving, and they try to move up the ramp. In backing the car up, Maria hits something, but they are not sure what has been struck. Back in Manhattan, the couple furtively repair to Maria's apartment, and filled with the endorphins of conquest over their foes in the Bronx jungle, they passionately make love. Sherman suggests that they call the police to report what may have been an accident, but Maria is more interested in sex, and she seduces Sherman.

Maria did indeed strike one of the two young men when she backed up the car. Henry Lamb suffers a concussion, and after a few hours of coherence during which he describes the white couple in the Mercedes and recalls its license number, he lapses into a coma. His mother knows a flamboyant and crusading Harlem minister, Reverend Bacon, and she enlists his help. Bacon approaches the police and the Bronx district attorney's office. Kramer alerts Weiss to the possibility of finally finding what Weiss (nicknamed Captain Ahab) has been after for so long: the Great White Defendant. Kramer and Weiss vow to "nail the WASP."

Meanwhile, Peter Fallow, a reporter for the sensationalistic tabloid *City Light*, is nearing rock bottom in his career. A transplanted Englishman, Fallow spends his days (the few hours he is awake) and his nights in alcoholic stupor, producing little that is ever published. After a warning from his fellow Brit, and publisher, Sir Gerald Steiner—whom the reporter has nicknamed "the Dead Mouse"—Fallow realizes his career is in desperate need of resuscitation. It comes in the form of a call from Al Vogel, a crusading liberal lawyer who became a national celebrity in the counterculture days of the late 1960s. Vogel, a friend of

Reverend Bacon's, passes on the tip about poor Henry Lamb and the mysterious and malicious white couple on a joy ride through Harlem who struck down this boy in the prime of life. Realizing it is the sort of story that could be easily sensationalized by his newspaper (which is known for such bizarre headlines as "Scalp Grandma, Then Rob Her"), Fallow talks to Bacon, then to one of Lamb's high school teachers. The teacher is at first unable to remember Lamb; the classrooms are over-crowded and a teacher can do little more than keep the students from killing each other in the trouble-plagued school. Though memory is dim, the teacher says Lamb was probably a good student. Only the trou-blemakers are memorable.

Fallow then creates a story about an honor student at death's door, owing to the irresponsibility of a rich, Mercedes-driving white couple from Manhattan. The Bronx district attorneys and the cops are also on the case. Sherman learns of Lamb's injury and police interest in the case when he happens to see a copy of the *City Light*. He learns from the story that the police know the make of the car and the beginning of the license-plate number. He makes arrangements to meet Maria at her love nest, a rent-controlled apartment she leases from a friend. They discuss whether to go to the police, but Maria talks Sherman out of it. While they are meeting, a workman comes to the door. He says he needs to paint the apartment, but he is actually on a mission to see if the friend Maria leases from does indeed live in the apartment. (The friend's rent is $331 a month; Maria pays her friend $750 for the convenience of having a home away from home.) After the workman leaves, Sherman is para-noid and unnerved that he would have shown up at the moment they were discussing their accident in the Bronx.

As Sherman learns from the next day's *City Light*, the police have determined that there are 124 cars in the city that could have been involved in the accident. Soon Sherman is visited by two detectives investigating the case. He feels the net closing and decides not to wait for Maria to come around. He calls a lawyer in his father's firm to ask for advice. After hearing Sherman's story, the attorney plants more doubts about Maria's honesty, suggesting that if they are discovered to be the couple, she will insist that Sherman was driving. The attorney then sug-gests that Sherman see Tommy Killian, an experienced criminal lawyer in another firm.

Sherman meets Killian, a fellow Yale graduate, but feels no kinship. Killian is a crude, rough-talking Irishman, offensive to Sherman's patrician sensibilities. Sherman tells Killian about the wrong turn in the Bronx and asks if he could just go to the police and explain the little mistake. Killian laughs at him. He tells Sherman about Weiss's quest for the Great White Defendant and notes how good a prosecution of Sherman and Maria would look when Bronx voters go to the polls that fall. Nailing a WASP would assure Weiss's election to the mayor's office.

Roland Auburn, Henry Lamb's companion the night they crossed paths with Sherman and Maria, has come forward to offer his eyewitness account of the accident in exchange for leniency on a drug charge. Sherman's arrest is now a certainty, Killian realizes. After some negotiations with the district attorney's office, Killian tells Sherman that he must surrender to authorities and face charges of reckless endangerment for the injury to Henry Lamb. Sherman informs his wife Judy that he will be arrested but in describing the incident tells her that Maria was only a flirtation, a woman whom he had known only three weeks and had offered to pick up at the airport. Judy responds coolly, but as her husband prepares to leave home the next day, she tells him to behave well and remember his place in society.

The surrender in the Bronx the next day does not go according to plan. Killian had been promised that there would be no sideshow and no press, but Weiss's staff cannot resist turning Sherman's appearance into a media event. Handcuffed, Sherman is led by an army of reporters—strangers with the audacity to call to him using his first name—and into the Criminal Courts Building. In the melee, Peter Fallow introduces himself to Sherman. Sherman thinks he should hate this tormentor, but he cannot find the necessary bile. He loathes himself so much more.

Jailed with violent offenders, Sherman spends time in the vile cell until his court appearance. Kramer appears on behalf of the district attorney's office and asks the judge to increase bail to $250,000. The judge refuses the request and releases Sherman on the bail amount already agreed to—$10,000. Spectators taunt Sherman in court and as he tries to leave the Criminal Courts Building. He feels oddly distant from it all. In his mind, Sherman is already dead.

Despite his failure to get the bail increased, Kramer's grandstanding accomplishes its dual purpose: it makes Weiss happy because it garners a lot of attention for the district attorney's office (and ensures that Weiss will not forget the name Kramer), and it makes Kramer happy because he becomes enough of a celebrity to develop the courage to ask out a pretty juror for whom he has been lusting. Kramer had been envious of

Sherman's home (it was featured in an *Architectural Digest* spread), his car, his clothes, and his mistress. Feeling a bit like a master of the universe himself, Kramer decides he wants an extramarital affair.

Although discouraged and resigned to his fate, Sherman still fights back. As he tries to take his daughter to school the next day, he slugs a female radio reporter—a scene photographed and dutifully presented on the front page of the *City Light*. As the purveyor of the hottest story in town, Peter Fallow is a restored human being. His newspaper tells readers of Sherman's companion on his drive through the Bronx, a "'foxy' brunette mystery girl" who is younger and a "'hotter ticket' than his forty-year-old wife."[12]

Sherman learns that Maria has gone to Italy, where she apparently is having an affair with an artist, according to a detective hired by Killian. Sherman has not disclosed Maria's identity publicly, so Fallow's major concern is finding the woman. One of Fallow's friends is a woman who had been having an affair with the artist Maria is with in Europe. Out of spite, she tells Fallow that both the artist and Maria had told her that it was Mrs. Arthur Ruskin who was with Sherman in the Bronx that night. Fallow arranges an interview with the elderly Mr. Ruskin on the pretense of writing a story about tycoons for his newspaper. During the interview luncheon, Ruskin suffers a fatal heart attack.

The young widow returns to New York for the funeral. Killian urges Sherman to confront Maria and to no longer feel that he has to protect her. Maria is a gold-digger, Killian tells his client, who married Ruskin for his bank account. Such a cold woman would give no thought to cutting Sherman loose. At the funeral home, Sherman pleads with Maria once again to come forward, but she begs off. Fallow approaches her when Sherman leaves, ostensibly to console her and tell her that he spent her husband's last moments on earth with him and that he did not suffer. Fallow then confronts Maria: "I gather you were in the car with Mr. McCoy when he had his unfortunate accident in the Bronx." Maria responds by calling Fallow "peckerhead."[13]

Identified in the next day's *City Light*, Maria is soon visited by the district attorney's office. Kramer instructs Maria to testify against Sherman or face charges herself. She then decides to call Killian and arrange to meet Sherman. On Killian's advice, Sherman goes to meet Maria wearing a concealed tape recorder in order to get Maria to incriminate herself. Before he can elicit any such comments from her, however, she discovers his tape recorder, and he runs from her "rent-controlled love nest," as it is now known in the press. Stories about Sherman and Maria's affair make good copy in the newspaper, and now Sherman realizes he has not just cheated on his wife, he has lied to her about his relationship with Maria.

Maria tells the grand jury that Sherman was driving when the car struck Henry Lamb and that she had begged to go to the police to report the incident but Sherman had refused. Infuriated and betrayed, Sherman is at a loss over what to do. Life as he knows it has ended.

The workman who had come to the apartment during one of Sherman and Maria's postaccident rendezvous had been installing a hidden microphone, which he intended to use to gather evidence against his delinquent tenant. Killian sends an investigator to find out whether any tapes have been made in the apartment, since landlords of rent-controlled apartments are often paranoid about their tenants. Killian therefore has a recording of Sherman and Maria in which she admits that she was driving the car and that it was Sherman who wanted to go to the police and report the incident, both direct contradictions of her grand jury testimony.

Unfortunately, the tape cannot be produced as evidence. Since the landlord obtained it surreptitiously, the tape is illegal. Too bad, Killian says. If Sherman had recorded the tape—even without Maria's knowledge—it could be admitted as evidence. Sherman then announces that he will lie. He will *claim* that he recorded their conversation that night with a hidden microphone because he feared something awful might happen—which it did.

The whole cast meets again in a Bronx courtroom. Reverend Bacon and his followers show up to jeer Sherman. Kramer is there to impale the Great White Defendant on the legal rotisserie. Fallow is there to record it all for the *City Light*, and presiding over the scene is Judge Myron Kovitsky. Killian asks to introduce the tape into evidence. Kovitsky is especially interested in the coercion Kramer used to help shape Maria's testimony. The second tape—the landlord tape—is then introduced, and Maria's candid account of the accident is heard, with her admission that she was driving the car.

Since Kovitsky has the authority to supervise the grand jury proceedings, he orders that the indictment against Sherman be dismissed "in the interests of justice."[14] Reverend Bacon's followers in the audience are displeased, and the courtroom collapses into pandemonium. Sherman and Killian join Kovitsky in fleeing the court and trying to escape the mob. Sherman, reduced by circumstances from his lofty position as a master of the universe, has learned how to fight.

In a brief epilogue, Wolfe sketches the final details of the story in a faux *New York Times* article a year later, covering a court appearance by Sherman McCoy. Henry Lamb has died, and Sherman has been arraigned on a manslaughter charge. His wife Judy is in court, apparently offering support. Reverend Bacon's troops are out in force to protest the "Wall Street murderer," although Sherman denies any connection to the financial center, describing himself as a "professional defendant." He represents himself in court, since he cannot afford to pay Killian. Kovitsky is not the presiding judge this day, since pressure brought by Reverend Bacon's forces cost him reelection. Kramer has also been replaced: it was discovered that he obtained Sherman and Maria's "rent-controlled love nest" for himself and the juror with whom he had begun an affair.

Peter Fallow is missing, however. The winner of a Pulitzer Prize for his coverage of the troubles of Sherman McCoy, he is on his honeymoon in the Aegean with the daughter of Sir Gerald "Dead Mouse" Steiner, publisher of the *City Light*.

A New Experience

Tom Wolfe had grown accustomed to scorn and abuse from certain quarters of the critical community. From the days of the *New Yorker* stories, through the feather ruffling of *Radical Chic* and *The Painted Word*, Wolfe was used to brickbats. Plus, he had attacked novelists for so many years, he expected abuse to be unleashed in his direction. He had made no secret of his intention to make his first major step into fiction: it was to be a realistic social novel of New York. Yet the critics were more than kind to the book, and readers enjoyed it as well. Though it took place entirely in New York City (with the exception of a brief scene in Southhampton), it was popular throughout the country and quickly became ensconced on the best-seller lists.

Nicholas Lemann, writing in the *Atlantic*, compared the book favorably with Fitzgerald's *The Great Gatsby* yet noted that Wolfe's playfulness with his cast of characters prevented the book from achieving the resonance that he so obviously wanted it to have. Nevertheless, Lemann noted, it was "a pleasure to read."[15] Frank Conroy, in the *New York Times Book Review*, summarized the plot succinctly: "Sherman screws up and the dark forces of the city close in on his rich white butt."[16] Conroy enjoyed Wolfe's manipulation of the book's pathetic characters but said, if the book had a fault, it was an overdose of malice. Indeed, criticism of the racial and ethnic stereotypes in Wolfe's book was widespread. The charges rankled the author, who said that he was merely reporting what he saw and the attitudes he felt were predominant in the streets of the city. He said that he did not, in writing the book, genuflect before the gods of political correctness. He wrote about what he saw. Not all of the critics, however, berated Wolfe on this point. R. Z. Sheppard, in *Time*, called Wolfe a "master of social satire" and commented that the book was "merciless" in its depiction of New York and its multicultural mix. Sheppard called the book itself "more than a tour de force."[17]

Other critics noted Wolfe's penchant for including what he called "status-life details." Each major character's clothing is described in extreme detail, right down to the shoes. The shoes, in fact, were a sore point with some. When the *Newsday* critic John Leonard learned that the book came close to receiving the National Book Critics Circle Award, he was incensed: "That the bailiffs almost gave their bauble to Tom Wolfe's catalogue of shoes—electric-blue lizard pumps! snow-white Reeboks! bench-made half-brogued English New & Lingwoods!—is scary."[18] Still other reviewers thought Wolfe's hyperbolic New Journalism style was irritating in a big novel. One critic condemned the book for its 2,343 exclamation points.

James Andrews, writing in the *Christian Science Monitor*, felt that Wolfe had succeeded in his stated goal and that *Bonfire* "invites comparison with Dickens." Andrews noted: "One has to be grateful to Tom Wolfe for producing a richly textured, contemporary novel whose epicenter is situated in the social concerns that so much of today's minimalist, self-absorbed fiction ignores."[19] Frank Rich disagreed. In the *New Republic*, Rich wrote that Wolfe had fallen short of his professed ambition: "He lacks the ability, or the desire, to visit every level, above and underground, of the metropolitan bleak house. . . . By failing to provide closeups of the denizens of the Bronx 'jungle' and the middle-class Manhattan 'ant colony' along with those of the Park Avenue 'hive,' Wolfe drains the blood out of the book—out of the half where the other half lives."[20]

The book was indeed a stunning achievement. If the critics were divided on whether it accomplished Wolfe's goal of writing a realistic novel of New York City that conveys the energy and essence of the times, most of them agreed that it was at least a tremendous technical achievement. (Even E. B. White and J. D. Salinger, who had attacked Wolfe over the *New Yorker* episode in 1965, commented on Wolfe's brilliance as a stylist.)

The book continued to attract attention even after the initial barrage of reviews upon its publication in the fall of 1987. The key phrase in the stories that circulated around *Bonfire of the Vanities* was "resonance." Wolfe noted Philip Roth's axiom that novelists cannot compete with the demented parade of events in the daily newspaper when they craft their books. Wolfe had carefully plotted the use of his character Larry Kramer as a frightened subway rider. In the original *Rolling Stone* version of the novel, Kramer is presented as somewhat paranoid about the young hoodlums who prey on subway riders. Wolfe had intended to show Kramer at the breaking point later in the serialization by having him lash out at two thugs who push him too far during his commute. However, before Wolfe could get to that point in his story, the demented parade passed by. Early in 1984, Bernhard Goetz, a frustrated subway patron beset by thugs, pulled out a .38 caliber revolver and shot his tormentors. The Goetz incident made news nationwide and left Wolfe in a tight situation. He had devoted a lot of space in the serialization to describing Kramer's subway attire (he dressed a certain way to discourage robberies) and mental state. Now that thread had to be dropped. As Wolfe said, "Now, how could I, four months later, in April of 1985, proceed with my plan? People would say, This poor fellow Wolfe, he has no imagination. He reads newspapers, he gets these obvious ideas. . . . So I abandoned the plan, dropped it altogether."[21]

The Goetz incident was not the only episode foreshadowed in *The Bonfire of the Vanities*, but the other realities for which the novel would serve as antecedent waited until after the book's publication. The book had begun with New York's Jewish mayor being booed from the stage by black activists during a press conference. In 1983 Mayor Ed Koch would endure such a confrontation, in a similar setting, although unlike his fictional counterpart, he would not end up yielding the stage. The major resonance, however, arose from Reverend Bacon's involvement in the Henry Lamb incident. In 1987 New York's real-life Reverend Al Sharpton would thrust himself into the abduction and rape case of a young girl named Tawana Brawley, situating himself in all of the city's newspapers and broadcasts on the subject.

Writers began calling Wolfe's book prophetic, a characterization from which he took satisfaction. The fact that ridiculous reality was outpacing the satire of his novel was vindicating him once again. As he told John Taylor of *New York* six months after the book's publication, and after the real-life events that authenticated his vision of New York in the novel:

There has been a lot of resonance, but I believe that if you make it your point to describe what's actually out there, this is what will happen. Two things that are so much a part of the eighties—and I couldn't believe nobody else was writing about this in book form somewhere—are the astounding prosperity generated by the investment-banking industry, and the racial and ethnic animosity.[22]

Soon to Be a Major Motion Picture

Hollywood beckoned. The book was a best-seller, so it was inevitable that producers would approach Wolfe with offers to buy the rights. The celebrated moviemakers Peter Guber and Jon Peters paid Wolfe $750,000 for the story.

The film became one of the major debacles of recent Hollywood history, a titanic failure. The *Vanity Fair* reporter Julie Salamon chose the *Bonfire of the Vanities* project as the subject of a long-planned study of the making of a film, from the acquisition of rights up through the movie's release. Filming Wolfe's book was a daunting task, as Salamon reports in her book, *The Devil's Candy* (1991). A breakfast conversation between Salamon and Wolfe runs throughout the book, and he steadfastly refused to be critical of the filmmakers. After all, he told Salamon, he had cashed the check.

The project had great promise. Brian DePalma was hired to direct the film, and his skills as a moviemaker were considerable. The studio, Warner Brothers, insisted that the film run no longer than two hours, a requirement that naturally posed problems with a story of such weight. The screenwriter Michael Cristofer decided to restructure the story so that it would all be seen from the perspective of Peter Fallow. With the story so framed, a two-hour limit was suddenly not an impossible burden.

One of the major problems the film faced was in casting. The likable comic actor Tom Hanks was widely scorned as the choice to portray Sherman McCoy, but the major botch was casting the action star Bruce Willis as Fallow. Because it was felt that moviegoers would not accept a British accent emanating from Willis's smirking mouth, Fallow became American. (Peter O'Toole or Jeremy Irons would have been great as Fallow, and DePalma had also sought out Daniel Day-Lewis, but Warner Brothers thought the film needed more "star clout" for the box office, even though Willis came with a $5 million price tag.) Nationalities were not the only thing Wolfe found changed about his characters. To assuage those who called Wolfe's book racist, Judge Myron Kovitsky was replaced by a black jurist portrayed by Morgan Freeman. The script called for this imposing black judge to deliver a homily about justice at the film's conclusion. This "justice speech" was based on a similar statement at the end of the serialized version of the book in *Rolling Stone*—a feature that Wolfe had thought was too forced and therefore had dropped from the finished book.

The author could only sigh over these changes. He had, after all, cashed the check. He was infuriated, however, to learn about the ending the producers had in mind for his story. Sharing a stage with the director Spike Lee at a charity forum, Wolfe was informed by Lee that the plan called for Henry Lamb to awake from his coma and walk out of the hospital, unnoticed. (Because Lee let this particular cat out of the bag and attracted a lot of media attention, that ending was dropped.) Lee asked Wolfe what he thought of that scene and other changes, but Wolfe demurred. He had not read the script. Lee was incredulous, accusing Wolfe of being irresponsible and greedy, but the author remained detached. "In actual life they never blame the writer [for bad films of their books]. It's always: Look what they did to his book! And if the movie is better than the book, the book gets caught in the updraft."[23]

The first part of Wolfe's statement became operative. Warner Brothers held a private screening for the author and his friends, and at dinner afterward, they came to the conclusion that the film stunk. Nevertheless, Wolfe did not violate his rule about silence on the subject of the movie. He suggested that the problem was with point of view: the director had not decided on one. It was, however, a noble effort. "DePalma took a chance," Wolfe told Salamon. "It really didn't pan out."[24]

The film was not without pleasures. A time-lapse opening shot of Manhattan photographed from beneath a Chrysler Building gargoyle is stunning. DePalma's virtuosity shines through in a long scene following the drunken Peter Fallow's arrival at a benefit. Lasting more than five minutes, this master shot was pronounced as one of the most spectacular shots of its kind. Yet these great technical achievements were outweighed by other poor choices, particularly the screenwriter's effort to make Fallow a likable, even heroic, character.

Wolfe may have been silent on the subject of the film, but many of the book's admirers were not so polite. Film critics who had read the book greeted the film with excoriating derision. Wolfe was right: "The great thing about selling a book to the movies is that no one blames the author."[25]

Not only did no one blame him, but his novel outlasted the monstrous flop that was the film version. Wolfe also found himself identified in the magazines simply as "novelist Tom Wolfe." As he considered his next project, Wolfe looked back on the arc of his career and decided to put it all into context.

Chapter Ten
Moralist of the Modern Age

You there! Don't let those multiple exclamation points fool you!!!!! Those prolific colons :::::::::: and extended ellipses . . . . are mere distractions! Exactly! Pay no attention to that man behind the curtain! He is *not* the Wizard of Odd! And those peculiar sounds, those bizarre *noises* that people make in his stories! (To wit: "Heeeeee-yuh-yuh-yuh-yuh-yuh-yuh-yuh . . . ," or, "Heh-heggggggggggggggggggghhhhh-hh-hhhhhhhhhh!") Or those nattering noises that *pop up* without warning ("hernia, hernia, hernia, hernia, hernia, hernia, hernia, hernia, HERNia, HERNia, hernia, hernia . . .") :::::::::: don't let all of that stuff divert you from this particular: Tom Wolfe is, morally speaking, a Good Old Boy. A traditionalist!

Tom Wolfe is without question a revolutionary stylist—William F. Buckley once called him "probably the most skillful writer in America"[1]—yet he traffics in a somewhat old-fashioned point of view. It is more than his white suits that sets him apart from the other writers of this part of the American Century. Some readers have been so blinded by the flat brightness of his characteristic clothing and the frenzy of his prose that they have been unable to see the social anarchy he has in mind. (Wolfe embodies Flaubert's advice to writers to be regular and orderly in their lives in order to be wild and original in their work. Wolfe follows Flaubert's creed: "Live life for art's sake.") Whatever the trend of the moment may be, Wolfe is against it. He may chronicle it vividly, brilliantly capture the madness of the craze in its full flower, and, in his breathless style, convey its essence—without in any way implying his approval. He is out to expose charlatans and mountebanks, like the boy-hero of "The Emperor's New Clothes." His use of satire in this mission is somewhat unusual. His writing does not convey brittle anger. He remains detached, smiling through the apocalypse du jour, using humor (often the gentle and subtle variety rather than heavy-handed barrel-house scorn) to illuminate the silliness of these times he has chosen to record.

Luckily for Wolfe, he has been a practicing writer during the phenomenon of the American crybaby culture, which has allowed grown adults to eschew all responsibility for their actions and invent new and fashionable varieties of neuroses in which to package and dispose of their accountability. A society that recognizes no obligations will soon descend into chaos, Wolfe nudges us. For example, a continuing theme in Wolfe's work is the tenuous nature of modern relationships. Through the cartoons and light verse in *In Our Time*, Wolfe repeatedly calls our attention to the dispensable wife, a casualty of late-twentieth-century America. Suddenly, responsibility is thrown out as so much garbage; the wife gets old . . . *throw her out!* The virulence of Wolfe's attack—in essays as well as in his treatment of the adulterous duo in *Bonfire of the Vanities*, Sherman McCoy and Larry Kramer—is veiled in humor, but it is virulence nonetheless.

Wolfe champions the eternal verities. During the carnal madness of the 1960s, smack-dab in the middle of the sexual revolution, Wolfe publicly pleaded, *Make them stop!* In an essay called "Down with Sin," Wolfe did not exactly come out against intercourse and all of its non-Euclidian variations; he just noted that it was a bit unseemly to talk about such things and to glamorize the weakening of moral standards. Another contemporary noted, in a different setting, "The Times They Are A-Changin'." As Wolfe lamented:

> I don't imagine there are more than two or three people in New York today—a couple of old Presbyterian preachers, maybe, but none of the younger ones—not more than two or three people in the whole town who would take a public stand against Adultery. I don't ever recall meeting a girl, over the last 10 years anyway, who would not be acutely embarrassed by any insinuation that she did not have as flaming a libido as the next girl.[2]

Wolfe saw this rampant lewdness as a subset of evil, which, in his view, the culture was embracing eagerly in the 1960s. The larger problem, Wolfe wrote, was that "the bourgeoisie is taking over sin. There has to be some other way out to avoid the terrible stigma of being bourgeois."[3] As recently as the end of the 1980s, Wolfe continued his plaint: "The sexual revolution—such a prim term—was a tremendous change in the '60s. Now we almost don't include it in discussions of morality. We don't think of it in moral terms. . . . There's been a sweeping aside of standards. Every kind of standard."[4]

The Right Stuff, in exploring heroism, forces us to contemplate the nature of modern idols. Largely, heroes have been reduced to entertainers or other self-promoters. The media have lauded persons (and even turned them into that curious commodity, "survivors") who have merely managed to overcome the self-induced problems (alcoholism, drug abuse, and so on) that are endemic to the crybaby culture.

Events have a way of momentarily putting things in perspective. After the 1986 *Challenger* disaster, which killed the whole crew, Wolfe wrote a moving essay on heroism for *Newsweek*. The schoolteacher Christa McAuliffe symbolized the shift in the role of the star voyagers: formerly the group was limited to possessors of the right stuff, the fighter jocks et al. Owing to the presence of the social studies teacher from New Hampshire, the *Challenger* mission represented the democratization of the space program. That set of new opportunities ended with an explosion in the sky above Cape Canaveral, yet another event in the sad and glorious spectacle of American life that Wolfe has recorded.[5]

In another unabashedly patriotic essay, about the Statue of Liberty (written to coincide with the restoration project of 1986), Wolfe used the occasion to note that, following the dictates of modern sculpture, the contemporary arts community would have laughed Lady Liberty off of her pedestal if they had been able to witness her original unveiling. Such is the state of exalted notions like heroism, freedom, and courage in the modern age.

Modern art has continued to be a target of Wolfe's ridicule. Replacing the less fashionable value of spirituality, modern art has emerged in the latter half of the twentieth century as a weapon to be used against the old, classic values. Wolfe notes that art has become a "new god," that it has largely displaced religion in modern life. In an essay called "The Worship of Art," Wolfe wrote:

> There was a time when well-to-do, educated people in America adorned their parlors with crosses, crucifixes or Stars of David. These were marks not only of faith or cultivation. . . . Today the conventional symbol of devoutness is—but of course!—the Holy Rectangle: the painting. . . .
>
> Today, what American corporation would support a religion? Most would look upon any such thing as sheer madness. So what does a corporation do when the time comes to pray in public? It supports the arts.[6]

Perhaps because he has held contemporary culture to a higher standard and been unwilling to adjust to the lower precepts and dogmatic intellectual fashions of his time, Wolfe has remained an outsider. He has become an independent contractor in the literary community. He prefers such a role, but the unyielding nature of his social criticism confines him to it anyway. Though largely identified with the New Journalism movement, he has retained his severe self-sufficiency, which allows him to stand back and jest at all participants in the social melee and to feel no affinity for a particular school, intellectual ideology, or literary fashion. As H. L. Mencken was in an earlier age, Wolfe is an iconoclast of the first order—a loose cannon on the deck of the ship of state. He is a moralist, and always has been.

He is a superb troublemaker, a smirker disguised by courtly manners and a gentle Virginia accent. William F. Buckley, Jr., in describing *The Painted Word*, said it was as if Wolfe had painted a moustache—in broad daylight, no less—on the *Mona Lisa*.[7] He likes taking the unpopular stance. One anonymous critic said, "No crueler writer ever lived."[8] "Cruel" seems harsh, but Wolfe has shown colossal acumen for nailing his subjects. A superb literary marksman, he has been relentlessly on-target with "Radical Chic," "The Me Decade," his criticism of the art world, and the social satire of *The Bonfire of the Vanities*.

Wolfe basked in the enormous success of his first novel and used the acclaim and generous sales (for seven months it rode in the higher reaches of the *New York Times* best-seller list and enjoyed a hugely profitable paperback rights sale) to rub his detractors' noses in what he had done. His "literary manifesto for the new social novel"—a novel, in short, much like *The Bonfire of the Vanities*—achieved its goal of stirring up trouble in the literary community, and it also allowed Wolfe, nearly 60 years old, to catalog his achievements and put his career in perspective. In a *Harper's* essay called "Stalking the Billion-Footed Beast," Wolfe claimed that all he had done was to reestablish the primacy of realism in modern letters. He had approached this task through the servants' entrance in the House of Letters: journalism. Yet by employing journalistic techniques in writing fiction (as he had once done the opposite), he single-handedly proved the point he had been arguing for so many years: that modern fiction was bankrupt and in desperate need of the social novel.

He had spent most of his career as a nonfiction writer, dishing out works like *The Electric Kool-Aid Acid Test* and *Radical Chic and Mau-Mauing the Flak Catchers*, assuming that the novelists of his generation were at his heels and writing the "big books" that would encapsulate the era and knock his little nonfiction books off the library shelves. It did not happen. Modern literary convention held that anything that could be understood by the rabble (that is, anyone not a member of the literary elite) could have no value. The realistic novel was a bastard stepchild of literature.

Centuries of great literature had compelled responsible writers to create art that was of their times, Wolfe said, but it did not happen in contemporary America. When Wolfe learned that Truman Capote intended to write a big novel of New York, he was pleased but also a bit disappointed, since he himself had decided, by the mid-1970s, that he wanted to write such a book. However, Capote's effort, *Answered Prayers*, was never completed; when early excerpts were published in *Esquire*, Capote was so distraught by the reaction from his friends that he was unable to finish the novel. It was left to Tom Wolfe to write the big book of New York, which he did.

In pursuing his goal, he was, of course, going against the grain, against the literary fashion dictating that realism was a destitute form. To forsake realism was folly, Wolfe said: "It is as if an engineer were to set out to develop a more sophisticated machine technology by first of all discarding the principle of electricity, on the grounds that it has been used ad nauseum for a hundred years."[9] Writers abandoned realism in part, Wolfe said, because it requires work. The self-indulgent modern fiction conveyed that the only valid experience was personal experience, an attitude that resulted in fiction dominated by meticulously detailed and therefore boring chronicles of the agonies of being a literary figure. To write his book, Wolfe realized, he would have to reach beyond his own experience. He would have to report on the experiences of others, exposure to which was the purpose of his missions to the courts of the South Bronx and the trading floors of Wall Street. Why, Wolfe wondered, were other novelists so reluctant to make such reconnaissance missions?

The novelist Philip Roth had said a generation before that the imagination of the novelist is powerless before the onslaught of carnalities in the daily newspaper, an observation that was cited by many writers as one reason for literature to turn its back with such finality on realism. Wolfe said that Roth's observation was perfectly valid, but that writers had drawn "precisely the wrong conclusion" from it. "The answer is not to leave the rude beast, the material, also known as the life around us, to the journalists, but to do what journalists do, or are supposed to do, which is to wrestle the beast and bring it to terms."[10]

Wolfe was, of course, excoriated by the literary community for his essay, and *Harper's* devoted several pages to letters of complaint, many from writers and literature professors who calmly stated, as if speaking to a small child, that the realistic novel Wolfe called for was a dead form. Others criticized the essay as pure self-promotion by the author. Wolfe responded to the attacks serenely and asked once again why writers were so afraid of the task of recording the bedlam of the modern age. "I have made one last attempt to give away the keys," Wolfe wrote. "I will merely leave them [the modern novelists] with a question that each can answer privately, in the solitude of the study: Why not at least try to . . . do it all?"[11]

The argument for relinquishing realism—that status details of modern life are conveyed much better through other media—renders the task of writing history difficult for our descendants. For several centuries, historians have been able to turn to each era's art and literature to supplement other sources of information. Historians who chronicle this era will find something sorely lacking when they attempt to construct a social tapestry. Future writers of our cultural history will also not have other resources that have been available to their predecessors; letters, journals, diaries, all these have now been supplanted by electronic storage systems. To those unfortunate twenty-first-century historians, the books of Tom Wolfe will be a godsend.

It will be the good fortune of future scholars that Wolfe focused so much of his early work on the tremendous affluence that descended on the United States after World War II. Postwar prosperity brought forth a new class of citizens—Wolfe called them "proles"—that created new and alternative lifestyles and were, of course, ignored by the literary and intellectual establishments. As one critic indelicately put it: "Wolfe's real beat is the American freakshow; the teenage netherworld, lower-class sports, and the poor rich."[12] That statement describes much of Wolfe's work up through *The Right Stuff*.

The arc of Wolfe's career has a nearly supersonic trajectory. His electric prose of the 1960s lit up the journalistic sky, illuminating new possibilities for nonfiction. He matured as a journalist and essayist in the 1970s, then showed in one brilliant example that he had mastered the form of the novel in the 1980s. In the 1990s he remains an essayist and writer of fiction—one sustained in reality.

Few journalists have a philosophy or anything remotely resembling a sense of direction in the daily accounts of living they are charged with creating. Yet from the start—even before the start of his career, as early as his dissertation—Wolfe's obsession was the nature of status in America. It has remained the defining theme in his work, through journalism, essays, and fiction.

Among his other achievements, Wolfe has served as the Great Emancipator of journalism. Journalists had long nourished themselves on the idea of graduating out of the daily grind to a higher calling: fiction. The work was merely the means to an end. Wolfe and his contemporaries made it a suitable end in and of itself. Wolfe liberated the form from its neuroses and from the inferiority complex that plagued its practitioners.

On the college lecture circuit, Wolfe almost always appears in a white suit so as to disappoint neither the admirers of his work nor those who would attend his talk just to see the character that he has become. Long a frequent visitor on college campuses, Wolfe is lecturing at universities more than ever in the 1990s.

While still basking in the glow of the *Bonfire*, Wolfe said he has begun to think of himself as a novelist and has begun the process of writing a second big book (presumably steeped in realism). He began *Bonfire* by deciding on the setting, New York City. The new book, he said, has its setting as well: the university. His trips to campuses, then, have had a twofold purpose: earning a hefty paycheck for an hour's worth of adoration or scorn, and research (perhaps) on his next book.

Yet the theme of his campus lectures is often not writing but the character of the era. The Great Phrasemaker has often been exhorted by reporters and lecture audiences to condense the 1990s into a two- or three-word rubber stamp. Wolfe demurs, although he is fond of saying that the money fever of the 1980s, which he wallowed in in his novel, has given way to the "moral fever" he hoped would dominate the agenda in the 1990s.

> People are starting to talk about morality and ethics, partly because there's such a hangover from what went on in the 1980s. But I have to caution you that a moral fever is only a fever. It doesn't mean that morals change. They could . . . if people are concerned about the topic enough. It doesn't necessarily mean that's going to happen. Harvard Business School right now has a tremendous emphasis on ethics because [it] became known as "greed central" in the 1980s.
>
> I get the impression that on campuses students are beginning to talk about such things as trying to construct a new morality for sexual behavior after the carnival of the 1970s and 1980s. It's something that's very much in the air.[13]

Wolfe admits that the task of writing is still as difficult as it was that evening in 1963 when he sat down to try to make some sense out of the custom-car rally he had witnessed in California. The *Esquire* editors, with their metaphorical gun at the writer's temple, allowed him to find the style that would characterize his prose and the era. Because that style was so frenetic and anarchistic, it looked easy. It was not, and it still is not. As Wolfe said during a campus visit for a speaking engagement:

> Writing's the hardest thing in the world. . . . Nothing makes me want to get up and want to write. It's so hard—it really is. I always look for a way not to write. I'll come to a campus and give a talk. Giving a talk is much better than writing. It all happens immediately. Usually the audience feels compelled to applaud. . . . Writing is a complicated business. Writers long for legitimate ways to avoid writing. You can usually find one.[14]

What, then, motivates him to get up each morning and brush his teeth?

Wolfe smiles, and in his soft Virginia gentleman's voice says, "Why, the possibility that I can then put on a white suit."[15]

Notes and References

Chapter 1

1. Tony Schwartz, "Tom Wolfe: The Great Gadfly," *New York Times Magazine* (20 December 1981): 46.

2. Ibid.

3. Elaine Dundy, "Tom Wolfe . . . But Exactly, Yes!" *Vogue* (15 April 1966): 124.

4. Michael Dean, "Pop Writer of the Period: Tom Wolfe Talks to Michael Dean," *The Listener* (19 February 1970): 250.

5. Schwartz, "Great Gadfly," 46.

6. Henry Allen, "The Pyrotechnic Iconoclast, Still Passing the Acid Test," *Washington Post*, 4 September 1979.

7. Toby Thompson, "The Evolution of Dandy Tom," *Vanity Fair* (October 1987): 118.

8. Allen, "Pyrotechnic Iconoclast."

9. Martin L. Gross, "Conversation with an Author: Tom Wolfe," *Book Digest* (March 1980): 19.

10. Dundy, "But Exactly, Yes!" 124.

11. Dean, "Pop Writer," 250.

12. Tom Wolfe and E. W. Johnson, *The New Journalism* (New York: Harper and Row, 1973), 4.

13. Dundy, "But Exactly, Yes!" 124.

14. Ibid.

15. Ibid.

16. Thompson, "Dandy Tom," 118.

17. Tom Wolfe, "The League of American Writers: Communist Organizational Activity among American Writers, 1929–1942" (Ph.D. dissertation, Yale University, 1957), 20.

18. Wolfe, *The New Journalism*, 5.

19. Gay Talese, *New York: A Serendipiter's Journey* (New York: Harper and Brothers, 1961).

20. Gay Talese, *Fame and Obscurity* (New York: World Publishing, 1970).

21. Wolfe, *The New Journalism*, 33.

22. Pat Sellers, "*Cosmo* Talks to Tom Wolfe, Savvy Social Seer," *Cosmopolitan* (April 1988): 189.

23. Philip Nobile, "Wolfe Foresees a Religious 'Great Awakening,'" *Richmond Times-Dispatch*, 17 August 1975.

24. Thomas Wolfe, interview with the author, Gainesville, Fla., 4 April 1991.

25. C. D. B. Bryan, "The SAME Day: heeeeeewack!!!" *New York Times Book Review* (18 August 1968): 2.

26. Hunter S. Thompson, *Hell's Angels: The Strange and Terrible Saga of the Outlaw Motorcycle Gang* (New York: Random House, 1967).

27. Robert Sam Anson, *Gone Crazy and Back Again* (New York: Doubleday, 1981), 258.

28. Schwartz, "Great Gadfly," 46.

29. Peter Gorner, "Tom Wolfe: In Big League as a Writer," *Chicago Tribune*, 7 December 1976.

30. Schwartz, "Great Gadfly," 46.

Chapter 2

1. Jane Clancy, telephone interview with the author, 27 January 1994.

2. Ibid.

3. This brief history of the *Washington Post* is drawn from David Halberstam, *The Powers That Be* (New York: Knopf, 1979). The story of the *Washington Post* is told in many books. *The Powers That Be* best merges the corporate history with the Meyer-Graham family history.

4. Chalmers Roberts, The Washington Post: *The First 100 Years* (Boston: Houghton Mifflin, 1977), 357.

5. Adrianne Blue, "The Earthling and the Astronauts," *Washington Post Book World* (9 September 1979): 9.

6. Richard Kluger, *The Paper: The Life and Death of the* New York Herald-Tribune (New York: Vintage, 1989), 672.

7. Thomas Wolfe, "The Dispensable Guide: In Rome Natives and Tourists Try to Flee Tourists [part 1]," *Washington Post*, 4 December 1959.

8. Thomas Wolfe, "The Dispensable Guide: Hospitable Greeks Swamp Their Guests with Kindness [part 7]," *Washington Post*, 14 December 1959.

9. Thomas Wolfe, "The Dispensable Guide: French Divide World: Parisians and Peasants [part 9]," *Washington Post*, 19 December 1959.

10. Thomas Wolfe, "Press Cards to Inaugural Stir Battle," *Washington Post*, 12 January 1961.

11. Allen, "Pyrotechnic Iconoclast."

12. *Washington Post*, 1 January 1960.

13. Roberts, *Washington Post*, 357.

14. Clancy interview.

15. Blue, "Earthling," 9.

16. Joe David Bellamy, *The New Fiction: Interviews with Innovative American Writers* (Urbana: University of Illinois Press, 1974), 75.

17. Nobile, "Wolfe Foresees 'Great Awakening.'"

18.   "Weenie roast" is a Wolfeism featured prominently in his "Great American Things," *Esquire* (December 1975): 83.

19.   Dundy, "But Exactly, Yes!" 124.

Chapter 3

1.   Wolfe interview.

2.   Tom Wolfe, *The Kandy-Kolored Tangerine-Flake Streamline Baby* (New York: Farrar, Straus and Giroux, 1965), ix.

3.   H. L. Mencken, *Newspaper Days* (New York: Knopf, 1940).

4.   "The Greatest Gamble," *Esquire* (August 1979): 5.

5.   Tom Wolfe, "Beatles! More Than Just a Word to the Wild," *New York Herald-Tribune*, 8 February 1964.

6.   Chet Flippo, "The *Rolling Stone* Interview: Tom Wolfe," *Rolling Stone* (21 August 1980): 30.

7.   Bellamy, *The New Fiction*, 75.

8.   Ibid.

9.   Wolfe, *Kandy-Kolored*, 68.

10.   Ibid., 47.

11.   Ibid., 48.

12.   Wolfe, "Las Vegas (What?) Las Vegas (Can't Hear You! Too Noisy!) Las Vegas!!!" *Esquire* (February 1964): 97.

13.   Wolfe, *Kandy-Kolored*, 206.

14.   Ibid., xiii.

15.   Ibid., 134.

16.   Ibid.

17.   Flippo, "*Rolling Stone* Interview," 30.

18.   Wolfe interview.

19.   Kurt Vonnegut, Jr., "Infarcted! Tabescent! [review of *The Kandy-Kolored Tangerine-Flake Streamline Baby*], *New York Times Book Review* (27 June 1965): 4.

20.   "The Wolfe-man," *Newsweek* (28 June 1965): 90.

21.   Emile Capouya, "The Kandy-Kolored Tangerine-Flake Streamline Baby," *Saturday Review* (31 July 1965): 23.

Chapter 4

1.   Tom Wolfe and E. W. Johnson, *The New Journalism* (New York: Harper and Row, 1973). *The New Journalism* contains four linked essays by Wolfe and selections made in consultation with E. W. Johnson. Wolfe also wrote most of the introductions to the pieces.

2.   Wolfe interview.

3.   Charles Dickens, *Sketches by Boz* (New York: Pan Books, 1947).

4.   Wolfe holds forth on the four characteristics of New Journalism in Wolfe and Johnson, *The New Journalism*, 30–32.

5. John Hersey, *Hiroshima* (New York: Knopf, 1946), 22–23.

6. Talese, *New York*, 2.

7. Gay Talese, "Frank Sinatra Has a Cold," *Esquire* (April 1966).

8. Talese wrote a compelling essay about the composition of the article. The piece was titled "When Frank Sinatra Had a Cold," *Esquire* (November 1987): 161. It appeared first in *The Best American Essays 1987* (New York: Ticknor and Fields, 1987).

9. Wolfe and Johnson, *The New Journalism*, 65.

10. Gay Talese, *The Kingdom and the Power* (New York: World Publishing, 1969); *Honor Thy Father* (New York: World Publishing, 1971); *Thy Neighbor's Wife* (New York: Doubleday, 1980); *Unto the Sons* (New York: Knopf, 1991).

11. Wolfe and Johnson, *The New Journalism*, 11.

12. Jimmy Breslin, *Can't Anybody Here Play This Game?* (New York: Viking Press, 1963).

13. Truman Capote, *In Cold Blood* (New York: Random House, 1966).

14. Norman Mailer, *The Armies of the Night* (New York: New American Library, 1968).

15. Norman Mailer, *The Executioner's Song* (Boston: Little, Brown, 1979).

16. Brendan Gill, *Here at the* New Yorker (New York: Random House, 1975), 317.

17. Truman Capote, *The Muses Are Heard* (New York: Random House, 1956).

18. Truman Capote, *Local Color* (New York: Random House, 1950).

19. Truman Capote, *Music for Chameleons* (New York: Random House, 1980), xiv.

20. Harper Lee, *To Kill a Mockingbird* (Philadelphia: Lippincott, 1960).

21. Capote, *In Cold Blood*, 54–55.

22. Wolfe and Johnson, *The New Journalism*, 116.

23. Truman Capote, *The Dogs Bark* (New York: Random House, 1973).

24. Truman Capote, *Answered Prayers: The Unfinished Novel* (New York: Random House, 1986).

25. Capote, *Music for Chameleons*, xix.

26. Norman Mailer, *The Naked and the Dead* (New York: Rinehart, 1948).

27. Norman Mailer, *An American Dream* (New York: Dial Press, 1965).

28. Mailer, *Armies of the Night*, 39–40.

29. Norman Mailer, *Of a Fire on the Moon* (Boston: Little, Brown, 1970); *The Prisoner of Sex* (Boston: Little, Brown, 1971); *The Fight* (Boston: Little, Brown, 1975).

30. Wolfe and Johnson, *The New Journalism*, 188.

31. Norman Mailer, *Marilyn: A Novel Biography* (New York: Grosset and Dunlap, 1973); *The Faith of Graffiti* (New York: Praeger, 1974).

32. Mailer, *Executioner's Song*, 223–24.

33. Norman Mailer, *Ancient Evenings* (Boston: Little, Brown, 1983); *Tough Guys Don't Dance* (New York: Random House, 1984); *Harlot's Ghost* (New York: Random House, 1984).

34. Joan Didion, *Run River* (New York: Obolensky, 1963); *Play It as It Lays* (New York: Farrar, Straus and Giroux, 1970); *A Book of Common Prayer* (New York: Simon and Schuster, 1977).

35. Joan Didion, *Slouching Towards Bethlehem* (New York: Simon and Schuster, 1968), 30–31.

36. Wolfe and Johnson, *The New Journalism*, 304.

37. Joan Didion, *The White Album* (New York: Simon and Schuster, 1979), 90–92.

38. Wolfe and Johnson, *The New Journalism*, 304.

39. James Atlas, "Slouching Towards Miami," *Vanity Fair* (October 1987): 56.

40. Joan Didion, *Salvador* (New York: Simon and Schuster, 1983); *Democracy* (New York: Simon and Schuster, 1984); *Miami* (New York: Simon and Schuster, 1987); *After Henry* (New York: Simon and Schuster, 1992).

41. Hunter S. Thompson, interview with the author, March 1990.

42. Hunter S. Thompson, *The Great Shark Hunt* (New York: Summit Books, 1979), 25–26.

43. Thompson interview.

44. J. Anthony Lukas, "The Prince of Gonzo," in *Stop the Presses, I Want to Get Off*, ed. Richard Pollack (New York: Random House, 1975), 184.

45. Hunter S. Thompson, *Fear and Loathing: On the Campaign Trail '72* (San Francisco: Straight Arrow Books, 1973); "Fear and Loathing at the Super Bowl," *Rolling Stone* (28 February 1974): 28–38; *Fear and Loathing in Las Vegas* (New York: Random House, 1972).

46. Tom Wolfe, "Tiny Mummies! The True Story of the Ruler of 43rd Street's Land of the Walking Dead!" *New York* [*New York Herald-Tribune* Sunday supplement] (11 April 1965): 8; and "Lost in the Whichy Thicket," *New York* (18 April 1965): 16.

47. Leonard C. Lewin, "Is Fact Necessary? A Sequel to the *Herald-Tribune–New Yorker* Dispute," *Columbia Journalism Review* 4, no. 4 (Winter 1966): 29–34.

48. The comments were summarized in the "Reports" section of the *Columbia Journalism Review* 4, no. 2 (Summer 1965): 42.

49. E. B. White, letter to John Hay Whitney, 12 April 1965, reprinted in *Letters of E. B. White*, ed. Dorothy Lobrano Guth (New York: Harper and Row, 1976), 530–31.

50. Wolfe and Johnson, *The New Journalism*, 24–25.

51. Nobile, "Wolfe Foresees 'Great Awakening.'"

52. John Hersey, "The Legend on the License," *Yale Review* 70, no. 1 (Autumn 1980): 1.

53.   In addition to nonfiction such as *Hiroshima* and *The Algiers Motel Incident* (New York: Knopf, 1968), Hersey published more than a score of novels, including *White Lotus* (New York: Knopf, 1965), *Under the Eye of the Storm* (New York: Knopf, 1967), and *My Petition for More Space* (New York: Knopf, 1974).

54.   Hersey, "Legend on the License," 3–5.

Chapter 5

1.   Lawrence Dietz, "Tom Wolfe on the Search for the Real Me," *New York* (19 August 1968): 42.

2.   Tom Wolfe, "The Author's Story," *New York Times Book Review* (18 August 1968): 40.

3.   Ron Reagan, "*GEO* Conversation: Tom Wolfe," *GEO* (October 1983): 14.

4.   Mary V. McLeod, "Tom Wolfe," *Contemporary Authors*, New Revision Series, vol. 9, ed. Ann Evory and Linda Metzger (Detroit: Gale Research, 1983), 536.

5.   Wolfe, "Author's Story," 41.

6.   Joe David Bellamy, "Sitting up with Tom Wolfe," *Writer's Digest* (November 1974): 22.

7.   Ibid., 22–23.

8.   John Taylor, "The Book on Tom Wolfe," *New York* (21 March 1988): 46.

9.   Thompson, "Dandy Tom," 160.

10.   Tom Wolfe, *The Electric Kool-Aid Acid Test* (New York: Farrar, Straus and Giroux, 1968), 5.

11.   Brant Mewborn, "Tom Wolfe," *Rolling Stone* (5 November–10 December 1987): 218.

12.   Allen, "Pyrotechnic Iconoclast."

13.   Flippo, "*Rolling Stone* Interview," 32.

14.   Wolfe, *Electric Kool-Aid Acid Test*, 9.

15.   Bellamy, *The New Fiction*, 75.

16.   Heath Hardage, "Never Try to Fit in: Tom Wolfe Advises Young Writers," *Richmond News-Leader* [Young Virginians Section], 3 November 1987.

17.   Thompson, "Dandy Tom," 118.

18.   Wolfe, "Author's Story," 41.

19.   Mewborn, "Tom Wolfe," 217.

20.   Wolfe, *Electric Kool-Aid Acid Test*, 37.

21.   Ibid., 17.

22.   Ibid., 411.

23.   Allen, "Pyrotechnic Iconoclast."

24.   Thompson, "Dandy Tom," 160.

25.   Reagan, "*GEO* Conversation," 14.

26. Bryan, "The SAME Day," 1, 2.

27. Joel Lieber, "The Electric Kool-Aid Acid Test," *Nation* (23 September 1968): 282.

28. Karl Shapiro, "Tom Wolfe: Analyst of the ———— Generation," *Washington Post Book World* (18 August 1968): 3.

29. Flippo, *"Rolling Stone* Interview," 30.

30. Reagan, *"GEO* Conversation," 16.

31. Ken Kesey, *The Further Inquiry* (New York: Viking Press, 1991).

Chapter 6

1. Apologies to Nora Ephron for appropriating the title of her *Wallflower at the Orgy* (New York: Knopf, 1973), a collection of her writings for *Esquire*.

2. Allen, "Pyrotechnic Iconoclast."

3. Tom Wolfe, *The Pump House Gang* (New York: Farrar, Straus and Giroux, 1968), 22.

4. John M. Glionna, "Are the Outsiders Now Insiders?" *Los Angeles Times*, 9 January 1991.

5. Ibid.

6. Wolfe, *Pump House Gang*, 63.

7. Ibid., 6.

8. Ibid., 84.

9. Dietz, "The Search for the Real Me," 43.

10. Lawrence Dietz, "Psychic Changes on the Social Landscape," *National Review* (27 August 1968): 866.

11. Jack Kroll, "Inside the Whale," *Newsweek* (26 August 1968): 84.

12. Jack Richardson, "New Fundamentalist Movement," *New Republic* (28 September 1968): 43.

13. Susan Walker, "First with Radical Chic," *New York Times*, 21 June 1987.

14. Tom Wolfe, *Radical Chic and Mau-Mauing the Flak Catchers* (New York: Farrar, Straus and Giroux, 1970), 51.

15. Ibid., 29.

16. Ibid., 54.

17. Nobile, "Wolfe Foresees 'Great Awakening.'"

18. Gross, "Conversation with Wolfe," 19.

19. Ibid.

20. Flippo, *"Rolling Stone* Interview," 34.

21. Wolfe and Johnson, *The New Journalism*, 378.

22. Timothy Foote, "The Fish in the Brandy Snifter," *Time* (21 December 1970): 74.

23. Wolfe, *Radical Chic*, 108–9.

24. Foote, "Brandy Snifter," 74.

25. Wolfe, *Radical Chic*, 120.

26. Peter Michelson, "Tom Wolfe Overboard," *New Republic* (19 December 1970): 17–18.

27. Melvin Maddocks, "Radical Chic and Mau-Mauing the Flak Catchers," *Christian Science Monitor*, 27 November 1970.

28. Joseph Epstein, "The Party's Over," *Commentary* (March 1971): 100.

29. Thomas R. Edwards, "Two Exercises in Elegant Minification," *New York Times Book Review* (29 November 1970): 4.

30. Thompson, "Dandy Tom," 118.

31. Tom Wolfe, "The Me Decade and the Third Great Awakening," *New York* (23 August 1976): 26.

32. Tom Wolfe, *Mauve Gloves and Madmen, Clutter and Vine* (New York: Farrar, Straus and Giroux, 1976), 145, 164.

33. Wolfe, "The Me Decade," 40.

34. Tom Wolfe, *In Our Time* (New York: Farrar, Straus and Giroux, 1980), 9.

35. Wolfe interview.

36. Wolfe, *Mauve Gloves*, 184.

37. Ibid., 200.

Chapter 7

1. Tom Wolfe, "The Courts Must Curb Culture," *Saturday Evening Post*, 3 December 1966.

2. Tom Wolfe, "The Worship of Art," *Harper's* (October 1984): 61.

3. William F. Buckley, Jr., "Firing Line" (PBS), 19 July 1975.

4. Flippo, "*Rolling Stone* Interview," 30.

5. Ibid., 32.

6. Hilton Kramer, "Seven Realists," *New York Times*, 28 April 1973.

7. Tom Wolfe, *The Painted Word* (New York: Farrar, Straus and Giroux, 1975), 6.

8. Gross, "Conversation with Wolfe," 19.

9. Wolfe, *Painted Word*, 58.

10. John Russell, "A Reputedly Clever Man, an Allegedly Dismal Book," *New York Times Book Review* (15 June 1975): 5.

11. Digby Diehl, "Jackson Pollock" (*Playboy* [February 1990]: 26), a review of Steven Naifeh and Gregory White Smith, *Jackson Pollock* (New York: Clarkson N. Potter, 1989).

12. Flippo, "*Rolling Stone* Interview," 34.

13. Russell, "Reputedly Clever Man," 5.

14. Flippo, "*Rolling Stone* Interview," 34.

15. Ruth Berenson, "The Painted Word," *National Review* (1 August 1975).

16. Allen, "Pyrotechnic Iconoclast."

17. "Tom Wolfe Examines Why the New Left Disappeared," *U.S. News and World Report* (5 November 1979): 68.

18. Gross, "Conversation with Wolfe," 19.

19. Tom Wolfe, *From Bauhaus to Our House* (New York: Farrar, Straus and Giroux, 1981), 7.

20. Ibid., 83.

21. Reagan, "*GEO* Conversation," 14.

22. Morley Safer (correspondent) and Tom Bettag (producer), "The Wrong Stuff," "60 Minutes" (CBS), 22 November 1981.

23. Lori Simmons Zelenko, "What Are the Social Pressures Affecting the Art World Today?" *American Artist* (April 1982): 86.

24. Wolfe, *In Our Time*, 31.

25. Ibid., 5.

26. Ibid., 13–15.

Chapter 8

1. Christian Williams, "The Making of 'The Right Stuff,'" *Washington Post*, 17 October 1983.

2. Blue, "The Earthling," 9.

3. [Associated Press], "'Moon Shot' Is the Real Stuff," *Gainesville* (Fla.) *Sun*, 16 May 1994.

4. Flippo, "*Rolling Stone* Interview," 30.

5. Tom Wolfe, "Big Daddy of the Skies," *Esquire* (August 1979): 35.

6. Williams, "Making."

7. "Two Views of the Tragedy," *U.S. News and World Report* (10 February 1986): 19.

8. Tom Wolfe, *The Right Stuff* (New York: Farrar, Straus and Giroux, 1979), 65.

9. "The Magnificent Seven," *The Economist* (1 December 1979): 113.

10. Wolfe, *Right Stuff*, 56.

11. Ibid., 58.

12. "This Week with David Brinkley" (ABC), 2 February 1986.

13. Wolfe, *Right Stuff*, 154–55.

14. Ibid., 121–22.

15. Flippo, "*Rolling Stone* Interview," 30.

16. Wolfe, *Right Stuff*, 168.

17. Ibid., 427–29.

18. "Two Views," 19.

19. Gross, "Conversation with Wolfe," 19.

20. Michael G. Sheldrick, "The First Astronauts: They Had What It Took," *Business Week* (15 October 1979): 10.

21. Ibid.

22. Gross, "Conversation with Wolfe," 19.

23. C. D. B. Bryan, "The Right Stuff," *New York Times Book Review* (23 September 1979): 1.

24. R. Z. Sheppard, "The Right Stuff," *Time* (24 September 1979): 81.

25. Gross, "Conversation with Wolfe," 20.

26. Williams, "Making."

27. Peter S. Prescott, "Tom Wolfe in Orbit," *Newsweek* (17 September 1979): 93.

28. Michael Collins, "So You Want to Be an Astronaut," *Washington Post Book World* (9 September 1979): 1.

29. Thomas Powers, "Wolfe in Orbit: Our Mercurial Interests," *Commonweal* (12 October 1979): 551.

30. John Romano, "Subcultural Chic," *Nation* (3 November 1979): 438.

31. Julie Salamon, *The Devil's Candy* (Boston: Houghton Mifflin, 1991), 23.

32. "Nightline" (ABC), 14 October 1983.

33. "This Week with Brinkley."

Chapter 9

1. Taylor, "The Book on Wolfe," 50.

2. Bellamy, *The New Fiction*, 75.

3. Taylor, "Book on Wolfe," 50.

4. Mervyn Rothstein, "Tom Wolfe Tries New Role: Novelist," *New York Times*, 13 October 1987.

5. Ibid.

6. Taylor, "Book on Wolfe," 52.

7. Rothstein, "Wolfe Tries New Role."

8. Patricia Leigh Brown, "The King of Pumping Irony Puts Torch to the Rich," *Chicago Tribune*, 2 September 1985.

9. Taylor, "Book on Wolfe," 52.

10. Ibid., 54.

11. Tom Wolfe, *The Bonfire of the Vanities* (New York: Farrar, Straus and Giroux, 1987), 44.

12. Ibid., 485.

13. Ibid., 578–79.

14. Ibid., 647.

15. Nicholas Lemann, "The Bonfire of the Vanities," *Atlantic* (December 1987): 104.

16. Frank Conroy, "The Bonfire of the Vanities," *New York Times Book Review* (1 November 1987): 1.

17. R. Z. Sheppard, "The Haves and the Have-Mores," *Time* (9 November 1987): 101.

18. Taylor, "Book on Wolfe," 48.

19. James Andrews, "The Bonfire of the Vanities," *Christian Science Monitor*, 3 November 1987.
20. Frank Rich, "The Bonfire of the Vanities," *New Republic* (23 November 1987): 42.
21. Tom Wolfe, "Stalking the Billion-Footed Beast," *Harper's* (November 1989): 54.
22. Taylor, "Book on Wolfe," 48.
23. Salamon, *Devil's Candy*, 191.
24. Ibid., 409.
25. Ibid., 408.

Chapter 10

1. Quoted in "Thomas Kennerly Wolfe, Jr.," in *Major Twentieth Century Writers* (Detroit: Gale Research, 1991).
2. Tom Wolfe, "Down with Sin!" *Saturday Evening Post*, 19 June 1965.
3. Ibid.
4. Bonnie Angelo, "Master of His Universe," *Time* (13 February 1989): 90.
5. Tom Wolfe, "Everyman vs. Astropower," *Newsweek* (10 February 1986): 40.
6. Wolfe, "Worship of Art," 63.
7. Buckley, "Firing Line."
8. *The Chelsea House Library of Literary Criticism: Twentieth Century American Literature*, Vol. 7, ed. Harold Bloom (New York: Chelsea House Publishers, 1988), 4456.
9. Wolfe, "Stalking Billion-Footed Beast," 51.
10. Ibid., 55.
11. Tom Wolfe, "Tom Wolfe's Novel Ideas," *Harper's* (March 1990): 9.
12. Joseph Epstein, "Rococo and Roll," *New Republic* (24 July 1965): 27.
13. Wolfe interview.
14. Ibid.
15. Ibid.

Selected Bibliography

PRIMARY WORKS

Books

The Bonfire of the Vanities. New York: Farrar, Straus and Giroux, 1987.
 Introduction by the author added to the 1990 reissue of the book.
The Electric Kool-Aid Acid Test. New York: Farrar, Straus and Giroux, 1968.
From Bauhaus to Our House. New York: Farrar, Straus and Giroux, 1981.
In Our Time. New York: Farrar, Straus and Giroux, 1980.
The Kandy-Kolored Tangerine-Flake Streamline Baby. New York: Farrar, Straus
 and Giroux, 1965.
Mauve Gloves and Madmen, Clutter and Vine. New York: Farrar, Straus and
 Giroux, 1976.
The New Journalism. New York: Harper and Row, 1973. Four essays by Wolfe,
 with an anthology of other writings edited by Wolfe and E. W. Johnson.
The Painted Word. New York: Farrar, Straus and Giroux, 1975.
The Pump House Gang. New York: Farrar, Straus and Giroux, 1968.
The Purple Decades. New York: Farrar, Straus and Giroux, 1982.
Radical Chic and Mau-Mauing the Flak Catchers. New York: Farrar, Straus and
 Giroux, 1970.
The Right Stuff. New York: Farrar, Straus and Giroux, 1979.

Magazine Articles

"The Author's Story." *New York Times Book Review* (18 August 1968): 40.
"Big Daddy of the Skies." *Esquire* (August 1979): 36.
"Big Daddy of the Skies." *Reader's Digest* (February 1980): 73.
"The Bonfire of the Vanities [part 1]." *Rolling Stone* (19 July–2 August [double
 issue] 1984): 16.
"The Bonfire of the Vanities [part 2]." *Rolling Stone* (16 August 1984): 15.
"The Bonfire of the Vanities [part 3]." *Rolling Stone* (30 August 1984): 24.
"The Bonfire of the Vanities [part 4]." *Rolling Stone* (13 September 1984): 31.
"The Bonfire of the Vanities [part 5]." *Rolling Stone* (27 September 1984): 65.
"The Bonfire of the Vanities [part 6]." *Rolling Stone* (11 October 1984): 29.
"The Bonfire of the Vanities [part 7]." *Rolling Stone* (25 October 1984): 37.
"The Bonfire of the Vanities [part 8]." *Rolling Stone* (8 November 1984): 49.
"The Bonfire of the Vanities [part 9]." *Rolling Stone* (22 November 1984): 53.
"The Bonfire of the Vanities [part 10]." *Rolling Stone* (6 December 1984): 41.

"The Bonfire of the Vanities [part 11]." *Rolling Stone* (20 December 1984–3 January [double issue] 1985): 90.

"The Bonfire of the Vanities [part 12]." *Rolling Stone* (17 January 1985): 25.

"The Bonfire of the Vanities [part 13]." *Rolling Stone* (31 January 1985): 43.

"The Bonfire of the Vanities [part 14]." *Rolling Stone* (14 February 1985): 37.

"The Bonfire of the Vanities [part 15]." *Rolling Stone* (28 February 1985): 47.

"The Bonfire of the Vanities [part 16]." *Rolling Stone* (14 March 1985): 35.

"The Bonfire of the Vanities [part 17]." *Rolling Stone* (28 March 1985): 89.

"The Bonfire of the Vanities [part 18]." *Rolling Stone* (11 April 1985): 51.

"The Bonfire of the Vanities [part 19]." *Rolling Stone* (25 April 1985): 47.

"The Bonfire of the Vanities [part 20]." *Rolling Stone* (9 May 1985): 67.

"The Bonfire of the Vanities [part 21]." *Rolling Stone* (23 May 1985): 43.

"The Bonfire of the Vanities [part 22]." *Rolling Stone* (6 June 1985): 48.

"The Bonfire of the Vanities [part 23]." *Rolling Stone* (20 June 1985): 51.

"The Bonfire of the Vanities [part 24]." *Rolling Stone* (4 July 1985): 43.

"The Bonfire of the Vanities [part 25]." *Rolling Stone* (18 July–1 August [double issue] 1985): 71.

"The Bonfire of the Vanities [part 26]." *Rolling Stone* (15 August 1985): 36.

"The Bonfire of the Vanities [part 27]." *Rolling Stone* (29 August 1985): 31.

"Columbia's Landing Closes a Circle." *National Geographic* (October 1981): 474.

"The Copper Goddess." *Newsweek* (14 July 1986): 34.

"The Courts Must Curb Culture." *Saturday Evening Post*, 3 December 1966.

"Crime." *Esquire* (December 1973): 137.

"Down with Sin!" *Saturday Evening Post*, 19 June 1965.

"Eulogy for the Twentieth Century." *Utne Reader* (March-April 1988): 32.

"Everyman vs. Astropower." *Newsweek* (10 February 1986): 40.

"Exploits of El Sid." *New York Times Book Review* (19 July 1981): 1. Review of *The Last Laugh* by S. J. Perelman.

"A Few Words about Rockefeller Center." *American Heritage* (October-November 1982): 106.

"From Bauhaus to Our House: Why Architects Can't Get out of the Box [part 1]." *Harper's* (June 1981): 33.

"From Bauhaus to Our House: Architecture for Architects Only [part 2]." *Harper's* (July 1981): 40.

"Great American Things." *Esquire* (December 1975): 83.

"Hayes and Company." *House and Garden* (October 1990): 156.

"Head of the Class." *National Review* (5 August 1988): 35.

"How You Can Be as Well-Informed as Tom Wolfe." *Esquire* (November 1967): 138.

"In Our Time: American Guernica." *Harper's* (December 1980): 70.

"In Our Time: The Birds and the Bees." *Harper's* (October 1978): 88.

"In Our Time: Dear Professor Emu." *Harper's* (September 1979): 75.

"In Our Time: Esperanto." *Harper's* (November 1980): 69.

"In Our Time: The Evolution of the Species: Growing Old Gracefully [part 1]."
    Harper's (June 1979): 99.
"In Our Time: The Evolution of the Species: The Eligible Bachelor [part 2]."
    Harper's (May 1980): 71.
"In Our Time: The Evolution of the Species: The Dress Designer [part 3]."
    Harper's (March 1981): 57.
"In Our Time: The Evolution of the Species: Dope Fiend [part 4]." *Harper's*
    (August 1981): 69.
"In Our Time: The Evolution of the Species: The Evening Promenade [part 5]."
    Harper's (September 1981): 82.
"In Our Time: Great Moments in Contemporary Architecture." *Harper's*
    (August 1979): 70.
"In Our Time: The Independent Woman." *Harper's* (February 1980): 61.
"In Our Time: The Invisible Wife." *Harper's* (January 1980): 57.
"In Our Time: The Jogger's Prayer." *Harper's* (December 1978): 84.
"In Our Time: The Long-Haul Trucker's Lament." *Harper's* (August 1980): 53.
"In Our Time: The Lord's Work." *Harper's* (July 1980): 76.
"In Our Time: The Lower Classes: The Down-Filled People [part 1]." *Harper's*
    (March 1980): 65.
"In Our Time: The Lower Classes: Victims of Inflation [part 2]." *Harper's* (June
    1980): 71.
"In Our Time: The Maternal Instinct." *Harper's* (April 1980): 117.
"In Our Time: Mens Sana in Corpore Sana." *Harper's* (April 1979): 61.
"In Our Time: The Modern Minister." *Harper's* (August 1978): 73.
"In Our Time: Modern Etiquette: The Coffee Break." *Harper's* (September
    1978): 83.
"In Our Time: Modern Martyrs: The Fiction Editor Confronting the Best-
    Selling Author's Latest Manuscript [part 1]." *Harper's* (May 1981): 56.
"In Our Time: National Health." *Harper's* (February 1979): 82.
"In Our Time: The National Pastime." *Harper's* (May 1979): 83.
"In Our Time: The New Cookie." *Harper's* (November 1978): 79.
"In Our Time: Political Science." *Harper's* (February 1981): 70.
"In Our Time: The Ringleader." *Harper's* (January 1981): 43.
"In Our Time: The Secret Heart of the New York Culturatus." *Harper's*
    (October 1979): 69.
"In Our Time: The Skateboy." *Harper's* (September 1980): 57.
"In Our Time: Style Note." *Harper's* (October 1980): 75.
"In Our Time: Sweet Mysteries of Life: Bliss Soho Boho [part 1]." *Harper's*
    (January 1979): 78.
"In Our Time: Women's Fate." *Harper's* (March 1979): 114.
"In Our Time: World Weary." *Harper's* (July 1979): 73.
"The Intelligent Co-ed's Guide to America." *Harper's* (July 1976): 27.
"Land of Wizards." *Popular Mechanics* (July 1986): 126.

"Las Vegas (What?) Las Vegas (Can't Hear You! Too Noisy!) Las Vegas!!!"
    Esquire (February 1964): 97.
"The Last American Hero Is Junior Johnson. Yes!" *Esquire* (March 1965):
    68.
"The Last American Hero Is Junior Johnson. Yes!" *Esquire* (October 1973):
    211. Reprint of the earlier article in a special anniversary issue of *Esquire*
    titled "The Best of 40 Years."
"Late Bloomers." *American Spectator* (November 1990): 32.
"Lost in the Whichy Thicket." *New York* [*New York Herald-Tribune* supplement]
    (18 April 1965): 16.
"The Marvelous Mouth." *Esquire* (October 1963): 146.
"A Master of the Universe." *Gentleman's Quarterly* (January 1989): 198.
"The Me Decade and the Third Great Awakening." *New York* (23 August
    1976): 26.
"The New Yellow Peril." *Esquire* (December 1969): 190.
"O, the Big Time, Game-Time, Show-Time Roll." *Esquire* (October 1974): 182.
"The Painted Word." *Harper's* (April 1975): 57.
"Pause Now and Consider Some Tentative Conclusions about Porno-Violence."
    Esquire (July 1967): 59.
"Post-Orbital Remorse." *Rolling Stone* (11 June 1992): 72. Reprint of selections
    from Wolfe's 1973 series for an anniversary issue of *Rolling Stone*.
"Post-Orbital Remorse: The Brotherhood of the Right Stuff [part 1]." *Rolling
    Stone* (4 January 1973): 24.
"Post-Orbital Remorse: How the Astronauts Fell from Cowboy Heaven [part
    2]." *Rolling Stone* (18 January 1973): 22.
"Post-Orbital Remorse: The Death of the Ego [part 3]." *Rolling Stone* (15
    February 1973): 26.
"Post-Orbital Remorse: The Last Great Galactic Flash [part 4]." *Rolling Stone* (1
    March 1973): 44.
"Proper Places." *Esquire* (June 1985): 194.
"Public Lives: Confidential Magazine—Reflections in Tranquility by the Former
    Owner, Robert Harrison, Who Managed to Get away with It." *Esquire*
    (April 1964): 87.
"Salvation." *Esquire* (December 1973): 201.
"Sex." *Esquire* (December 1973): 169.
"Sissy Bars Will Be Lower This Year." *Esquire* (February 1971): 60.
"Stalking the Billion-Footed Beast." *Harper's* (November 1989): 45.
"Summing up the Seventies." *Esquire* (June 1983): 368. Reprint of "Tom
    Wolfe's Seventies" (*Esquire*, December 1979).
"There Goes (Varoom! Varoom!) the Kandy-Kolored Tangerine-Flake
    Streamline Baby." *Esquire* (November 1963): 114.
"The Tinkering of Robert Noyce: How the Sun Rose over the Silicon Valley."
    Esquire (December 1983): 346.

"Tiny Mummies! The True Story of the Ruler of 43rd Street's Land of the Walking Dead!" *New York* [*New York Herald Tribune* supplement] (11 April 1965): 22.

"Tom Wolfe Examines 'Why the New Left Disappeared.'" *U.S. News and World Report* (5 November 1979): 68.

"Tom Wolfe's Novel Ideas." *Harper's* (March 1990): 4. Criticism of Wolfe's "Stalking the Billion-Footed Beast" essay and his response.

"Tom Wolfe's Seventies." *Esquire* (December 1979): 36.

"The Truest Sport: Jousting with Sam and Charlie." *Esquire* (October 1975): 156.

"2020 A.D." *Esquire* (January 1985): 88.

"The Wayward Reader: Force of Circumstance." *Holiday* (August 1965): 14. Review of Simone de Beauvoir's *Force of Circumstance*.

"Why They Aren't Writing the Great American Novel Anymore." *Esquire* (December 1972): 152.

"The Worship of Art." *Harper's* (October 1984): 61.

Newspaper Articles

"1,500 Movie Extras Vie for Glory." *Washington Post*, 31 August 1961.

"Abduction Try Is Laid to Three Here." *Washington Post*, 4 June 1961. First appearance of *"Tom* Wolfe" byline; a collaboration with the reporter Susanna McBee.

"Agency Here Wages Battle on Glaucoma." *Washington Post*, 8 October 1959. Includes sketch by Wolfe.

"Area Basks in 70-Degree Sunshine as Potomac Rises with Rapid Thaw." *Washington Post*, 20 February 1961.

"Area Tobacconists Hurt, Saddened by Decline in Smokers' Tastes." *Washington Post*, 19 July 1959.

"Area-wide Planners Reject D.C. Board as Authority." *Washington Post*, 21 February 1961.

"Arlington Salesgirl Slain at Party; Alexandria Laborer, 19, Arrested." *Washington Post*, 2 November 1959.

"Balky New FAA System Embarrasses in Debut." *Washington Post*, 2 March 1961.

"Beatles! More Than Just a Word to the Wild." *New York Herald-Tribune*, 8 February 1964.

"Big Cosmos Meeting Set for Today." *Washington Post*, 15 January 1962.

"Bishop Ousted from Cuba to Celebrate Mass Here." *Washington Post*, 4 February 1962.

"Boy Scientists Study Future by Computer." *Washington Post*, 6 March 1961.

"Byrd Scales Old Rag Mountain at 74 for Dedication." *Washington Post*, 11 June 1961.

"Cars and Brains and Girls Featured at New Auto Show." *Washington Post*, 14 January 1960.

"Children on Panel Reveal How They Beat TV Habit." *Washington Post* [date uncertain].

"Chinese Authors Stifled by Reds." *Washington Post*, 17 January 1961.

"Cigar Smokers! (Including JFK) Help on the Way." *Washington Post*, 4 February 1962.

"Critic Says DeGaulle Has Literary Bug." *Washington Post*, 13 January 1960.

"Cuba May Fall but (the) Havana Will Live Forever." *Washington Post*, 6 July 1961. Includes illustration by Wolfe of cigar-smoking fat cats studying Castro's picture on magazine cover.

"D.C. Army Tenor Gains Met Opera Finals." *Washington Post*, 21 January 1962.

"Dieting Franklin Holds Fatter Hand Out." *Washington Post*, 12 October 1961.

"The Dispensable Guide: In Rome Natives and Tourists Try to Flee Tourists [part 1]." *Washington Post*, 4 December 1959. Includes sketch by "Tom Wolfe." Article credited to "Thomas Wolfe."

"The Dispensable Guide: Black Market Money Replaces Slave Girls in Ankara Trading [part 2]." *Washington Post*, 6 December 1959. Includes sketch by "Thomas" Wolfe.

"The Dispensable Guide: Karachi Is 'Heaven' for Camel but No Other Creature [part 3]." *Washington Post*, 7 December 1959. Includes sketch by Wolfe.

"The Dispensable Guide: 'Tureh' (Courage) True Virtue in Afghanistan [part 4]." *Washington Post*, 8 December 1959. Includes sketch by Wolfe.

"The Dispensable Guide: New Delhi Called Versailles and Bureaucrats' Paradise [part 5]." *Washington Post*, 9 December 1959. Includes sketch by Wolfe.

"The Dispensable Guide: Cosmopolitan Tehran Lacks Middle East Table [part 6]." *Washington Post*, 13 December 1959. Includes sketch by Wolfe.

"The Dispensable Guide: Hospitable Greeks Swamp Their Guests with Kindness [part 7]." *Washington Post*, 14 December 1959. Includes sketch by Wolfe.

"The Dispensable Guide: Tunisians Get Deadline to Adopt Last Names [part 8]." *Washington Post*, 17 December 1959. Includes sketch by Wolfe.

"The Dispensable Guide: French Divide World: Parisians and Peasants [part 9]." *Washington Post*, 19 December 1959. Includes sketch by Wolfe.

"The Dispensable Guide: Proper Bostonians, Properly Attired, Feel at Home in Madrid [part 10]." *Washington Post*, 21 December 1959. Includes sketch by Wolfe.

"The Dispensable Guide: Moroccans' Virility Legendary and It Is Carefully Cultivated [part 11]." *Washington Post*, 22 December 1959. Includes sketch by Wolfe.

"The Dispensable Guide: In Washington the Illustrious Are Rated at a Dime a Dozen [part 12]." *Washington Post*, 23 December 1959.

"District's 'Crime Doctor' to Retire after 26 Years." *Washington Post*, 1 May 1961.

"District Really Does Get into Politics as Democrats Open 'Prep School.'" *Washington Post*, 7 January 1962.

"Doctors' 7-Hour Battle Fails to Save Worker Suffocated in Manhole Heat." *Washington Post*, 13 June 1961.

"Dr. Terry Is an Enzyme Researcher." *Washington Post*, 16 January 1961.

"Dog Hunting Master for Six Weeks Enlists Connecticut Ave. Sympathies." *Washington Post*, 11 January 1960.

"Ducks, Assigned to Rural Life, Come out of the Wilds to White House." *Washington Post*, 13 April 1961.

"Eberhart Sees Poets Aided by Space Age." *Washington Post*, 16 May 1961.

"Elegantly Clad Beatnik Chief Beats Band for Business Boom." *Washington Post*, 31 July 1959.

"Engineer in Fatal Bowie Crash Tells Hearing the Brakes Failed." *Washington Post*, 15 February 1961.

"His Cup Runneth over: Constituents Pay a Visit." *Washington Post*, 26 February 1961.

"Holiday Gets Cold Start, Mild Finish." *Washington Post*, 29 May 1961.

"Hopeless Horror of Cystic Fibrosis Battled in Research Backed by UGF." *Washington Post*, 15 October 1959.

"Inaugural Floats Are 'Something.'" *Washington Post*, 8 January 1961.

"Iranians Jailed, Freed in Row over Passports." *Washington Post*, 11 July 1961.

"Jim Makes Holidays Drab and Proud: For Once, He's Sober and out of Jail." *Washington Post*, 27 December 1959.

"Jaycees Tonight Pick 1959 Men of the Year." *Washington Post*, 1 January 1960.

"Kearns Takes Time out to Attend Game While Police Guard His Office." *Washington Post*, 2 October 1961.

"King of Hoaxers Deals His Jokers Like a Real Ace." *Washington Post*, 14 January 1962. This full-page feature is illustrated with sketches by Wolfe.

"Lightning Hits 7 Homes in Fairfax." *Washington Post*, 24 August 1959.

"Lincoln 'Too Human' for Throne." *Washington Post*, 12 February 1962.

"Local Restaurateur Will Feed King of Arabia." *Washington Post*, 11 February 1962.

"Loud Speakers Help in Reducing Confusion on First All-Bus Day." *Washington Post*, 30 January 1962.

"MacKay Circle Cock-a-doodle-doo Called Fowl Blow by Neighbor." *Washington Post*, 10 January 1962.

"Math Group Is Told of Shortage." *Washington Post*, 26 January 1961.

"Modern Art Group Plans Gallery Here." *Washington Post*, 8 January 1962.

"Modern Craftsmen Delight in Pioneers' Careful Skills." *Washington Post*, 30 January 1962.

"Moonshiner's Sleek Auto Now Used to Carry 'Revenooer' around Town." *Washington Post*, 25 July 1961.

"Morning Paper Lands Right at His Bedside." *Washington Post*, 11 January 1960.

"Mt. Vernon Fans Cheer at Park Plan." *Washington Post*, 31 January 1962.

"Mrs. Woodrow Wilson Is Buried at Cathedral." *Washington Post*, 2 January 1962.

"Mysterious Blotches on Monument Probed." *Washington Post*, 14 February 1960.

"New 7th St. Bus Run Still down to a Walk." *Washington Post*, 6 January 1960.

"Of Things Dedicated Walkers Want, Mass Transport's at Foot of the List." *Washington Post*, 12 November 1959.

"Old-fashioned Idea Works Fine for Calomiris." *Washington Post*, 28 January 1962.

"Pan American Pedaler Sells Wanderlust." *Washington Post*, 5 October 1959.

"Pandemonium Reigns Supreme Here in Capital of Confusion." *Washington Post*, 20 January 1961.

"Poet Frost's Coffee Hour Gives Strong Taste of His Ideas." *Washington Post*, 2 May 1961.

"Poet Joaquin Miller's Meridian Hills Cabin Being Restored." *Washington Post*, 2 January 1962.

"Poles Still Refuse to Bow to Masters." *Washington Post*, 2 August 1959.

"Press Cards to Inaugural Stir Battle." *Washington Post*, 12 January 1961.

"Red Latin-Poet's Fame Laid to Communist Ties." *Washington Post*, 31 January 1961.

"Red Writers Circulate Works Underground." *Washington Post*, 10 January 1961.

"Rep. Evins Protests Bitterly That Tennessee Ave. Fails Dismally to Do Honor to His Home State." *Washington Post*, 4 October 1961.

"Rich Nobility Loved Leningrad." *Washington Post*, 29 July 1959.

"Science, It's Wonderful—Hear This: A Snail's Pace Is 24.7 Ft. an Hour." *Washington Post*, 21 June 1961.

"Scotsman Takes a Fling at Pert Aussie 'Invasion.'" *Washington Post* [date unknown].

"Ship Convoys to Crack Bay Freeze." *Washington Post*, 30 January 1961.

"Smithsonian Building Biggest Whale Ever." *Washington Post*, 7 January 1960.

"A Sneeze Can Buy a Carload of Tobacco." *Washington Post*, 26 April 1961.

"State Department Messenger Ends 44 Years of Rubbing Elbows." *Washington Post*, 27 April 1961.

"Sticky Stuff Which Once Stuck D.C. Now British 'Cure.'" *Washington Post*, 10 May 1961.

"Sunday Monkey Chasers Put Quietus on Cute Capuchin Cutting Capers." *Washington Post*, 27 July 1959.

"Switchman Describes Crash of Bowie Train." *Washington Post*, 16 February 1961.

"Telegrapher Comes to End of Line 8 Years after Express Forgot to Stop."
     Washington Post, 12 January 1961.
"To Him 'Rhythmic Rhyme' Is Just Fine." *Washington Post*, 14 August 1961.
"Tourists in Unprecedented Numbers Are Here to See Blossoms, Shrines."
     Washington Post, 6 April 1961.
"UGF Brings Hope to Exiles of Deafness." *Washington Post*, 11 October 1959.
     Includes sketch by Wolfe.
"UGF Finds Love for Terror's Children." *Washington Post*, 6 October 1959.
     Includes sketch by Wolfe.
"UGF Unit Saves Arthritics from Preying Quacks." *Washington Post*, 3
     November 1959. Includes sketch by Wolfe.
"Visitor Here Gets 'Dope' on City from an Old Pro." *Washington Post*, 30 May
     1961.
"Wails Greet Order to Sell Market." *Washington Post*, 5 April 1961.
"Welfare Unit Beats Child Noise Problem." *Washington Post*, 14 March 1961.
"Well-Stacked Sverdlovsk Has Glitter amid Grime." *Washington Post*, 30 July
     1959.
"Wows and Woolies Advised for Siberian 'Chicago.'" *Washington Post*, 28 July
     1959.
"Yanks and Rebs Hated Officers, Says Scholar." *Washington Post*, 9 March 1961.
"You Can So Beat the Gambling House at Blackjack, Math Expert Insists."
     Washington Post, 23 January 1961.

Miscellaneous Writings

"The League of American Writers: Communist Organizational Activity among
     American Writers, 1929–1942." Ph.D. dissertation, Yale University,
     1957.
"The Angels." In *The Literary Journalists*, edited by Norman Sims (New York:
     Ballantine Books, 1984), 87.
"The Bonfire of the Vanities [excerpt]." In *20 Years of Rolling Stone: What a Long,
     Strange Trip It's Been*, edited by Jann Wenner (New York: Friendly Press,
     1987), 432.
"Funky Chic." In *20 Years of Rolling Stone: What a Long, Strange Trip It's Been*,
     edited by Jann Wenner (New York: Friendly Press, 1987), 209.
"Great American Things." In *Mom, the Flag and Apple Pie: Great American
     Writers on Great American Things*, compiled by the editors of *Esquire* (New
     York: Doubleday, 1976), 1.
Introduction. In *Marie Cosindas: Color Photographs*. Boston: New York Graphic
     Society, 1970.
"Post-Orbital Remorse: The Brotherhood of the Right Stuff [part 1]." In
     Reporting: The Rolling Stone Style, edited by Paul Scanlon (Garden City,
     N.Y.: Doubleday, 1977), 327.
"Post-Orbital Remorse." In *The Best of Rolling Stone*, edited by Robert Love
     (Garden City, N.Y.: Doubleday, 1993), 72.

"The Pump House Gang." In *The Sixties*, edited by Linda Rosen Obst (New York: Random House/Rolling Stone Press, 1977), 142.

Recorded Interviews

"Tom Wolfe." Interviews conducted for Tapes for Readers, a Washington, D.C. audiocassette service. Drawn from 1973 and 1978 interviews with Stephen Banker, the tape includes Wolfe's discussion of the writing of *Radical Chic and Mau-Mauing the Flak Catchers* and *The Painted Word*.
"This Week with David Brinkley." ABC Television, 2 February 1986. Wolfe joins host David Brinkley, Sen. John Glenn, and the writer Isaac Asimov in discussing the future of the American space program in the aftermath of the *Challenger* disaster.
"Firing Line." PBS Television, 19 July 1975. Wolfe discusses *The Painted Word* with William F. Buckley, Jr.
"Nightline." ABC Television, 14 October 1983. Hosted by Ted Koppel, this broadcast includes a discussion between Wolfe and the producers of the film *The Right Stuff*, Robert Chartoff and Irwin Winkler, of the effect the film might have on Sen. John Glenn's campaign for the presidency. The actor Gene Hackman and the director Costa-Gavras also debate the worth of films with political meaning.
"The World of Ideas." PBS Television, 26 January 1988 and 27 October 1988. Both programs, hosted by Bill Moyers, review Wolfe's impact on contemporary writing.
"60 Minutes." CBS Television, 22 November 1981. In a segment called "The Wrong Stuff" (Tom Bettag, segment producer), Wolfe discusses with Morley Safer the subjects of architecture in general and *From Bauhaus to Our House* in particular.
"Tom Wolfe with Peter York." Conducted for ICA Video (London) and distributed by the Roland Collection, Northbrook, Ill. In this 1989 video interview with Peter York, Wolfe discusses the birth of New Journalism, experimental fiction in America, and the use of journalistic techniques in writing a novel.

SECONDARY WORKS

Books

Anderson, Chris, ed. *Literary Nonfiction: Theory, Criticism, Pedagogy*. Carbondale and Edwardsville: Southern Illinois University Press, 1989.
Bellamy, Joe David. *The New Fiction: Interviews with Innovative American Writers*. Urbana: University of Illinois Press, 1974.

Capote, Truman. *Answered Prayers: The Unfinished Novel*. New York: Random House, 1986.

——. *The Dogs Bark*. New York: Random House, 1973.

——. *In Cold Blood*. New York: Random House, 1966.

——. *Local Color*. New York: Random House, 1950.

——. *The Muses Are Heard*. New York: Random House, 1956.

——. *Music for Chameleons*. New York: Random House, 1980.

——. *Selected Writings*. New York: Random House, 1962.

Dennis, Everette E., and William L. Rivers. *Other Voices: The New Journalism in America*. San Francisco: Canfield Press, 1974.

Didion, Joan. *After Henry*. New York: Simon and Schuster, 1992.

——. *A Book of Common Prayer*. New York: Simon and Schuster, 1977.

——. *Democracy*. New York: Simon and Schuster, 1984.

——. *Miami*. New York: Simon and Schuster, 1987.

——. *Play It as It Lays*. New York: Farrar, Straus and Giroux, 1970.

——. *Run River*. New York: Obolensky, 1963.

——. *Salvador*. New York: Simon and Schuster, 1983.

——. *Slouching Towards Bethlehem*. New York: Simon and Schuster, 1968.

——. *The White Album*. New York: Simon and Schuster, 1979.

Fishkin, Shelley Fisher. *From Fact to Fiction: Journalism and Imaginative Writing in America*. Baltimore: Johns Hopkins University Press, 1985.

Fletcher, Angus, ed. *The Literature of Fact*. New York: Columbia University Press, 1976.

Halberstam, David. *The Powers That Be*. New York: Knopf, 1979.

Hellmann, Jerome. *Fables of Fact*. Urbana: University of Illinois Press, 1981.

Hersey, John. *Hiroshima*. New York: Knopf, 1946.

Hollowell, John. *Fact and Fiction: The New Journalism and the Nonfiction Novel*. Chapel Hill: University of North Carolina Press, 1977.

Johnson, Michael L. *The New Journalism*. Lawrence: University of Kansas Press, 1971.

Kluger, Richard. *The Paper: The Life and Death of the* New York Herald-Tribune. New York: Vintage, 1989.

Mailer, Norman. *An American Dream*. New York: Dial Press, 1965.

——. *Ancient Evenings*. Boston: Little, Brown, 1983.

——. *The Armies of the Night: History as a Novel; the Novel as History*. New York: New American Library, 1968.

——. *The Executioner's Song*. Boston: Little, Brown, 1979.

——. *The Faith of Graffiti*. New York: Praeger, 1974.

——. *The Fight*. Boston: Little, Brown, 1975.

——. *Harlot's Ghost*. New York: Random House, 1984.

——. *Marilyn: A Novel Biography*. New York: Grosset and Dunlap, 1973.

——. *Miami and the Siege of Chicago*. New York: New American Library, 1968.

——. *The Naked and the Dead*. New York: Rinehart, 1948.

————. *Of a Fire on the Moon*. New York: Little, Brown, 1970.

————. *The Prisoner of Sex*. Boston: Little, Brown, 1971.

————. *Tough Guys Don't Dance*. New York: Random House, 1984.

Roberts, Chalmers. The Washington Post: *The First 100 Years*. Boston: Houghton Mifflin, 1977.

Salamon, Julie. *The Devil's Candy: "The Bonfire of the Vanities" Goes to Hollywood*. Boston: Houghton Mifflin, 1991.

Scura, Dorothy, ed. *Conversations with Tom Wolfe*. Jackson: University Press of Mississippi, 1990.

Sims, Norman, ed. *Literary Journalism in the Twentieth Century*. New York: Oxford University Press, 1990.

————, ed. *The Literary Journalists*. New York: Ballantine, 1984.

Talese, Gay. *Fame and Obscurity*. New York: World Publishing, 1970; New York: New American Library, 1974.

————. *Honor Thy Father*. New York: World Publishing, 1971.

————. *The Kingdom and the Power*. New York: World Publishing, 1969.

————. *New York: A Serendipiter's Journey*. New York: Harper and Brothers, 1961.

————. *Thy Neighbor's Wife*. New York: Doubleday, 1980.

————. *Unto the Sons*. New York: Knopf, 1991.

Thompson, Hunter S. *Fear and Loathing in Las Vegas: A Savage Journey to the Heart of the American Dream*. New York: Random House, 1972.

————. *Fear and Loathing: On the Campaign Trail '72*. San Francisco: Straight Arrow Books, 1973.

————. *Generation of Swine: Gonzo Papers, Volume 2*. New York: Summit Books, 1988.

————. *The Great Shark Hunt: Gonzo Papers, Volume 1*. New York: Summit Books, 1979.

————. *Hell's Angels: The Strange and Terrible Saga of the Outlaw Motorcycle Gangs*. New York: Random House, 1967.

————. *Songs of the Doomed: Gonzo Papers, Volume 3*. New York: Summit Books, 1990.

Weber, Ronald. *The Literature of Fact*. Athens: Ohio University Press, 1980.

————. *The Reporter as Artist: A Look at the New Journalism Controversy*. New York: Hastings House, 1974.

Articles and Parts of Books

Allen, Henry. "The Pyrotechnic Iconoclast, Still Passing the Acid Test." *Washington Post*, 4 September 1979.

Alter, Jonathan. "Two Cheers for Tom Wolfe." *Washington Monthly* (March 1988): 42.

Amiel, B. "Society's Monitor." *Maclean's* (6 November 1978): 4.

Angelo, Bonnie. "Master of His Universe." *Time* (13 February 1989): 90.

Atlas, James. "The Case for Tom Wolfe." *New York Times Book Review* (2 December 1979): 3.

Bada, Peter. "Holding 'Bonfire' up to a Mirror." *New York Times Book Review* (28 April 1988): 24.

Barrett, A. "Akond of Swock." *The Reporter* (12 August 1965): 50.

Bellamy, Joe David. Introduction to Tom Wolfe, *The Purple Decades: A Reader.* New York: Farrar, Straus and Giroux, 1982.

———. "Sitting up with Tom Wolfe." *Writer's Digest* (November 1974): 22.

———. "Tom Wolfe Is Not Always There." *Writer's Digest* (June 1973): 16.

Berkowitz, Harry. "The Author as Activist." *Newsday*, 12 January 1989.

"Between Fact and Fiction." *Maclean's* (14 December 1987): 1.

Blades, John. "Vanity Fare: On Tom Wolfe on the Great American Novel by Tom Wolfe." *Chicago Tribune*, 21 November 1989.

Blue, Adrianne. "The Earthling and the Astronauts." *Washington Post Book World* (9 September 1979): 9.

Brown, Patricia Leigh. "The King of Pumping Irony Puts Torch to the Rich." *Chicago Tribune*. 2 September 1985.

Brown, Doug. "Author Who Rewrote the Way Journalists Write Talks about First Novel at Chapman." *Los Angeles Times*, 16 May 1985.

Broyard, Anatole. "New York Is Worth a Novel—Are You?" *New York Times Book Review* (10 January 1988): 11.

Bryan, C. D. B. "The Right Stuff." *New York Times Book Review* (23 September 1979): 1.

———. "The SAME Day: Heeeeeewack!!!" *New York Times Book Review* (18 August 1968): 1.

Buckley, William F., Jr. "Mau-Mauing Wolfe." *National Review* (12 January 1971): 51.

Coleman, Terry. "How to Wolfe a Tangerine at a Tangent." *Manchester Guardian Weekly* (10 March 1966): 12.

Compton, Neil. "Hijinks Journalism." *Commentary* 47, no. 2 (February 1969): 76.

Coyne, John R., Jr. "Sketchbook of Snobs." *National Review* (26 January 1971): 90.

Davis, David. "Crying Wolfe." *Newsweek* (9 June 1975): 88.

Dawson, Roslyn. "Tom Wolfe Comments on Being a Social Commentator." *Dallas* (December 1979): 26.

Dean, Michael. "Pop Writer of the Period: Tom Wolfe Talks to Michael Dean." *The Listener* (19 February 1970): 250.

DeVries, Hilary. "The Police Reporter at the Garden Party." *Christian Science Monitor*, 14 December 1987.

Dickstein, Morris. "The Working Press, the Literary Culture, and the New Journalism." *Georgia Review* 30, no. 4 (Winter 1976): 855.

Dietz, Lawrence. "Psychic Changes on the Social Landscape." *National Review* (27 August 1968): 865.

————. "Tom Wolfe on the Search for the Real Me." *New York* (19 August 1968): 42.

Dundy, Elaine. "Tom Wolfe . . . But Exactly, Yes!" *Vogue* (15 April 1966): 124.

Eason, David. "New Journalism, Metaphor and Culture." *Journal of Popular Culture* 15, no. 4 (Spring 1982): 142.

Edwards, Thomas R. "The Electric Indian." *Partisan Review*, no. 3 (1969): 535.

————. "Two Exercises in Elegant Minification." *New York Times Book Review* (29 November 1970): 4.

Epstein, Joseph. "The Party's Over." *Commentary* (March 1971): 99.

————. "Rococo and Roll." *New Republic* (24 July 1965): 27.

Erlanger, Steve. "Bonfire in the Bronx!!! Wolfe Catches Flak!!!" *New York Times*, 11 March 1988.

Fernand, Deidre. "The World According to Tom Wolfe." *Times* [London], 31 March 1991.

Flippo, Chet. "The *Rolling Stone* Interview: Tom Wolfe." *Rolling Stone* (21 August 1980): 30.

Foote, Timothy. "The Fish in the Brandy Snifter." *Time* (21 December 1970): 72.

"For Better or for Worse, These 30 People Changed Our Styles." *People* (20 September 1982): 32.

Frankel, H. "Author." *Saturday Review* (31 July 1965): 23.

Gilder, Joshua. "Creators on Creating: Tom Wolfe." *Saturday Review* (April 1981): 40.

Gingrich, Arnold. "Anatomy of a 21-Day Wonder." *Esquire* (January 1976): 8.

Glionna, John M. "Are the Outsiders Now Insiders?" *Los Angeles Times*, 9 January 1991.

————. "New 'Pump House' Generation Still Battles the Outsiders." *Los Angeles Times*, 26 November 1990.

Gordon, J. "Tom Wolfe: Reactionary Chic." *Ramparts* (January 1972): 58.

Gorner, Peter. "Tom Wolfe: In Big League as a Writer." *Chicago Tribune*, 7 December 1976.

"The Grandest Gamble." *Esquire* (August 1979): 5.

Gray, Paul. "Mauve Gloves and Madmen." *Time* (27 December 1976): 62.

Grier, Peter. "Wolfe: Tilting His Lance at the Glass Box." *Christian Science Monitor*, 14 December 1981.

Gross, Martin L. "Conversation with an Author: Tom Wolfe." *Book Digest* (March 1980): 19.

Grunwald, Lisa. "Tom Wolfe Aloft in the Status Sphere." *Esquire* (October 1990): 146.

Hardage, Heath. "Never Try to Fit in: Tom Wolfe Advises Young Writers." *Richmond News-Leader*, 3 November 1987.

Harvey, Chris. "Tom Wolfe's Revenge." *American Journalism Review* (October 1994): 40.

Hersey, John. "The Legend on the License." *Yale Review* 70, no. 1 (Autumn 1980): 1.

Hillis, R. K. "Art and the Car." *Design* (Midwinter 1968): 24.

Hughes, Robert. "The Painted Word." *Time* (23 June 1975): 40.

———. "White Gods." *Time* (19 October 1981): 69.

"In Chic's Clothing." *Time* (2 July 1965): 59.

"In Wolfe's Clothing." *National Review* (8 December 1989): 13.

Koncius, Jura. "Tom Wolfe, the Stiff-Colored Scribe." *Washington Post*, 23 October 1980.

Kramer, Hilton. "Revenge of the Philistines." *Commentary* (May 1975): 35.

Kroll, Jack. "Inside the Whale." *Newsweek* (26 August 1968): 84.

Lehman, David. "An Unleashed Wolfe." *Newsweek* (26 October 1987): 84.

Levine, Martin. "An Interview with Tom Wolfe." *Book Digest* (November 1981): 60.

Lewin, Leonard C. "Is Fact Necessary? A Sequel to the *Herald-Tribune–New Yorker* Dispute." *Columbia Journalism Review* 4, no. 4 (Winter 1966): 29.

Macdonald, Dwight. "Parajournalism, or Tom Wolfe and His Magic Writing Machine." *New York Review of Books* (26 August 1965): 3.

"The Magnificent Seven." *The Economist* (1 December 1979): 113.

Maslin, Janet. "Behind the Best Sellers." *New York Times Book Review* (28 October 1979): 54.

Mewborn, Brant. "Tom Wolfe." *Rolling Stone* (5 November–10 December 1987): 214.

Michelson, Peter. "Tom Wolfe Overboard." *New Republic* (19 December 1970): 40.

Mok, Michael. "*PW* Interviews: Tom Wolfe." *Publishers' Weekly* (18 June 1973): 203.

Murphy, James E. "The New Journalism: A Critical Perspective." *Journalism Monographs*, no. 34 (May 1974).

Nobile, Philip. "Wolfe Foresees a Religious 'Great Awakening.'" *Richmond Times-Dispatch*, 17 August 1975.

Nocera, Joseph. "Tom Wolfe at the Keyboard." *Washington Monthly* (March 1980): 20.

Overend, William. "Down to Earth with Tom Wolfe." *Los Angeles Times*, 19 October 1979.

Powers, Thomas. "Cry Wolfe." *Commonweal* (24 October 1975): 497.

———. "Lives of Writers." *Commonweal* (3 March 1978): 142.

Reagan, Ron. "*GEO* Conversation: Tom Wolfe." *GEO* (October 1983): 14.

Richardson, Jack. "New Fundamentalist Movement." *New Republic* (28 September 1968): 30.

Roberts, Sam. "Mau-Mauing the Flak Catchers on the East Side." *New York Times*, 12 January 1989.

Rose, Barbara. "Wolfeburg." *New York Review of Books* (26 June 1975): 26.

Ross, Charles S. "The Rhetoric of 'the Right Stuff.'" *Journal of General Education* 33, no. 2 (Summer 1981): 113.

Rothstein, Mervyn. "Tom Wolfe Tries New Role: Novelist." *New York Times*, 13 October 1987.

Salamon, Julie. "The Vanities of the 'Bonfire.'" *Vanity Fair* (November 1991): 206.

Sanoff, Alvin P. "Tom Wolfe's Walk on the Wild Side." *U.S. News and World Report* (23 November 1987): 57.

Schwartz, Tony. "Tom Wolfe: The Great Gadfly." *New York Times Magazine* (20 December 1981): 46.

Sellers, Pat. "*Cosmo* Talks to Tom Wolfe, Savvy Social Seer." *Cosmopolitan* (April 1988): 186.

Shapiro, Karl. "Tom Wolfe: Analyst of the ———— Generation." *Washington Post Book World* (18 August 1968): 1.

Sheed, Wilfred. "A Fun-House Mirror." *New York Times Book Review* (3 December 1972): 2.

Sheldrick, Michael G. "The First Astronauts: They Had What It Took." *Business Week* (15 October 1979): 10.

Sheppard, R. Z. "The Haves and the Have-Mores." *Time* (9 November 1987): 101.

————. "The Right Stuff." *Time* (24 September 1979): 81.

"Shuttle Disaster Surprised Wolfe." United Press International dispatch, 15 April 1987.

Simmonds, C. H. "Popcult Orgy." *National Review* (2 November 1965): 989.

"'Sly, Cruel, Poisonous.'" *Columbia Journalism Review* 4, no. 2 (Summer 1965): 42.

Swertlow, Frank S. "Wolfe Tells Why Novel Is Outmoded." *Los Angeles Times*, 18 July 1973.

"Talk of the Town." *National Review* (4 May 1965): 359.

Taylor, John. "The Book on Tom Wolfe." *New York* (21 March 1988): 46.

"That Party at Lenny's." *Time* (15 June 1970): 80.

"Thomas Kennerly Wolfe, Jr." In *Major Twentieth Century Writers*. Detroit: Gale Research, 1991.

Thompson, Toby. "The Evolution of Dandy Tom." *Vanity Fair* (October 1987): 118.

"Tom Wolfe." In *Contemporary Literary Criticism*, vol. 35, ed. Daniel G. Marowski, Roger Matuz, and Jane E. Neidhardt (Detroit: Gale Research, 1985), 448.

"Tom Wolfe." In *Twentieth-Century American Literature*, vol. 7, ed. Harold Bloom (New York: Chelsea House, 1988), 4456.

"Tom Wolfe." Interview with Mary V. McLeod. In *Contemporary Authors*, New Revision Series, vol. 9, ed. Ann Evory and Linda Metzger (Detroit: Gale Research, 1983), 536.

"Tom Wolfe Examines Why the New Left Disappeared." *U.S. News and World Report* (5 November 1979): 68.

Towers, R. "The Flap over Tom Wolfe." *New York Times Book Review* (28 January 1990): 15.

Trachtenberg, Alan. "What's New?" *Partisan Review* 16, no. 2 (1974): 296.

Tuchman, Mitchell. "Writings of Tom Wolfe." *New Republic* (25 October 1975): 21.

"Two Views of the Tragedy." *U.S. News and World Report* (10 February 1986): 19.

Van Dellen, Robert J. "We've Been Had by the New Journalism: A Put Down." *Journal of Popular Culture* 9, no. 1 (Summer 1975): 219.

Vonnegut, Kurt, Jr. "Infarcted! Tabescent!" [review of *The Kandy-Kolored Tangerine-Flake Streamline Baby*]. *New York Times Book Review* (27 June 1965): 4.

Webb, Joseph M. "Historical Perspective on New Journalism." *Journalism History*, no. 1 (Summer 1974): 38.

Weber, Ronald. "Journalism, Writing and American Literature." Gannett Center for Media Studies Occasional Paper No. 5, Columbia University, April 1987.

———. "Tom Wolfe's Happiness Explosion." *Journal of Popular Culture* 8, no. 1 (Summer 1974): 71.

"Whisperer." *Time* (16 April 1965): 60.

"William and the Wolfe." *Newsweek* (19 April 1965): 62.

Williams, Christian. "The Making of 'The Right Stuff.'" *Washington Post*, 17 October 1983.

Williamson, C., Jr. "Intelligent Co-ed's Guide to Tom Wolfe." *National Review* (18 February 1977): 212.

"Wowie!" *Newsweek* (1 February 1965): 44.

Zelenko, Lori Simmons. "What Are the Social Pressures Affecting the Art World Today?" *American Artist* (April 1982): 12.

Unpublished Works

McCord, Phyllis Frus. "News and the Novel: A Theory and a History of the Relation between Journalism and Fiction." Ph.D. dissertation, New York University, 1985.

Meyers, Paul Thomas. "The New Journalist as Culture Critic: Wolfe, Thompson, Talese." M.A. thesis, Washington State University, 1983.

Index

169

The Author

William McKeen earned his bachelor's and master's degrees at Indiana University and his doctorate at the University of Oklahoma. He is professor of journalism and communications at the University of Florida. He was a newspaper reporter and editor in Indiana, Florida, Oklahoma, and Kentucky. While working for the *Saturday Evening Post,* he was assistant editor of the anthology *The American Story* (1975). His books include *The Beatles: A Bio-Bibliography* (1989), *Hunter S. Thompson* (1991), and *Bob Dylan: A Bio-Bibliography* (1993). He has three children, Sarah, Graham, and Mary, and lives in Gainesville, Florida.

The Editor

Frank Day is a professor of English and head of the English Department at Clemson University. He is the author of *Sir William Empson: An Annotated Bibliography* (1984) and *Arthur Koestler: A Guide to Research* (1985). He was a Fulbright lecturer in American literature in Romania (1980–81) and in Bangladesh (1986–87).